SELF-PORTRAIT BY DANIEL WADSWORTH COIT

Digging For Gold Without A Shovel

The Letters of

DANIEL WADSWORTH COIT

From Mexico City to San Francisco

1848–1851

Edited, with an Introduction by

GEORGE P. HAMMOND

FRED A. ROSENSTOCK
OLD WEST PUBLISHING COMPANY
MCMLXVII

©COPYRIGHT 1967
FRED A. ROSENSTOCK
OLD WEST PUBLISHING COMPANY
1228 EAST COLFAX AVENUE
DENVER, COLORADO

LIBRARY OF CONGRESS CATALOGUE CARD NO. 67-18460

1250 COPIES
DESIGNED AND PRINTED BY LAWTON AND ALFRED KENNEDY
SAN FRANCISCO

PENCIL DRAWINGS BY DANIEL WADSWORTH COIT

Self-Portrait *Frontispiece*

MEXICAN DRAWINGS, 1848

The Noble Presence of Mexico City *Between pages*

The Great Plaza (Zócalo) and the Cathedral 32-33

Interior of the Cathedral

A Town Residence

Street Scene

View from Drusina's Hacienda, San Antonio 48-49

Priest Reading in Convent of San Francisco, Mexico City

Loafers Eating in Market Place, Mexico City

Two Sketches: Burro and Charro on Pony

CALIFORNIA DRAWINGS, 1849–1851

San Francisco in the Golden Spring of 1849

North Bay and the Golden Gate 80-81

Portsmouth Square above Yerba Buena Cove

Yerba Buena Cove from Upper Clay Street

Yerba Buena Cove and Mission Bay from Telegraph Hill

The Jetty at Benicia, 1850 96-97

"Benicia, California, Looking down the River," 1850

"Sketch above Benicia—Government Property," 1851

Clay Street at Montgomery, San Francisco, 1851

Introduction

Nearly every '49er came to California with pick and shovel—pack on his back or sea chest filled with necessaries—some enthusiasts even provided with an elaborate gold-washing machine. The cross-country trek or ocean voyage, begun in holiday mood by most of the gold-seekers, too often turned into a tough struggle in which the lucky ones survived and reached journey's end, stripped of most of their baggage, jettisoned along the way.

Daniel Wadsworth Coit was not this kind of '49er. He was a man of different mold, intelligent and shrewd, who toted up a balance sheet before plunging into a project. He brought no shovel, no pick, no gold-washing invention. In fact, when he went to Mexico in January, 1848, on a business trip, he had probably never dreamt of California, for this was before the gold discovery. There was then no magic in the name California. Coit meant only to stay in Mexico one year, according to his agreement, and then return to his family in Connecticut.

But fate intervened. The month of August, 1848, brought the startling gold news to Mexico City, authentic news, carried by Lieutenant Edward F. Beale of the United States Navy, official dispatches from the highest California officials. Moving in the upper echelon of the American colony, Coit learned the news at once, and almost as quickly developed a project for profiting by the discovery. True to his instincts and training as a businessman, he stuck to his last, aiming to supply Californians with gold and silver coin, of which there was only a miserly amount on that frontier, in exchange for gold dust which he would sell at a good commission.

In time, the plan matured. Coit reached San Francisco in April, 1849, at the very height of the gold excitement, when that city, Benicia, and other towns were in a frenzy of real estate speculation brought on by the steady stream of gold from the placers and the mass of humanity that descended on California almost overnight.

Of these fantastic events, Coit proved a faithful recorder. From Mexico, he wrote regularly to his wife, giving a pen picture, in letters and sketches, of that country and its people during the turbulent aftermath of war. And when he came to San Francisco, he was one of the few to make it his base of activity, instead of seeking a will-of-the-wisp fortune in some remote mining camp. In the burgeoning city of San Francisco, which grew from a few hundred residents to scores of thousands in four or five years, he witnessed an endless procession of gold-seekers, successful or unsuccessful, trudging the streets in search of a job, stifling their disappointment or sating their luck in drinking and gambling, happily booking passage home with a substantial pile of dust in their bags; or dying in loneliness, of disease, hardship, or frustration, their hopes blasted, their lives ruined.

All the while, Coit kept close to his business of trading, investing, buying gold, gold that the other fellow had mined with back-breaking labor. This gave him relative leisure, a chance to become a sort of professional reporter, an opportunity to cultivate friendships.

As the curtain goes up on Coit's adventure, the United States and Mexico are at war, a war that has aroused violent emotions among partisans both for and against it. The immediate pretext for the struggle between the United States and Mexico was the annexation of Texas in 1845. Spanish settlers had first come into that area about 1690, but effective occupation dated from 1718 with the founding of San Antonio and its famous mission, commonly called the Alamo. There was only a handful of colonists then, farmers and soldiers, stationed near the missions to help the friars keep order among their flocks and especially to protect them from hostile Indians.

The pioneer settlements in Texas, whether missions or presidios, were strung along an arc extending from Nacogdoches near the Sabine River at the Louisiana border to San Antonio. Isolated from Mexico by hundreds of miles of desert and wild country, they formed a lonely outpost, where life had few comforts or pleasures, and many dangers. Chief among these were raids from the north by Apaches or Comanches, who rustled cattle or horses and even attacked the missions and surrounding settlements. These beleaguered centers of Spanish power survived, however, becoming the nuclei of modern cities.[1]

Soon after 1800, Americans took a greater interest in this land, partly because of the national and irresistible westward movement and partly because of the belief that Texas was embraced in the Louisiana Purchase of 1803, callously given back to Spain in 1819 when the United States acquired Florida.[2] Aroused by these developments, frontiersmen had taken matters into their own hands, led their friends and neighbors into Texas, set up an independent Republic, and gained annexation to the United States, all by the end of 1845. Mexico blustered, threatening that annexation meant war. When the United States sent General Zachary Taylor into Texas, war came in May, 1846, each side having special reasons for encouraging it. For the United States it was part of an inexorable movement of westward expansion. For Mexico, defending her soil against an aggressor, it gave Santa Anna, that ambitious, deceitful, and vainglorious opportunist, another chance to seize power and again become the leader of his nation. Indeed, he promised to drive the invader from Mexican soil and to lead his people to glorious victories.[3]

This is not the place to re-tell the story of the Mexican War. Rather, we are concerned with preparing a background for understanding Daniel Wadsworth Coit's sojourn in Mexico in 1848 and his trip to California the following year. The war itself—the brilliant campaigns over deserts and mountains—ended in September, 1847, for all practical purposes, with General Winfield Scott's capture of Mexico City and Santa Anna's flight into exile. Defeated and discouraged, his country was without leadership. None of Santa Anna's successors wished to assume responsibility for making a treaty that would dismember the country; none wanted to pay for his costly errors.[4]

Yet the situation was desperate. The Mexican armies had been decimated or dispersed; responsible government had come to an end, both in the nation and in the individual states; lawless groups roamed the countryside. "The roads are filled with bands of robbers under the names of guerillas, who are as ready to plunder and murder the Mexicans as they are to attack us," an American officer commented.[5] No place was safe, least of all the route from Vera Cruz to Mexico City, the lifeline of communication and supply for some eight to ten thousand American troops occupying Mexico City.

The temporary national government under the acting president, Manuel de la Peña y Peña, which had established the capital at Querétaro, was at a loss to find a way out of the dilemma. The president could not count on foreign aid—England having positively refused to intervene

1. Cf. Herbert E. Bolton, *Texas in the Middle Eighteenth Century* (Berkeley, 1915), pp. 1–41; C. E. Castañeda, *Our Catholic Heritage in Texas* (Austin, 1936), Vol. II; Odie B. Faulk, *The Last Years of Spanish Texas, 1778–1821* (The Hague, 1964).
2. Samuel F. Bemis, *A Diplomatic History of the United States* (New York, 1950), pp. 180–195. In this treaty, Spain recognized her hold on Florida was no longer tenable. In exchange for recognition of $5,000,000 worth of claims against the United States, she gave up the Floridas and title to any land beyond the Sabine, the Red, and the Arkansas rivers, to the 42nd parallel of north latitude, as far as the Pacific Ocean. See *ibid.* for further details.
3. *Ibid.*, pp. 232–240; Nathaniel W. Stephenson, *Texas and the Mexican War* (New Haven, 1921); H. H. Bancroft, *History of Mexico* (San Francisco, 1885), Vol. V, pp. 307–367.
4. There were several major studies of the Mexican War about fifty years ago, which will be cited in these notes, but fewer since then. See Peter T. Harstad and Richard W. Resh, "The Causes of the Mexican War; a Note on Changing Interpretations," in *Arizona and the West*, Winter issue. 1964.
5. E. Kirby Smith, *To Mexico with Scott* (Cambridge, 1917), p. 153.

—nor could he follow the delaying tactics so dear to a politician. Time for such action had run out. Nicholas P. Trist, the American agent in Mexico, was making progress in negotiating an end to the war, aided by General Scott at the head of his troops.

In the meantime, while Mexico lay prostrate—an open invitation to anarchy—astute observers in the United States felt that there must be excellent commercial opportunities for those willing to take the chance, if they acted quickly. Some firms, like Hargous & Co., which had been in Mexico for many years, though out of favor during the war, resumed their activities. Others prepared to come in, among them Howland & Aspinwall of New York.

This company, under the direction of William Edgar Howland and William H. Aspinwall, had succeeded to a business established in the early 1800's by two brothers, Gardiner Greene Howland and Samuel Shaw Howland of Norwich, Connecticut. The activities of this company had been widespread, extending into much of Latin America, and its management now turned to a cousin, Daniel Wadsworth Coit, to represent it in Mexico.

Coit had first served the firm in 1818, when he went to Peru as supercargo on the ship *Boxer* with a shipment of firearms, munitions of war, and other merchandise. Immediately after his arrival in Lima, and discharging the cargo, he witnessed Lord Cochrane's attack on the city. Then he sent the *Boxer* back, staying on as representative of his employers to collect the sums due for his goods. These he had sold at a profit of 150%. But to collect the money proved another matter, as the government was without funds! In the end, through the influence of friends, he got permission to export a substantial load of cocoa, free of duty, in payment for the munitions. Subsequently he sold the cocoa in Gibraltar and Bordeaux to good advantage. These activities extended over a two-year period, September, 1818, to September, 1820.[6]

Instead of returning to his home in New England, Coit visited France and England, keeping in touch with businessmen in both countries. These contacts led to an offer from Frederick Huth & Co., a German firm long established in London, of a six-year partnership to transact business in Valparaiso and Lima. Coit's share of the profits was to be 32%. Lima would be his place of residence, and he would have complete control of the business, a very tempting offer for a man of 35. After he and Huth had made the appropriate purchases, Coit sailed from London in June, 1822, aboard the ship *Catharine*, for the coasts of Chile and Peru.

Imagine this young New Englander, a bachelor, occupying a large and well-staffed house in Lima, after the fashion of the country, and keeping extremely busy. Expenses were heavy, commissions large. Nor did he lack for enough to do. "Our business keeps our house constantly thronged with captains and supercargoes," he wrote home, "who give me not a moment's leisure or peace except when I am in bed."

In February, 1825, he had eight vessels in port consigned to him with cargoes valued at $400,000. In August, eleven more came; and in the following January, he was overwhelmed with business amounting to more than a million dollars. By April, 1826, he did not think his firm ever could have another three months so profitable, but after a year and a half he wrote, "the present year is the best we have ever had."[7] This success came in spite of the revolutions and political instability that plagued the South American countries, testimony to their great need for the vitalizing commerce with other nations.

Two months after his contract with Huth & Co. expired, Coit succeeded in freeing himself from the pressure of business. In June, 1828, he closed his private affairs, made some remittances of funds, carried a goodly measure of specie, gold and silver bullion, and other treasures, and took leave of South America forever. Ten years abroad and what an experience! He had

6. For an excellent summary of Coit's early life, see *A Memoir of Daniel Wadsworth Coit of Norwich, Connecticut, 1787-1876* (Cambridge, 1909); *Autobiography of Daniel Wadsworth Coit, of Norwich, Conn.* (Grand Rapids, 1887).
7. Coit, *Memoir*, p. 89.

learned to know the Spanish people, their language, their way of doing business, and he had made a stunning personal success. The financial reward, too, had been substantial. But he had no plans to return to Spanish America. To the delight of his family, he went home, with many tales of Latin American life, often illustrated with his own charming sketches.

After spending the winter in the bosom of family and friends, Coit sailed for Europe in May, 1829, to confer with Huth regarding affairs in Lima, and to enjoy the sights of the continent. He delighted, particularly, in European art, and continued to indulge his passion for sketching from nature. Fascinated by this, a life-long hobby, he studied under the best teachers. Three years later, returning to New England, he brought well-filled portfolios of his sketches, as well as paintings by old masters which he had purchased with his customary acumen. In his travels, when some scene took his fancy, he would jump out of the carriage, sketch-book and pencil in hand. For a time he thought of devoting himself to the study of art and remaining in Italy, but returned instead to his family in America in the summer of 1832.[8]

Up to this time, Coit had traveled through life without a mate, despite efforts of friends and relatives, especially his sister Maria, to find one for him. Then, in September, 1834, he married Harriet Frances Coit, daughter of Levi Coit and granddaughter of Joseph Howland, both long-established New York merchants. Harriet's mother, Lydia Howland Coit, being his own cousin, Harriet was his second cousin. Maria, herself happily married, had been promoting this match for some time.

The newly wedded couple settled at Washington Place, near Broadway, then the center of fashion in New York. Within a couple of years Coit bought an estate at New Rochelle, seventeen miles from the city. Here were born their first two children, Elizabeth Bill and Charles Woolsey. But the good fortune he had experienced for about twenty years was too good to last, and when depression came with the Panic of 1837, ravaging the economy of the entire nation, it carried away most of Coit's resources. Under the circumstances, he accepted the invitation of his mother to bring his family to live with her (his father having died). In 1841, he moved into the parental home at Norwich, Connecticut, where he cultivated the family orchards and gardens and gained a reputation for growing choice fruits and vegetables.[9]

In making this move, Coit did not give up some property acquired in 1833 along the rapids of the Grand River in Michigan Territory, when on a shooting excursion to the west. An old Indian trader had aided him in the selection of desirable land, which Coit purchased for a few thousand dollars. The place (now the city of Grand Rapids) became the county seat and an important manufacturing town. In later years, Coit journeyed several times to the western territories. Among other ventures, he tried sheep-raising on the prairies of Iowa,[10] but the Grand Rapids property proved his best investment.

In January, 1848, the wheel of fortune took an unexpected turn when Coit's cousins and friends in New York, Howland & Aspinwall, telegraphed him an invitation to engage in a confidential enterprise for them in the city of Mexico. He accepted the offer—it must have been very tempting—and left home hurriedly to take ship for Vera Cruz. The exact nature of the mission is not described in Coit's correspondence, but is given in his published Autobiography.[11]

At the moment of Coit's departure for Mexico, the American Army held the city of Mexico,

8. *Ibid.*, pp. 104–114.
9. *Ibid.*, pp. 119–121.
10. *Ibid.*, p. 122.
11. See Coit's letters of April 7 and July 22, 1848; and *Autobiography*, p. 48. The latter he prepared for his children, and his brother Joshua had it printed in 1877 (reprinted in 1887). In these reminiscences, he wrote: "My business in Mexico, wholly a monied one, was conducted through the house of Drusina & Co., one of the most prominent in that city. It consisted in negotiating bills on England and the United States, and remitting to the Pacific Coast for the use of our Government." The firm of Howland & Aspinwall was evidently engaged in shipping supplies to Mexico for the American Army, and perhaps in other trading operations.

captured in September, 1847, after the savage battles of Churubusco, Molino del Rey, and Chapultepec, and Commissioners of the two countries were trying to hammer out an armistice or peace agreement. Presumably Howland & Aspinwall sensed that peace was near and the moment was ripe for venturesome capital. So Coit left home on short notice, boarded a sailing vessel in New York early in February, 1848, and soon found himself bound for Mexico, via Jamaica.[12]

Coit found agreeable companions aboard. His cabin party consisted of five men, of whom he names only "Stevens," actually John Lloyd Stephens, author of several "best-sellers"—one on his travels in Arabia and the Holy Land (1837), and another on the discovery of the Maya ruins, graphically told as *Incidents of Travel in Central America, Chiapas, and Yucatan* (1841). J. L. Baldwin, a skillful and experienced engineer, was also in the party.[13] While Stephens and Baldwin went on to the Isthmus "to carry out some project of our cousin W. A. in connection with his steamboat contract with government for the Pacific," as Coit wrote to his wife, he himself continued on to Vera Cruz. "Cousin W. A." was of course William H. Aspinwall, whose Pacific Mail Steamship Company was about to launch steam navigation on the Pacific Ocean from Panama to San Francisco. At almost the same time, Aspinwall became deeply involved in a scheme for building an Isthmian railroad, a project that was closely related to his steamship venture.[14]

Steam navigation on the Pacific, to be a business success, required better transit across the Isthmus of Panama than the combined mule-back and river-boat trip, then the only means available, not only for passengers and freight but for military and naval purposes. Improved communication across the Isthmus had been projected at least as early as 1835, when President Andrew Jackson appointed Charles Biddle to investigate and report on the best method and to negotiate with the government of Colombia for a permit. After visiting Panama, Biddle went to Bogotá, obtained an agreement to construct a railroad over the Isthmus, returned in 1837 in the depth of the financial collapse of that year, but died soon afterward. His project for an Isthmian Railway died with him.[15]

In the wake of the Mexican War, the Congress of the United States passed an act on March 3, 1847, authorizing the Secretary of the Navy to make contracts for mail steamship service on both the Atlantic and Pacific oceans. This was subsidized by the government, the first line to run from New York and New Orleans to Chagres at the mouth of the Chagres River, and the latter from Panama as far north as Oregon, with service to ports on the way. The subsidy for the Pacific mail service was to be $199,000 per year. Arnold Harris was awarded the Pacific contract in 1847, but he immediately assigned his rights to Aspinwall and associates (named as Messrs. Henry Chauncey, Gardiner Greene Howland, and Edwin Bartlett). Aspinwall was the manager. They incorporated the Pacific Mail Steamship Company with a capital of $500,000 under the laws of the State of New York, April 12, 1848, and began construction of three steamers, all launched in 1848, the *California*, May 19; the *Panama*, July 29; and the *Oregon*, August 5.[16]

The spectacular project came to a head at a most auspicious moment, just in time to reap a golden harvest from the surging migration of 1849 to the gold fields of California—and from a

12. Coit to his wife, February 10, 1848.
13. F. N. Otis, *Isthmus of Panama. History of the Panama Railroad; and of the Pacific Mail Steamship Company* (New York, 1867), p. 17. On the career of Stephens, see letter of February 10, 1848.
14. John Haskell Kemble, *The Panama Route, 1848–1869* (Berkeley, 1943), pp. 22–28. See also his study, "The Genesis of the Pacific Mail Steamship Company," in California Historical Society *Quarterly*, Vol. XIII (1934), pp. 240–254, 386–406.
15. H. H. Bancroft, *History of Central America* (San Francisco, 1887), Vol. III, p. 699; Ernesto J. Castillero, *El Ferrocarril de Panamá y su Historia* (Panamá, 1932), p. 1.
16. Otis, *op. cit.*, pp. 16–17; Kemble, *The Panama Route*, p. 27 ff.

stream of travelers returning home, successful or unsuccessful in their quest for riches. This fabled event was still hidden in the womb of time, however, as gold was not discovered until January, 1848, and it was many months before the news reached the outside world.

At such a moment in history, Coit's traveling companion, John Lloyd Stephens, pursuing Biddle's dream of a decade earlier, was on his way to Chagres, accompanied by engineers, to make final arrangements for a railway across the Isthmus of Panama to provide transporation between the two great oceans. Meantime, the steamer *California* sailed from New York on October 5, 1848, for the long voyage around the Horn, to begin mail service between Panama and California, with but a handful of passengers, before valid news of the gold discovery reached the Atlantic seaboard. When the vessel arrived at Panama on January 17, 1849, it was greeted by a mob of adventurous gold seekers clamoring for space on its decks, space that was inadequate to accommodate more than a fraction of those who fought to get aboard. As a consequence of the gold discovery, and the many passengers stranded on the Isthmus who would pay almost any price for transportation to San Francisco, the company got off to a fine start—one of the great success stories of American business. The advantageous transport of both passengers and freight continued for many years.

Almost equally fortunate, after experiencing enormously greater difficulties, was the Panama Railroad, for which the government of New Granada in 1845 had entered into a 99-year agreement with a group of French capitalists, but which foundered on the fall of the French government in 1848. The shrewd Aspinwall, aware that a railroad across the Isthmus would be an important feeder for his Pacific steamship operations, made a contract in December, 1848, to take over the French rights. This was confirmed by legislation of the government of New Granada in 1849, a decree that was duly signed on April 15, 1850, with John L. Stephens representing the American company.[17]

Construction of the railway across the Isthmus began almost as soon as legal rights had been arranged. By October, 1851, the road reached Gatun, eight miles from the Atlantic, marking a triumph over swamps, tropical terrain, and disease that had decimated the labor force. Soon, passengers were traversing this part of the line and, as additional rails were laid, transit across the Isthmus became faster and less disagreeable. By January, 1855, the entire railroad was finished, and travelers could look forward to a commodious trip from New York to San Francisco.[18] It was not, to be sure, comparable to present-day supersonic flights by air at speeds of five or six hundred miles per hour, but to the generation of the 1850's, even more of a miracle. At first the steamer run from San Francisco to Panama required about 20 to 22 days; the trip over the Isthmus before the railroad, from three to five, and the voyage to New York about nine or ten more. On completion of the railroad, the Isthmus could be crossed in three to five hours. Improvement in ship construction and rivalry of competing lines gradually cut down the number of days at sea.

On his voyage to Mexico, Coit had met John Lloyd Stephens purely by chance, and had learned a good deal from him about the ambitious schemes of their employer, Aspinwall. Coit's mission was not on the Isthmus, however, but in Mexico, where he hoped to mend his shattered fortunes as well as to serve his superiors with his customary zeal. To undertake such a responsibility at sixty-one years of age indicates that he enjoyed good health, courage, and self confidence, all in good measure.

Coit wrote his wife with regularity, usually every two weeks. The letters preserved by his

17. The authoritative account of the building of this railroad is Kemble, *The Panama Route*, pp. 183–195. See also Bancroft's *Central America*, Vol. III, p. 701; and Charles T. Bidwell, *Isthmus of Panama* (London, 1865), p. 90 ff.
18. Otis, *op. cit.*, pp. 31–36; and Kemble, *The Panama Route*, p. 71.

DIGGING FOR GOLD—WITHOUT A SHOVEL

family reflect an educated, experienced traveler, knowledgeable in the ways of life in a Latin country. He was a keen observer and, though his language is moderate, he gives a dramatic insight into the conditions of the peoples and lands he visited. His letters may seem too reserved, yet their very conservatism assures the reader that Coit was writing not an unreal or imaginative story of a "never-never" world, but a practical account of what went on about him. One gets a real understanding of his character, integrity, sense of duty, and responsibility to his family and his employers, and also to the people among whom he lived and carried on his business.

Coit's voyage to his post was delightful—most of the way—the warmth of both weather and water in strong contrast to the January chill of New England. "I had a bucket of sea water drawn up for bathing my feet early in the morning," he wrote on February 12, "and could hardly realize that it had not been warmed over the fire." Between Jamaica and Vera Cruz, the vessel experienced rough weather, and the author's description of the sea-sickness that prevailed would be comic were it not so real. The last Sunday aboard Coit remained in his berth, seeking solace in the 107th Psalm, "They that go down to the sea in ships . . .," but found little comfort in its verses. His description of a wallowing ship heading into contrary winds is classic, but after a day or two of this turmoil, the vessel reached its destination in Vera Cruz late in February, 1848.[19]

In Mexico, life was in a continual state of chaos, as a new government sought to re-establish order. The road from Vera Cruz to Mexico City, as usual, was beset by guerrilla bands, and every supply caravan had to be guarded by troops. Soon after Coit's arrival, one of these United States military supply trains, comprising eighty wagons with goods for the American troops, escorted by two hundred cavalry and infantry, set out for Jalapa and the interior.

Coit joined the party, having provided himself with a horse, Mexican saddle, blankets and other necessaries. But he found little enjoyment in the company of these men. The teamsters were a rough lot, the discomforts of the road severe, as everyone was assailed by "mosquitoes, flies, ticks, and other equally noxious insects." To cap it all, his horse was shot one night by a nervous guard who suspected that some "guerrilleros" were infiltrating the camp! Coit got another mount, reached Jalapa, and left there very suddenly when a small pack train, hurrying through to Mexico City, came along, under the command of Colonel William H. Emory. Coit was able to join it, though unhappy about perfunctory treatment by the Colonel. The party experienced only the usual tribulations incident to travel on horseback, and Coit soon found himself at his destination—the great City of Mexico.[20]

From his fertile pen, under date of April 7, 1848, immediately after arrival, we learn of Coit's first reaction to the city, occupied by soldiers of the United States Army with little or nothing to do, marking time until a peace treaty could be ratified, a process that was to require several months. The first day or two he stayed at the Gran Sociedad Hotel. The lower story, called the Astor House, was in fact a licensed gambling place run on a very large scale. Coit suspected that some of the Army officers connived at or participated in its operation. The effect on troop morale, together with excessive drinking, Coit thought very bad, a state of affairs encouraged by the inactive life of the soldiers.

From this depressing situation at the hotel Coit escaped when Mr. Drusina, owner of the firm through which he carried on his business affairs in Mexico, invited him to take lodging in his establishment, "where I am delightfully situated, having all the quiet and security I could desire."[21] He was to remain in the midst of Mr. Drusina's family, with his own quarters,

19. Letters of February 25 and 28, 1848.
20. Letter of April 1, 1848.
21. Letter of April 7, 1848.

throughout his year-long stay in the capital, a fortunate opportunity for a gentleman of conservative temperament.

In Mexico City, Coit found himself in a favored social and business environment, able to move among the elite of the community, including the top officers of the United States Army, though with little spare time to improve this opportunity. While the Army waited for the peace negotiations to bear fruit, a spectacular discord developed among some of the officers, largely over who should receive credit for the recent military victories.

The difficulties had begun at Puebla, when Scott's army was on its way to the valley of Mexico. General William J. Worth's division, in the advance, occupied Puebla on May 15, 1847, as Santa Anna retreated. When Scott came up a little later, he found that Worth had committed various indiscretions, such as issuing a "scare circular" to the troops, warning them that the Mexicans were mixing poison with the food being sold to the American soldiers. Worth demanded a court of inquiry, which was held and which found him in error, but Scott, out of consideration for a life-long friend, made the censure light and gave it minimum publicity. The sting rankled, however, and prepared Worth for participation in the Pillow scandal that broke out in Mexico City as soon as the battles were over. Chief offenders were Gideon J. Pillow, commander of the Third Division, and Lieutenant Colonel James Duncan.

Pillow was one of those who in the World War of 1914–1918 would have been called a "30-day wonder," a civilian who, with more influence than training, had obtained a commission in the Army. Before the war, Pillow had been a law partner of James K. Polk and was in some measure responsible for his nomination. Later, Pillow obtained from Polk an appointment as brigadier general of volunteers and took part in many battles of the war. He evidently considered himself a confidential agent of the President, kept him informed of what went on, and especially praised his own achievements and minimized those of General Scott, who was after all a Whig, a member of the wrong political party. Naturally inclined to enjoy intrigue, Pillow operated behind Scott's back with complete freedom and audacity.

One incident in particular led to a major scandal. This was the publication of an article in the *New Orleans Delta* on September 19, 1847, later reprinted in other papers, including the *American Star* in Mexico City, written by "Leonidas," claiming that Pillow really was responsible for the victories at Contreras and Churubusco, and that Scott as commander-in-chief had virtually nothing to do with them. To most officers of the Army in Mexico, this was too ridiculous to be taken seriously, but not so in Washington, where Pillow achieved his purpose of belittling Scott and of enhancing his own reputation as a conquering hero—for it was indeed he who had inspired the article in the *Delta*.

General Worth and Colonel Duncan acted in much the same manner. When Scott called the officers to account, they were defiant, and he then preferred charges against them. President Polk of course favored his old friends, forcing Scott to submit to a court of inquiry, after which the President relieved him of his command and appointed William O. Butler in his stead.[22]

The court of inquiry began its sessions in Mexico City in mid-March, 1848, which afforded Coit an opportunity to attend. To one who had just arrived in the capital, this must have been very interesting. The hearings were indeed closely followed by both Mexicans and Americans. To most of the American army, the whole show was an outrage, but it was a reflection also of Scott's character—"he was one of the biggest men in great things and one of the smallest men in little things I ever saw..."[23]

Pillow's character, too, stood out for all to see. To Coit, "the evidence against him [Pillow] of endeavoring to arrogate to himself by underhanded means the credit of successes which

22. Robert S. Henry, *The Story of the Mexican War* (Indianapolis, 1950), pp. 382–388.
23. Arndt M. Stickles, *Simon Bolivar Buckner* (Chapel Hill, 1940), p. 18.

belonged clearly to General Scott, General Smith, and others, will be established beyond all controversy. His manner, too, in the courtroom is most exceptional, and in my opinion the court does not understand what belongs to its own dignity or it would not hesitate to put the mark of its disapprobation and reproof to conduct which disgusts every well-bred man who observes it." Later he commented, "I could not help thinking, however, that they might still further have maintained their dignity and the respect due them as a military court by requiring of the general [Pillow] that he should desist from cutting up the tables, as materials for the use of his penknife, while with his legs crossed on top of the tables he was addressing them. The dignity and gentlemanly deportment of General Scott was in striking contrast with this."[24]

Late in April, these court proceedings were transferred to the United States, where the quarrel with Worth and Duncan was dropped. Pillow, on the contrary, though held guilty of claiming a larger share of the final victories of the war than was justified, was given a mere slap on the wrist, and further proceedings against him were dropped, in "the interest of the public service."[25] Polk stood by his old friend, and hoped he had buried the political ambition of General Scott as a presidential candidate. Instead of being accorded a hero's welcome on returning at the head of his troops, Scott came home in relative obscurity.

Amid this turmoil, President Polk and the United States Senate were deeply enmeshed in consideration of the treaty draft negotiated by Nicholas P. Trist, whom Polk had sent to Mexico as peace commissioner. Though he had lost the confidence of the President and had been officially recalled—in view of his controversy with General Scott—Trist remained in Mexico. Communications between Washington and Mexico were so slow that by the time Trist received the papers of recall, the situation in Mexico had changed, he and Scott had become reconciled and were acting in harmony, and both saw the possibility of squeezing some action out of the Mexican government.

With Scott's veiled warnings of occupying other parts of the country, Trist's threat of breaking off negotiations unless the government came to terms, and the efforts of the British secretary of legation, Percy W. Doyle, to induce the Mexicans to accept the proffered treaty, the peace commissioners could no longer quibble over details. With the backing of President Peña y Peña, the negotiations were concluded and a treaty signed. Out of respect for Mexican pride, the act was performed not in Mexico City, but at the village of Guadalupe Hidalgo, immediately north of the capital, on February 2, 1848.[26]

By its terms, the treaty embodied virtually all of the requirements originally laid down by President Polk to Trist, including the recognition of Texas as a part of the United States and the cession of New Mexico and California (but not of Lower California, which many expansionists in the United States desired). For the ceded territory, the United States agreed to pay $15,000,000, and to assume certain old claims of American citizens against Mexico to the amount of $3,000,000.

Polk and the government were immediately plunged into a controversy over acceptance of the treaty. Some wanted more of northern Mexico, in the hope that it would provide a field for expansion of the slave area, while others objected to the acquisition of so much. Despite his own doubts, Polk recommended ratification, and the Senate approved, with minor modifications.

To explain these changes to the Mexican government the President appointed A. H. Sevier, chairman of the Foreign Relations Committee of the Senate, and then added Nathan Clifford,

24. Letter of April 7, 1848.
25. Henry, *op. cit.*, p. 383.
26. George L. Rives, *The United States and Mexico, 1821–1848* (New York, 1913), Vol. II, pp. 589, 593–613; George P. Hammond, ed., *The Treaty of Guadalupe Hidalgo, February Second, 1848* (Berkeley, 1949), p. 8 *et seq.*

the Attorney General, as associate commissioner, since Sevier had been taken ill. Sevier's health, indeed, was delicate, but he was able to journey to Mexico and to participate in the conferences with the Mexican government that led to acceptance of the modifications in the treaty and to the exchange of ratifications on May 30, 1848.[27]

With peace established, the American Army, which had kept order in Mexico City and surrounding towns, held its last review in the Zócalo, or great plaza, in the center of the city, on June 12. The Stars and Stripes were lowered and the Mexican flag hoisted, whereupon the troops went off to Vera Cruz for embarkation to ports in the United States. Though it was in the middle of summer when the *vómito*, or yellow fever, was most dangerous in the hot lowlands around Vera Cruz, nothing could restrain the troops, volunteers and regulars alike, from a pell-mell rush for home. Coit, who had reached Mexico in time to witness these exciting events, had a ring-side seat from which to describe them. In fact, he became extremely homesick when the troops left, and he would have joined them had not business obligations checked him.

With the departure of the American troops, life assumed a somewhat different pattern for Coit. He still took tea or dinner at the Gran Sociedad Hotel, or some other favorite spot formerly thronged with Americans. Now, the bars and gambling rooms all but deserted, Coit seems to have been thrown more into the company of business associates and to have had greater opportunity to visit the surrounding country. His week-end visit in May, 1848, to Mr. Drusina's country estate at San Antonio, a few miles south of the Churubusco battlefield, excited him. "What think you of a farm requiring 400 yoke of oxen permanently to do the work, with as many young cattle coming on, constantly in training, and with 250 milch cows, half of which are generally in milking at once, the milk from which is sent to town? But the main product of the place is corn and wheat, of which immense quantities are raised...."[28]

Not only the fields of the ranch impressed the visitor, but its mass of buildings, "resembling rather a small castle than a private residence," its private chapel, its "hovel-looking dwellings of the Indians," the granaries, thrashing floors, and barns. The interior of the owner's house was in harmony with the exterior, with lofty halls and large apartments opening off from a central, open court, with corridors leading to the wings, and the floors all tiled. It was a scene that must have taxed the mind of his New England family to appreciate; while he, the fortunate visitor, reveled in the lap of luxury, moving in the company of people with great houses or castles, and with servants to do one's slightest bidding.

Visits to such spectacular places revived Coit's interest in sketching, and his letters reveal that he was busy with pencil and easel, once again. In May, he confided that he had a new subject, the court of a convent (evidently the convent of San Francisco), which had been occupied by some American troops, and that he was progressing tolerably well.[29] As time hung heavy on his hands, when business duties were not demanding, he enjoyed his sketch book and pencil more than ever. Indeed, what could have been more relaxing for a sixty-one-year-old, compelled to stay abroad another six or eight months, than to indulge such a delightful hobby.

Coit never wearied of entering the multitude of rich churches of Mexico City, "and noticing their magnitude, their architecture, and the rich gilding and ornament with which their interior abounds and to which much additional effect is given by the gorgeous and imposing ceremonies, the form of worship, as well as the picturesque exteriors and groups of the monks and worshipers."[30] Some of this magnificence Coit sought to capture in his drawings. With

27. Henry, *op. cit.*, pp. 389–390.
28. Letter of May 25, 1848.
29. Letters of May 17 and October 12, 1848.
30. Letter of July 23, 1848.

patience, skill, and perception, he recorded many scenes of great interest. Of the quality of his sketches he had no doubt. He was certain they were worth while, and might even bring a handsome pecuniary reward.

In writing home on October 31, 1848, he stated that he had made nearly thirty views, and had written to an old acquaintance in London, Thomas Sidney Cooper, to learn if he would undertake their publication, afterward furnishing Coit the lithograph stones for use in a similar publication in the United States. Though not sanguine of Cooper's acceptance of this idea, Coit thought the result might net him from $2,000 to $3,000. He even toyed with the idea of going to London or Paris to arrange for their publication.[31]

From these delightful reveries, days of ease and relaxation, Coit was aroused by the news of gold in California. How soon the first intimation of this discovery reached him he does not say, but on August 21, 1848, he wrote his wife what might be called an official report. The day previous, Lieutenant Edward F. Beale (he calls him Beals) had arrived in Mexico City with official dispatches from Commodore Thomas ap C. Jones—and also from Consul Thomas O. Larkin—which were used by President Polk in his startling message to Congress on December 5, announcing to the world the truth of the fabulous discovery.

The adventurous lieutenant, making a forced trip, had taken the steamboat *Ohio* to La Paz in Lower California, and then had crossed the Gulf to Mazatlán. There he took a Mexican schooner to San Blas, a five-day voyage, and thereafter went by horse to Mexico City, traveling almost day and night. This was partly to escape the gangs of bandits still infesting the country, and partly due to the urgent nature of his mission. Beale told Coit that he rode the 350 miles from San Blas to Mexico City in three and one-half days, sleeping only "from 15 to 20 minutes at a time" while changing horses, and that he expected to reach Vera Cruz, a distance of 270 miles, in another two days.[32]

The excitement created by Beale's heroic ride and the tale he had to tell, aroused even the staid Coit to visions of a gilded future. If these tales were true, he wrote home on August 21, "we may soon have gold in such abundance as to be overstocked with it." The streams of California are so rich with it "that a common laboring man in a very rude manner of working readily obtains an ounce of pure gold per day, and such as have greater facilities, twice as much." He described the tremendous extent of "the mine," the depopulation of whole villages, and the desertion of sailors and government troops to get their share. Nor did he fail to tell of the sums gathered by some of the more fortunate, especially those employing Indians.

One can only imagine what Coit's wife thought of all this but she must have suspected that he, too, was getting the gold fever. In fact, the infection had taken hold. Coit resented not receiving his wife's letters more regularly, giving some hint of her reaction to his suggestions; but he kept writing, mostly about his daily routine.[33] When Louis Hargous left for New York on November 1, in company with Clifford, the United States minister, and other officials, Coit seized the opportunity to send his wife a letter, assured of an early and safe delivery since Clifford merited a cavalry escort to Vera Cruz.

Coit was homesick, but "I must bide my time," he wrote, as he still had two long months before the expiration of his contract with Howland & Aspinwall. Time hung heavy on his

31. Letter of October 31, 1848. Coit's younger brother, Joshua, gives some additional notes about this English artist (1803–1902). Cooper, then struggling for recognition, had finally become well known "as perhaps the most distinguished landscape, figure and animal painter of the English school." Coit studied under Cooper's direction, and his work so nearly approached that of his master in quality that it could be distinguished from his only by skillful judges. Joshua Coit in *Autobiography of Daniel Wadsworth Coit*, pp. 60–61.
32. Letter of August 21, 1848.
33. From July to November, 1848, Mrs. Coit's letters to her husband were greatly delayed or lost; we now understand why.

hands; maybe he was dreaming of California's riches, fearful that his wife might object to his joining the gold seekers. In the absence of word from her, he busied himself with sketching—his one absorbing hobby.

By November, more details of the incredible gold desposits in California had reached Mexico, and Coit relayed some of the wonderful tales to his wife, revealing the basis of the project that was now taking shape in his mind. Not only was it possible for one person to harvest one or two ounces per day of the yellow dust (much more with the help of Indians), but there was such a desperate shortage of coin in California that "by bringing the gold to a Mexican port, [a man] could realize 50 per cent more for it in coin than it was worth in California, or could exchange it very advantageously for the necessaries he was in need of." Gold dust had sold as low as $8 per ounce, half of its real value. Since Mexico "is full of gold and silver coins," there should be an excellent opportunity for an enterprising merchant to ship such coins to California, there to be exchanged for gold at a substantial profit.

The lack of coinage was no idle dream, but a serious deterrent to business or trade, as miners flocked to California and gathered gold from the mountain streams. At best, the use of the dust as a medium of exchange was inefficient and inaccurate. Coit's recognition of this situation, and his scheme for profiting by it, suggests that he was in close touch with the business community in Mexico—and with events in the gold country.

The nature of the profits to be made, not only in exchanging gold for coin but for other goods, is indicated by the experience of Antonio Coronel, a Californian who visited the Southern Mines. One evening, several Indians came to camp, much interested in "several ordinary blankets that were used as saddle blankets." They were old and dirty and valued at only two pesos each, but the Indians wanted them so much that one Indian gave Coronel seven and one-quarter onces of gold dust for one of these blankets, and a second Indian gave a little over nine ounces for another.

Very soon thereafter, one of the successful miners offered to sell Coronel gold for silver coins. "He proposed to sell me clean gold at *twenty reales* [two and one half pesos] *per ounce*. I bought six ounces at this price; I did not have silver for any more." Purchases at such a rate of exchange would have excited any businessman. That Coit already had formulated a plan to profit by it shows how fast the California news reached Mexico and how alert he was.

Very soon Coit broached the news to his wife: "I have the prospect of going to California, the 'El Dorado' of the present times, on business which promises great pecuniary advantages and which, I think, it would be wrong for me to decline. . . . The object in view is the purchase of gold dust, which has become so abundant in that country, owing to its easy acquisition, that the price, as compared with dollars or coin of any kind, is exceedingly low." He had already reached an understanding with Mr. Drusina relative to submitting the scheme to Howland & Aspinwall, which he did in "a very full, private letter to William on the subject, offering my services. . . ."

Coit's plan was to go to San Francisco with $200,000 in coinage to be exchanged for gold dust. The gold would be shipped to Mazatlán or other Mexican ports where persons wishing to make remittances to England or the United States could make the appropriate exchange. To carry out this scheme, Coit would make the purchases in San Francisco, while Drusina in Mexico City and George W. P. Bissell, Howland & Aspinwall's agent on the Coast, would handle the business elsewhere. His earnings would be 5 per cent. If successful, the profit would be substantial.[34]

To Coit the scheme seemed logical for all concerned, especially for Howland & Aspinwall,

34. Letter of November 12, 1848; see also *The Annals*, pp. 214–215.

whose steamers would soon be running every month between San Francisco and Mexican ports. "Here is all the machinery in a nutshell and it only requires one word from William to set it in motion. It appears to me that he can hardly decline an operation offering such advantages, but still it may be."

As for the journey to California, Coit had no fear. So many parties were going through that it would not be difficult to find a congenial group. Nor would it be difficult to get aboard a merchant ship at Acapulco, though steamers would be out of the question.

Coit's anxiety to embark on this project was so keen that he hoped to receive a reply from Howland & Aspinwall by the first packet, expected early in January, 1849. If they did not accept, he had a tentative agreement with Mr. Drusina, though he pinned his expectations on the former. To his great vexation, his cousins kept him in suspense, while "men are continually arriving here in parties of six, eight, or ten from Vera Cruz on their way to Mazatlán or San Blas to embark...."[35]

Early in February, 1849, the expected letter from Cousin Aspinwall finally came, dashing Coit's rosy hopes and throwing him into a gloomy mood. Howland & Aspinwall would have nothing to do with the scheme. Instead, they gave Coit leave to come home, bringing his Mexican employment to an end. Deeply depressed, Coit reported the news to Drusina, who revived his spirits by making him an offer to represent that firm in San Francisco on the same business—buying gold. "Since we talked this matter over, certain parties in Europe with whom you know I have extensive operations . . . have just placed $100,000 at my disposal for such a transaction, and in some respects it offers better advantages than what was anticipated from your friends." Indeed, Drusina had agreed to send Coit all the gold and silver coin he could invest in gold dust, allowing him a three per cent commission on the investment. To his wife, Coit wrote, "Was not this noble?" Without delay he set about making plans for the trip to the fabled El Dorado.[36]

After so many exasperating delays, Coit was on the way to California before he had time to tell about it, merely sending his wife a short note from Guadalajara on March 15. There were eighteen to twenty men in the party, besides muleteers and servants, all well armed, to guard against attack by bandits. Fortunately, a group had come through Mexico City, including a Mr. Meredith,[37] cousin of Louisa Howland, who invited Coit to join them. He promptly obtained "a suitable Mexican horse, and an extra mule," and was on his way. The party went to San Blas, not Acapulco, a longer ride, but these were all young men and well armed.

"You would have laughed to see our motley group," he wrote, "with two wagons loaded with washing machines, sieves, tin pans, and every apparatus for use in the mines." The men, after a few days on the trail, were equally grotesque—bearded, dirty, wearing odd-shaped hats of all colors, rifle slung at the back and a pair of large revolvers in holsters, and a pair of smaller ones at the waist. "No wonder that the entire population came out to stare at us whenever we entered a town or village, and that the big children caught up the little ones and ran indoors to save them from our clutches."[38]

The appearance of the men at the start of the trip was more elegant. As far as Querétaro, the party had carretas, or two-wheeled carts, for the baggage, but at Guadalajara it had to give up this luxury and use pack mules. To Coit, the carts, drawn by three animals harnessed abreast, made an amusing sight. He was much impressed with Querétaro, where the peace treaty had been so recently negotiated. The lofty domes and steeples of its churches and con-

35. Letter of January 30, 1849.
36. Letter of February 12, 1849; *Autobiography*, p. 49.
37. Gilmor Meredith. See Kemble, *The Panama Route*, pp. 61, 149, 152 and 164.
38. Letter of April 11, 1849.

vents lent its architecture a distinctive grace and beauty, and he regretted that the speed of travel denied him the pleasure of sketching them for his collection of Mexican scenes.

All went well, save for the hardships of the trip. Food was scant, and sleep difficult, usually on the ground, except for "the old man"—Coit, to whom all deferred because of his age. "I seem to be considered the father of the party and am treated with all the attention and respect from everyone that I could possibly desire." His friend, Drusina, moreover, had provided him with "a nice, portable, jointed iron bedstead, with sacking bottom, which folded up in a trunk." This proved a luxury, not only on the road, but on board ship. Nor would his younger companions let him stand guard at night. When they reached San Blas, he was able to repay some of these courtesies by obtaining deck space on the *Oregon* for Meredith and several others. The vessel made a quick trip of seven days to San Francisco, whence he wrote a long report on his adventures.[39]

San Francisco, at last! Headquarters of the Land of Gold. First, Coit must find a place to stay. Through Howland & Aspinwall's office, he obtained temporary lodging with one of their employees, a Mr. Probst, whereas "many respectable people [are] living in tents." As for the city, "the situation of the town, together with the noble bay, and the hilly or mountainous country by which it is surrounded, is infinitely more picturesque and beautiful than I had been led to suppose." He promised to give a more vivid idea of it in the form of sketches. Shortly after his arrival he had made three, but he had felt compelled to give away two, one to General Persifor F. Smith, the military governor, "whose friendship is not to be slighted," and another to the General's wife. Coit had an eye to business even while enjoying his hobby, his avocation.

The principal inducement that had brought Coit to San Francisco was "the exchange business," carried on through Drusina & Co. Since he did not arrive until the beginning of April, 1849, the ripest fruit already had been harvested. No longer was gold selling at such discounts as at first reported. The price was now much higher, and he doubted how successful the exchange business might be. Coit had brought with him only $8,000, which he invested immediately and forwarded the dust to Drusina, hopeful that it was of such quality as to encourage his principals to go on.

In view of the slowness of communication, not till October, 1849, did Coit learn what Drusina & Co. might be prepared to do. Then he received $26,000 in coin, for investment, "a larger sum than any one else received" by that particular steamer. "Still," he confided to his wife, "even this is far short of what was anticipated." In May of the following year, he had good news, when Drusina & Co. sent him bills of lading of $70,000 in gold and silver coin, making him again the largest consignee on the steamer's manifest. Coit was elated. His employer not only had found no fault with him but on the contrary had expressed "the most entire satisfaction." He was happier than he would have been under the thumbs of Howland & Aspinwall, who would certainly have expected more of him. Under the new company, he was his own master, "and in a pecuniary point of view I certainly have lost nothing."

Within a year he had invested nearly half a million, before the price of gold advanced so much that it could no longer be bought to advantage.[40] How changed everything was now, he wrote, in what was for him unusual self-praise. "Enjoying the unlimited confidence of mercantile houses of very high standing ... with the control of large specie funds and credits on different parts of the world, handling gold coin and gold dust with as much *sangfroid* as a little

---

39. Letters of April 11 and 9, 1849. The *Oregon* reached San Francisco on April 1, 1849. H. H. Bancroft, *History of California* (San Francisco, 1888), Vol. VI, pp. 134, 137.
40. *Autobiography*, p. 49.

time ago I did my garden seeds or the very soil that received them. I say, are not these rapid changes and contrasts truly astonishing?"[41]

At the time he confided these thoughts to his wife, Coit was one of the successful financiers of the city. The business acumen and reputation for integrity built up over a period of three decades, much of the time in Latin American countries, was bearing gratifying fruit.

In his letters, Coit tells relatively little of those intimate details of daily life that would have enlightened his family and gratified posterity, and his wife duly complained of his negligence. In response to one complaint, he penned a letter on February 28, 1851, giving a point by point summary of his daily routine—he enjoyed unusual good health, which he attributed to the good climate and his own regular habits; he had rooms in the Post Office Building, "on the public square [Portsmouth Square], consisting of a small parlor, which serves at the same time for an office, with a bedroom adjoining." The cost, unfurnished, was $50 per month. For breakfast, he either took a cup of tea at home or went to Delmonico's "for a cup of coffee, bread and butter, which, with a mutton chop or some like simple thing, costs a dollar." Here he found a half dozen daily papers—but he does not name them.

Having learned the news, he would drop in at one of the banking houses, usually Wells & Company, to observe the world of finance. If he had any writing to do, he attended to this next, or dropped in at one of the auction houses to gauge the market and observe the sacrifices being made. If several cargoes of goods arrived simultaneously, they were frequently offered at auction to cover costs, flooding the market at ruinous prices, sometimes selling for one-fourth of their value in New York.[42]

At two o'clock in the afternoon, Coit dined at one of the thirty or forty restaurants, where dinner could be had from $1 to $10, but "I don't go in for luxuries; indeed, one may dine perfectly well for a *single* dollar upon fresh salmon, wild geese and ducks and venison, with all the domestic meats, and a tolerable dessert." Poultry, however, was costly. After dinner he would read or take a stroll, "and ten o'clock generally finds me in bed."[43] Late in 1851, he lived at a boarding house, which proved neither so comfortable nor so satisfying.

Innumerable details of the hectic character of life in California, and especially in San Francisco, are pictured in Coit's letters, but it is possible to touch on only a few of them.

He noted the flimsy, combustible character of "The City's" buildings, and the extreme hazard of fire. Streets were mere trails, mudholes when it rained, dusty and dirty when the weather was dry. Prevailing westerly winds would blow the sand into every nook and cranny during the long summer days, so that if the pedestrian or the man with buckboard and horse was not mired down when he ventured out, he had to cope with the wind and dust. Later, as the city grew and sand hills were leveled, the streets were paved with wooden planks, which in turn gave way to paving blocks and other improvements.

In case a fire started, there was truly nothing to stop it. With prophetic foresight, Coit wrote, on August 19, 1849: "I consider the risk alone of fire here exceedingly great. The town is but one great tinder box, and a fire once commenced at the windward side would be certain to burn the whole of it to ashes, and this I predict will sooner or later be its fate. The material

41. Letters of October 30, 1849, and May 23, 1850.
42. Letters of May–June, 1849, and March 15 and April 14, 1851. Etienne Derbec, French journalist in San Francisco, wrote on February 15, 1850: "How many there are who, hoping to triple their fortunes, had put the whole of it in cargoes which are auctioned off in the public squares and whose sale price can not even pay the freight costs! The crisis, who would believe it? has raised the interest on loans to 20% per month...." A. P. Nasatir, *A French Journalist in the California Gold Rush; the Letters of Etienne Derbec* (Georgetown, California, (1964), p. 84.
43. Letter of February 28, 1851.

is all of combustibles, very dry pine, with a large proportion of canvas roofs; no engines, I mean fire engines; no hooks or ladders, and in fact no water (except in very deep wells) available where it might be most required. Many people have their all at stake under these circumstances. Is it not enough to make a prudent man tremble?"

The great need for housing when the miners returned to San Francisco from the mountains to escape the winter cold had led to feverish building. "What was wanted above all else was a roof under which one might find shelter, no matter what its form. . . ." Lacking adequate materials, the miners used whatever they could obtain—canvas, wood, sheet iron, tin, zinc— anything that would provide shelter, although lumber and brick gradually replaced these substitutes. Virtually everything had to be brought from the Eastern seacoast or from Europe. Prefabricated houses were not as novel then as one might suppose, and many of these were shipped to California.[44]

Coit, alert to what was needed, had ordered some "iron warehouses" in England to be delivered in San Francisco in 1851. They arrived and were soon erected, with the United States Government as chief tenant. Coit evidently had a one-third interest in this project. Set up outside the business district, to minimize the danger of fire, the warehouse project went well until the bluffs above crumbled and slid down, causing damage both to buildings and contents. This blow, and the greater competition for the purchase of gold dust, caused Coit finally to leave California and return to his home in Norwich.[45]

Coit's foreboding about fire was soon realized, for on Christmas Eve, 1849, an entire block, between Washington and Clay, Kearny and Montgomery, went up in flames, the first great fire of the period. The loss was estimated at a million and a quarter dollars.

Even greater was the fire of May 4, 1850, which burned three blocks—Montgomery to Dupont (Grant) and Jackson to Clay, with a loss of 300 houses, valued at about $4,000,000. Six weeks later, on June 14, the area from Clay to Sacramento and from Kearny to the waterfront was burned. The financial loss was almost as great as in May.

Rebuilding went on at a feverish pace, without much improvement in materials. When the fourth great fire broke out three months later—September 17, 1850—it ravaged a part of the same area, from Montgomery to Dupont and Washington to Pacific. The loss this time was smaller, about a half million dollars. Another fire on December 14 burned some iron buildings, shaking the faith of merchants even in this type of construction.

The greatest fire of the Gold Rush period came on the anniversary of the second conflagration, May 4, 1851, consuming the entire business district from Pine to Pacific and from Kearny to Battery, at the water's edge. Out of an area of 22 blocks, only a few houses remained. The loss was estimated at $12,000,000. From then on, merchants used better materials and greater care in construction, so that no comparable loss by fire took place again, in the early days.[46]

In spite of these fires, life went its normal course, if anything in San Francisco could be called normal during the booming years of Coit's stay.

On Sundays, he attended church services and visited friends. In writing home, he gave his wife a picture of the law-abiding, spiritual side of the city's life. The habit of church-going fitted well his conservative nature, and reflected no doubt the customs of a lifetime. This Sunday enjoyment he had not found in Mexico, a Catholic country, but in one of his first

44. Coit letter of March 15, 1851; see also Nasatir, *op. cit.*, pp. 85–86, and 207.
45. *Autobiography*, pp. 51–52.
46. Bancroft, *History of California*, Vol. VI, pp. 201–207; Kenneth M. Johnson, *Gleanings from the Picayune* (Georgetown, California, 1964), pp. 47–52, 99–107, and 129–130; George P. Hammond, *The Larkin Papers* (Berkeley, and Los Angeles, 1951–1964), Vol. VIII, pp. xiv, 228–229, 329, 420; and Vol. IX, pp. 15, 23, 49.

letters from San Francisco, dated April 29, 1849, Coit comforted his wife that there was a regular Congregational service, with two meetings each Sabbath, and a lecture on Wednesday nights, given by a Mr. Hunt.

This was the Reverend Timothy Dwight Hunt, who had been sent to the Hawaiian Islands in 1844 by the American Board of Commissioners for Foreign Missions to work among the natives. With the news of the gold discovery, and the need for religious services among the incoming population in California, his church in Honolulu gave him leave of absence to go to San Francisco to minister to the needs of its people, virtually without Protestant services of any kind. He reached San Francisco by the clipper schooner *Honolulu*, October 29, 1848, and preached his first sermon in the city in the little school house on the public square on Sunday, November 5. Meantime, on November 1, he had been chosen "Protestant chaplain to the citizens" for a year at an annual salary of $2,500. As other denominations sent out ministers, the need for a city chaplain waned, and Hunt formally organized "the Mother Church of Congregationalism in California" on July 29, 1849.[47]

Coit met another clergyman, Mr. Williams—the Reverend Albert Williams, a Presbyterian—who had come out on the steamer *Oregon* on April 1, 1849. The next month, May 20, 1849, this gentleman organized the First Presbyterian Church in the city, "in the public school house, then standing on the southwest corner of Portsmouth Square." There he also maintained a public school for some months, by permission of the alcalde and ayuntamiento.[48]

Coit must have attended the first meeting of the newly organized Congregational church, whose building was a spacious tent, for on that day, July 29, 1849, he wrote his wife, with some comment on Mr. Hunt's sermon. The subject was gambling, which flourished on a seven-day-a-week basis in San Francisco.

At this particular time, there was a great public outcry against the "Hounds," or "Regulators," an organized band of desperadoes who were terrorizing the city and who had recently attacked some peaceful Chileans and other Latins who lived on the slope of Telegraph Hill, killing and wounding some, and burning their humble shacks. There was a tremendous reaction against this violence. Alcalde Leavenworth called a public meeting in Portsmouth Square, W. D. M. Howard was elected chairman, and Sam Brannan and others denounced the recent outrages, demanding justice and restitution for the injured parties. A grand jury was impaneled, trials held, and many of the guilty convicted and sentenced.[49] This incident was a harbinger of the greater disorders of 1851 and 1856, which led to the formation of the famous citizen Vigilante committees to combat them.

The gold rush brought in other religious leaders too, including the Reverend O. C. Wheeler, a Baptist, who arrived in February, 1849, and established a church on Washington Street, near the corner of Stockton.[50] The Methodists also had their meetings, especially with the coming in September, 1849, of the Reverend William Taylor, who began organized religious work in San Francisco for this denomination, though he had been preceeded by the Reverend

47. William Warren Ferrier, *Congregationalism's Place in California History* (Berkeley, 1943), pp. 13–14; ——— *Ninety Years of Education in California, 1846–1936* (Berkeley, 1937), pp. 51–52; Frank Soulé, John H. Gihon, and James Nisbet, *The Annals of San Francisco* (1855), pp. 207 and 688 (hereafter cited as *The Annals*); William Taylor, *California Life Illustrated* (New York, 1858), pp. 62–63. See also Coit's letters of July 15, 1849, and January 14, 1850.
48. Albert Williams, *Farewell Discourse delivered Sunday, October 8th, 1854* (San Francisco, 1854), pp. 14–16; Taylor, *op. cit.*, pp. 66–67.
49. See Coit's letter of July 15, 1849, and references cited therein.
50. Sandford Fleming, "Selected Letters of Osgood Church Wheeler," California Historical Society *Quarterly*, Vol. 27 (1948), pp. 9–18; O. C. Wheeler, *The Story of Early Baptist History in California* (n. p., 1889), pp. 11–15.

Elihu Anthony and the Reverend William Roberts. The first Methodist church to be established in San Francisco was located at Washington and Powell Streets.[51]

Samuel Brannan had brought the first company of Mormons to San Francisco as early as July 31, 1846, on the ship *Brooklyn*. On one occasion, a November Sunday in 1849, Coit had a curious experience when he went to hear the Reverend Mr. Hunt, but somehow found himself instead among the Mormons, listening to a discourse on the "new revelation," an hour he disliked very much. But he does not explain how he came to be among them that day.

Located near the Reverend Hunt's Congregational Church was another, the Episcopal Trinity Church, with the Reverend Flavel S. Mines, rector. He had arrived in California in the summer of 1849.[52] Both of these structures, the Congregational and Episcopalian, were situated on the slope of a steep hill, giving a beautiful view of the town below, stretching out toward the Bay. All the church buildings of these early days were flimsy, some only tents, unpleasant on rainy days when services might be postponed due to the weather. At first, Coit preferred the sermons of Mr. Williams, but the Presbyterian Church was housed in a tent and most uncomfortable during the wet season, so he changed to the Congregational. Mr. Hunt, however, he found an unbearable windbag, his sermons poorly prepared, in striking contrast to Mr. Mines, the Episcopalian, whose sermons were solemn, impressive, and delivered with power and eloquence.

By January, 1851, Coit met another Congregational minister, a young man by the name of the Reverend Samuel H. Willey, and spent an evening with him and Mrs. Willey at a "donation visit." Willey represented the Congregationalists and New School Presbyterians of New England, who had sent him and Reverend John W. Douglas to California, under the auspices of the American Home Missionary Society.[53] Reverend and Mrs. Willey were good friends of the Gilmans, especially of Edward Gilman, all acquaintances from Norwich.

In such a widening circle of congenial spirits, Coit spent his last months in San Francisco. Business demands on his time were seemingly not oppressive, yet had to be attended to with precision on occasion. Clearly, he was no gambler, not joining in the frantic real estate and other speculations.

All through Coit's life, an artistic vein appears in him, even though it was forced to take second place to "duty," that sense of obligation to support his family and to provide a substantial hedge against the vagaries of fortune. Coit longed to be an artist, for which he had a decided talent, but he never was able to give it free rein. The number of drawings and sketches he made is not known, for he gave away many to friends; and these, if preserved, are scattered. Coupled with his sense of the beautiful and dramatic was a deep feeling for the historical. In Peru and Chile, he had observed not only the Spanish culture, several centuries old, but also the more ancient, aboriginal civilizations. During his travels in Europe, he had probed the depth and extent of Western civilization through study of its art forms. And in America, he had watched his own New England grow; then had been drawn to the Far West to observe the birth of a new society, the richness and future potential of which he could scarcely estimate. Yet he lived long enough to know that it was no fleeting mirage, but something that was to become a solid and fundamental part of the American heritage.

---

51. Taylor, *op. cit.*, pp. 24, 52–57; and Charles P. Kimball, *The San Francisco City Directory* (San Francisco, 1850), p. 127. (Cited hereafter as Kimball's *Directory*.)

52. Taylor, *op. cit.*, p. 67; and Coit's letters of November 11, 1849, and January 14, 1850. Coit gives his name also as Miles and Milne.

53. Samuel H. Willey, *Thirty Years in California* (San Francisco, 1879), pp. 37–40; and his *The History of the First Pastorate of the Howard Presbyterian Church, San Francisco, California, 1850–1862* (San Francisco, 1900), Ch. 1; W. W. Ferrier, *Pioneer Church Beginnings and Educational Movements in California* (Berkeley, 1927), pp. 15–18, 45–52; and his *Congregationalism's Place in California History*, p. 16 *et seq.*

DIGGING FOR GOLD — WITHOUT A SHOVEL

Coit's absence from his family lengthened to four years, whereas he had contemplated only one when he set out for Mexico so hurriedly in January, 1848. Meantime, one of his daughters, only a few months old when he left home, had died; and Elizabeth, or "Libby," had grown to be a young lady. As a loving father, Coit talked about the children in nearly all his letters, often apologizing for his absence, but feeling that the pecuniary reward he was attaining for them by his prolonged stay abroad was worth the cost. In one of his last letters from San Francisco, December 13, 1851, he wrote his wife affectionately, "Keep up your courage but a little longer, and I promise you a very experienced beau for the future." At that time, he planned to return the following April.

The date of Coit's departure from San Francisco is not definite, but it is probable that he was back home by the summer of 1852. On March 1 of that year he wrote his brother-in-law, William C. Gilman, "I shall use every endeavour to get away from here in a couple of months from the present time, & think at present I shall accomplish it. . . . It seems clear that he did. The remaining days of a rich life he spent in the grand old home at Norwich amid old friends—and in his garden. He died in 1876, in his 89th year. What a rich store of experience, knowledge, and travel in other lands he left behind as a family inheritance!

The Mexican sketches in this book, and the letters, are reproduced through the courtesy of a grandson, Dr. Charles G. Coit, longtime friend of the University of California. The San Francisco sketches were given to the University by Daniel Coit Gilman, a nephew of Daniel Wadsworth Coit, in 1899. Gilman, then president of Johns Hopkins University, had occupied the same position at the University of California from 1872–1875. To Dr. Charles G. Coit, I wish to express my deep appreciation and affection as I bring this work to fruition in book form.

In editing these letters and sketches, I would be remiss if I did not express my gratitude to a dear friend, the late Miss Edith Coulter, who asked me to continue the task she had hoped to do after publishing a selection of Coit's sketches, with short extracts from his letters, *An Artist in El Dorado; the Drawings and Letters of Daniel Wadsworth Coit*. Miss Coulter's lovely book was printed for the Book Club of California in 1937 by the Grabhorn Press in a small edition. In the present work, I have omitted certain passages in the letters of a wholly personal nature.

Perhaps I should note that the Gilman collection of Coit sketches in the Bancroft Library consists of a portfolio of ten mounted pencil drawings of California scenes (to which has been added a water color of a Mexican subject). Only five of these ten drawings were reproduced by Miss Coulter. To round out her attractive group of eight plates she added, from an unknown source, three San Francisco views, captioned: "Portsmouth Plaza & the Bay 1850," "View of Portsmouth Plaza Looking Westward 1850," and "View of Portsmouth Plaza Looking Eastward 1850." Possibly the first of these, her Plate IV, derives from an early sepia-toned photographic copy mounted on stiff paper which has been found among her collections. Her Plates V and VI may have a similar provenance, derived from photographic versions in private possession, rather than from original drawings. Eight of Coit's ten California sketches in the Gilman collection are reproduced in the present work, including two views of Benicia and one of "San Francisco 1849" (looking northeasterly across the Bay), which were not used by Miss Coulter. Two other drawings in the collection were not reproduced by Miss Coulter, nor are they used now; one is a sketchy view of Benicia labeled "The Gov[t] property & Col. Allen's residence 1851," and the other is a portrayal of a rather featureless "Valley near San Joseph, Cal.," not dated.

As I close this study, it is gratifying to remember those who helped me check references, find information on obscure points, and with their assistance encouraged me to continue a chore that, seemingly endless, had to be sandwiched in between my duties as Director of the

Bancroft Library and my teaching. To the entire reference staff of the Bancroft Library, I am grateful—to Dr. John Barr Tompkins, Helen Harding Bretnor, Lee Chase, Fred Lynden, and Assistant Director Robert H. Becker, originally a member of this group. Marie Byrne, Estelle Rebec, and Victory Van Dyck gave many an assist. Ruth Rodriguez typed the manuscript, and Dale L. Morgan and Susanna Bryant Dakin offered fruitful suggestions and constructive ideas. To each, my deepest thanks. I am appreciative also of help from the American Antiquarian Society, the New-York Historical Society, New York Public Library, and others named in the body of the work. Lastly, I wish to pay tribute to the printer and publisher, Lawton and Alfred Kennedy and Fred A. Rosenstock, friends of long standing, with whom I have worked on many projects. It has always been a delight to be associated with them.

GEORGE P. HAMMOND

The Letters

My dear wife   *At sea Lat. 20° N. Long. 70°*
                                             February 10, 1848

I have been waiting quite a number of days for a favourable combination of circumstances for writing you: this morning at length presents them in some considerable degree. Altho' the stomach & head are not exactly right, neither the vessel particularly steady, yet these things are so very much more satisfactory than they have heretofore been, that I would at least make a beginning at the only intercourse which for a considerable period of time we are permitted to enjoy.

Let me first go back to the commencement of our voyage & narrate to you how it has gone with us up to the present time. When I wrote the postscript to my last letter off Sandy Hook, the pilot was just ready to leave us, having performed his duty of putting us to sea. It was just the commencement of a N. West gale & we went careening our way before it for two days together, on our course it is true, but with anything but agreeable sensations. I hardly left my berth or took nourishment during the time, & altho' from knowing how to manage myself not so deadly sick as some of our passengers, yet with quite sufficient nausea. After this N. West gale abated we had more moderate weather & continued to make good progress on our voyage up to nearly or quite a week from our sailing. We had besides got into a very different climate —we no longer required blankets to our berths nor fire in the cabin. In fine we had the temperature & fair weather of May or June, in exchange for that of January, & moreover the winds had so far favoured us that we anticipated being in the trade winds in a day or two more & thus securing our voyage to Jamaica in the shortest possible time; but in this we were, as the result has shown, quite too sanguine. Instead of meeting the trade wind as is common in 27° or 28° North, to waft us on our way, we encountered there the wind in exactly the opposite direction, & of course dead ahead, with mild & pleasant weather, it is true, but turning us aside from the course we wanted to go & giving us an easterly direction instead of a southern one. Now this for a day or two would have been supportable, but when nearly a week succeeded with little change, & we found ourselves some ten degrees east of our proper course, it occasioned Mr. Stevens [Stephens][1] & our Jamaica passengers great anxiety, for their aim being to meet the steamer at Jamaica by a certain date, they were now like to be disappointed, & the object of their mission might be greatly interfered with.

You will perhaps be amused to trace out our position on the map or chart at this time; find there the 22° of latitude & [by] observing where the 65th parallel of longitude intersects it, you will have our location yesterday morning. There we lay rolling about in a dead calm, the sails thrashing themselves uselessly against the masts & yards, & altho' the weather was otherwise delightfully pleasant, yet our breakfast parties were unusually dull & desponding. We were, however, for a moment aroused by the cry from deck of fish. This brought us all quickly there where we found the mate tugging over the stern at a fine dolphin, which in a moment after was flapping on deck & we were for a while amused in noticing the rich & varied colors of gold, blue, green, &c., by which this fish is distinguished.

This event over, the next question was what has become of the trade winds? Had they ceased to exist, or what event had occurred to disturb their usual course? The captain had

---

1. See note 3, below.

made more than thirty voyages to the Islands before, & had never known anything like it; thus passed the forenoon in anxious watching of the heavens & particularly the eastern horizon, where our wind should come; now, when patience was almost exhausted, a slight ripple is seen on the water in the right direction. It increases to a slight breeze, the sails begin to fill, the vessel again comes up to her course & moves slowly on; now the breeze freshens, it grows stronger and stronger, until at length every sail is swelled to its utmost, & the gallant vessel walks off like a thing of life, running to spurn the waves, as now gathering in masses they roll up under the stern or rush foaming along the sides. What a delightful change even a few moments brings about at sea. Every countenance is now lighted up with joy, & should not every heart go out in corresponding emotions of gratitude to the great source of all good, who freely giveth us all things richly to enjoy?

The trade wind once obtained here our voyage may be deemed as secure. We have been going for the last 24 hours at the rate of eight miles per hour, running along the coast of Santo Domingo toward its west end, & tomorrow, if our wind continues as strong as at present, we shall keep away, passing between that & the island of Cuba, & within 48 hours' sail of our port of destination, Kingston in Jamaica.

Our dolphin has furnished us some good dishes for breakfast & dinner & altho' rather a dry fish, is not to be despised on board ship. Besides our fishing has been quite successful in adding two other kinds for our table, one of which, the barracota [barracuda?], is said to be excellent, the merits of which, however, will soon be amply discussed over the dinner table.

February 11th.

I resume my pen to tell you how much we continue to be favoured both by wind & weather. We have had a delightful run thro' the night & having now arrived at the extreme west end of Santo Domingo, are keeping away for Jamaica where it is presumable we may arrive day after tomorrow.

We have now to complain of the weather being too hot. The thermometer ranges from 75° to 84° during the day & does not fall much below that at night, so that thick clothes are quite oppressive & I already regret that I have not supplied myself with more of a thin description.

I have been very much surprised by the great size of the island of Santo Domingo. The notice I had formerly taken of it on maps (& the same remarks will apply equally to Cuba) never gave me a proper idea of it, but now, having sailed along its shores a distance of 400 miles or nearly half the length of our Atlantic coast, I begin to have a just appreciation of it. Altho' with a Republican form of government there is, I believe, here little of the security to person & property which that term would indicate.

February 12th

Our trade winds have continued through the last twenty-four hours without material change & with a continuance of the same delightful weather. I had a bucket of sea water drawn up for bathing my feet early in the morning & could hardly realize that it had not been warmed over the fire. Our atmosphere on deck is of corresponding temperature, the mornings & evenings alone being bearable there. I mean on deck.

I am happy to say that our cabin party, which I believe I have before told you, consists of five persons besides the captain, proves a very pleasant one.[2] Indeed, whether in the cabin or the forecastle, the most perfect harmony, cheerfulness & good feeling has uniformly prevailed, not an oath or anything approaching to it have I heard since I came on board, & the officers & men have conducted themselves, among themselves, & towards one another, with all the order & propriety of a well-ordered family.

2. These men are not named in the correspondence that has survived. Besides Coit and Stephens, Baldwin, an engineer, was one of the group. Otis, *Isthmus of Panama*, p. 17.

DIGGING FOR GOLD—WITHOUT A SHOVEL

Stevens is, as I anticipated, an excellent fellow. The more I see of him the better I like him. He is one of those men of whom you do not tire on acquaintance—cheerful, affable, intelligent, with a fund of interesting conversation & never descending from the proprieties of a true gentleman. I only wish he was to accompany me to Mexico; it would add greatly to my enjoyment, & indeed to his too, for he would infinitely prefer that course to that where his duty calls him. I believe I have not told you what the object of his voyage is. It is also to carry out some project of our Cousin W. A. in connection with his steamboat contract with government for the Pacific. It is of importance that there should be a good & convenient mode of communication across the Isthmus somewhere in the vicinity of Panama on the Pacific & Porto Bello in the Gulph of Mexico, & it is with reference to this survey that Stevens goes with engineers & all things necessary to select the most feasible route which will afterwards have to be made available by a great outlay of money upon it, tho' he will not wait to see this accomplished but will probably return to the U. S. at a period not differing materially from that fixed for my return, say in June next.[3]

Stevens, who knows everybody, has kindly given me letters to Genl. Worth,[4] Genl. Cush-

3. Coit was in good company. John Lloyd Stephens (1805–1852) was a celebrity in his own right, then at the height of his fame. Educated at Columbia College and Tapping Reeve's Law School, he decided to spend a year in travel before settling down to the task of a lawyer's life. With a friend, he toured the Ohio and Mississippi valleys in 1824, then returned to New York and engaged in the practice of law. A decade later, after a political campaign, his doctor recommended a year abroad to recover from a throat infection. It was a turning point in his life. On his return, after visiting and studying the civilizations of the East, he wrote *Incidents of Travel in Egypt, Arabia Petraea, and the Holy Land*, published by Harper and Brothers of New York in 1837. The book was hailed by the most eminent literary critics. Edgar Allan Poe wrote a twelve-page article about it for *The New York Review* that made Stephens famous.

For Stephens, this was only the beginning of a literary career. Other books followed, all an outgrowth of his European travels, but somehow these aroused the possibility of exploration and travel in the jungles of Central America, a subject in which others, including William H. Prescott and Washington Irving, were becoming interested.

Stephens set out for Central America in 1839, accompanied by Frederick Catherwood, an Englishman already noted as architect, artist, draughtsman, and lecturer, who was also intensely interested in archaeology. What a team! Stephens the gifted writer, Catherwood the talented artist, cooperating in one of the most exciting discoveries of their generation. In the next few years, these men explored the Maya ruins of Guatemala and southern Mexico, and Stephens wrote them up, in books beautifully illustrated by Catherwood. In 1841 came *Incidents of Travel in Central America, Chiapas and Yucatan*, two volumes; in 1843, *Incidents of Travel in Yucatan*, also in two volumes, and these were followed by articles and other writings on the same theme. On the basis of these books, Stephens became one of the celebrated writers of the time.

From literary work, Stephens turned to business, associating himself with William H. Aspinwall and Henry Chauncey, and became vitally interested in building a railroad across the Isthmus of Panama, a subject of such importance that it had been considered by the President and top members of the Government.

Stephens disappeared from his customary haunts in New York in the spring of 1848. Coit's matter-of-fact statement explains what had happened. Stephens was on his way to Porto Bello on the Isthmus of Panama, evidently accompanied by engineers, to survey a route for a railroad. For this reason he left the ship at Jamaica, there to take passage to the Isthmus, while Coit continued on his way to Vera Cruz. In December, 1848, Congress received a "Memorial of Wm. H. Aspinwall, John L. Stephens and Henry Chauncey in reference to the Construction of a Railroad across the Isthmus of Panama." Coit was delighted with Stephens, so famous for his wit, sociability, and literary attainments. See Victor Wolfgang Von Hagen, *Maya Explorer; John Lloyd Stephens and the Lost Cities of Central America and Yucatan* (Norman, 1947), *passim*.

4. William J. Worth (1794–1849), after service in the War of 1812, became one of Scott's top officers in the war with Mexico, in which he gained distinction for bravery, energy, and efficiency. Off the battlefield he was said to be narrow and self-centered. Toward the end of the Mexican campaigns, he entered into a cabal with Pillow and Duncan against Scott, for which he was placed under arrest and his reputation suffered from the controversy. He died of cholera in 1849. See Edward S. Wallace, *General William Jenkins Worth, Monterey's Forgotten Hero* (Dallas, 1953); and *Dictionary of American Biography* (New York, 1928–1936). This work will hereafter be cited as *DAB*.

ing,[5] Mr. Trist, our government agent,[6] & sundry other officers & private individuals in Mexico, which may be very useful as aiding the objects of my business as well as giving me useful information & conducing to my personal gratification.

What I have said in regard to Mr. Stevens' business movements you will keep to yourself, as Cousin W. does not like to have his plans become public talk, & indeed I may say as much of my own objects. We were very much amused in N. York at the notice taken of my movements in your *Norwich Courier*.[7]

Sunday Eve, February 13th
Kingston Harbour, Jamaica

We have just come to anchor in the grand & picturesque harbour after 16 days' passage; we made the Island at daylight in the morning. The mountains being very high can be seen at a great distance at sea, & it was noon before we approached near the shore.

Kingston, Monday 14th February

These will be my last words at bringing my long letter to a close. We were up bright & early this morning to receive the visits of health physician, customs officers, &c., &c., & after breakfast had permission to go on shore. A boat man'd by four Negroes, the sternsman a polite smart fellow soon rowed us up from our anchorage four miles to town & landed us with our luggage (that of the Panama passengers) on the customhouse wharf & after some customhouse formalities passing luggage, &c., we sallied out into the streets to look up a hotel or lodging house & to call on some merchants to whom we had letters. On calling on the English house of Write & Co., I was quite surprised in meeting Mr. Armstrong, who I met in N. York a few years since at Ed Woolsey's.[8] His grandfather, Mr. Chas. Roberts, as also his father, I had previously known very well. I wish I had time to give you my impressions of the place, its situation, as well as the style of the building & the inhabitants. All are peculiar & would alone make an amusing letter but I have no time now to go into particulars.

I dine with the gentlemen who have us here at four o'clock by invitation & shall put to sea again early tomorrow morning. I mean to take with me on board a good lot of these fine oranges & bananas, & only wish I had an opportunity of sending you some at the same time. And now, my dear wife, once more adieu. Embrace all our dear little ones for me. I trust they do not forget their promises to be good obedient children during my absence. This will go by a North Carolina vessel to sail in a day or two. Very soon after its receipt you may expect ad-

---

5. Caleb Cushing (1800–1879), a native of Massachusetts, served his country long and faithfully. He organized a volunteer regiment in the Mexican war, served at Matamoros, was promoted to brigadier-general, and then proceeded to Vera Cruz and Mexico City. The war had ended when he got there.

6. Nicholas P. Trist (1800–1874), diplomat and administrator, was sent to Mexico in 1847 by President Polk as a special agent to negotiate a treaty of peace. Though he quarreled with Scott, chiefly due to inadequate information of the administration's policy, he and Scott became friends, and despite being recalled to Washington, Trist remained in Mexico to negotiate the treaty signed on February 2, 1848.

7. At this time, the *Norwich Evening Courier* was a weekly. The article Coit refers to appeared in the issue of January 22, 1848, p. 2. It read: "We understand that a heavy Commercial House in New York has just fitted out a trading expedition to Mexico—the object being the establishment there of a mercantile concern on a large scale. A gentleman of Norwich well qualified by his familiarity with the Mexican language, and his ample experience in the commercial affairs of that part of the world, has been employed as the agent in the accomplishment of this enterprise; and this week he took his departure for New York, whence he was to sail immediately for Mexico. The arrangement under which the gentleman in question has gone out, does not, we believe, contemplate his stay in that country beyond the limited period requisite for putting the projected establishment in operation."

8. Mr. Charles Armstrong was admitted to the firm of Elin, Wright & Co. of Jamaica in January, 1841. In that year he is listed also as an ensign of the Kingston Militia, in 1842 as lieutenant, and in 1854 as justice of the peace. (Courtesy of Miss Rema Falconer of the West India Reference Library, Kingston, Jamaica.)

vises from me at Vera Cruz, where by the blessing of Providence we should arrive in two days or so. Remember me to all friends who may inquire after me, believing me, Ever faithfully & affectionately yours,
D. W. Coit

Mrs. Daniel W. Coit
Care of Messrs. Howland & Aspinwall, New York

At sea, Gulph of Mexico, February 25, 1848

I have for some days been desirous of holding a little chat with you, my dear wife, but the movement of our vessel has been so unsteady that I have had neither legs nor arms at sufficient command to do so. Not that we have had bad weather. On the contrary, ever since we left Jamaica we have had a succession of clear bright summer days with favouring breezes which have now brought us within a single day's sail of our destined port, but the wind having for the most part been directly astern, and our brig rather a small one, we have had more of a disagreeable rolling motion than I have before experienced under like circumstances. We are within a single day's sail of our port, that is, if we are favoured with strong and fair winds, but there is many a slip between the cup and the lip.

We are peculiarly liable here at this season of the year to those gales called Northers, which come up frequently at the shortest possible notice and blow with great force, so that although now in the enjoyment of perfectly clear bright weather and delightful temperature we may before midnight be hove to or scudding before a violent tempest. You may fancy then with what anxiety I am looking forward to the results of the succeeding day or two. . . .

Feb. 28 and still at sea. How prophetic were my remarks of Friday morning last at the commencement of this letter in regard to the weather! I had hardly finished writing the foregoing when there were evident appearances of a change of weather; first our fine fair wind gradually died away and left us. Then a long swell from the north set in with an almost entire calm. Soon gentle breezes from this quarter, which in short soon progressed to a gale, and we were in the midst of the dreaded Norther. Fortunately, we had plenty of sea room—no low shore near, nor reefs nor shoals, and we had only to battle out the storm in the clear open sea. True, this is nothing to the true sailor. What will not education, training, and habit do in making things naturally disagreeable passable and even desirable? But with the landsman, truly such as I am, notwithstanding my not unfrequent and long voyages, oh how fatiguing, how nauseating, how in every way unpleasant is a long hard gale at sea!

Let me try to give you some faint idea of it. Just fancy yourself in a large cradle with just room enough for the body to move freely about. Next fancy that some strong hand has hold of the cradle, determined if possible to throw or rock you out of it. Now you are rolled first on one side, then on the other. Perhaps when you are at the very brink of going out on the very edge of the cradle comes two or three hard shakes to get you over but it does not succeed and the cradle falls back and recovers its equilibrium. These motions failing, you are now lifted by the wind as if to throw you head over heels, but it does not succeed, and then as quick as thought the motion is reversed and you are raised at foot instead of head. At length the couch comes back into a natural position and you have a moment's comparative quiet, but it is only to lull your suspicions to rest, for immediately you are in motion again and all the variety of movement I have so imperfectly depicted are repeated ad infinitum.

Now this would be tedious for a half day in your own pleasant chamber, in health and without any disagreeable accessory, would it not? But suppose exhaustion of body for need of food, the most aggravated nausea, and this in an atmosphere compounded of the most repulsive odors, from dirty cooks, dirtier pantry, a closet filled with paints, tarred rope and codfish, and a scuttle, vomiting up from time to time. The confined air of the hold, bilge water, and what not, and to cap the climax, the everlasting tobacco smoke. I say, suppose all this, and not for a single half day but for nearly three days together, and you will be able to form some estimate of what I have endured ever since I laid down the pen on Friday last. During the period referred to I have passed over the Sabbath in my berth the whole day, and as you will readily imagine, rather a gloomy one.

I thought much of you, of your quiet enjoyment of the day and of delight I should have felt, in joining with you in your worship. In lack of this, I read some portions of Scripture with more than usual interest, particularly the 107th Psalm, an exhortation to praise God which you will recollect is a favorite with me at home, but how much more varied are the emotions created, in realizing for oneself at sea the graphic descriptions of the Psalmist. "They that go down to the sea in ships, that do business in great waters; these are the works of the Lord and His wonders in the deep. For He commandeth, and raiseth the stormy wind, which lifteth up the waves thereof. They mount up to the heaven, they go down again to the depths; their soul is melted because of trouble. They reel to and fro, and stagger like a drunken man, and are at their wit's end. Then cry they unto the Lord in their trouble, and he bringeth them out of their distresses. He maketh the storm a calm, so that the waves thereof are still. Then are they glad because they be quiet; so he bringeth them unto their desired haven."

This last verse describes my present state of feeling. The storm has passed away, favoring breezes have succeeded, and we are actually being wafted into our desired haven. The walls of the heretofore thought impregnable castle are proudly lifting themselves out of the waters. The line of shipping extends itself on either hand and the famous city of the True Cross (Vera Cruz) forms the background and makes a truly beautiful picture. How feelingly then can I appropriate the concluding verse of the Psalmist's exhortation, "Oh that men would praise the Lord for his goodness and for his wonderful works to the children of men!"

Vera Cruz, Mar. 2

I have only time to add I am safely here and will write you in a few days.

In great haste, yours affectionately,
D. W. Coit

My very dear Wife,   *Vera Cruz, March 6th, 1848*
On arrival here about a week since I forwarded under cover to Howland & Aspinwall, N.Y., a letter for you which had been written on the voyage from Jamaica here, not having found time to add after I came on shore. I am now having pretty well got through my business here about proceeding towards Mexico. I say proceeding towards Mexico, for there is no [pack] train going through for a considerable time and I am therefore obliged to avail [myself] of a dispatch of government waggons going to Jalapa only about 90 miles on the way, but by being there I shall be more likely to get on to my destination than if I remained here waiting on uncertainties.

I hope you will have no uneasiness for my safety. Be assured that I shall endeavor to use all due precaution and for the rest we must leave it with that kind Providence which has heretofore watched over and shielded me from a thousand dangers, seen and unseen. We suppose that an armistice is ere this concluded at the seat of Government and they will do away with all apprehension for the present from regular troops,[1] and as for guerrillas, the trains go well protected with regular troops to guard against their attacks.[2]

The train to leave tomorrow has a sufficient military force for all purposes, and I have the advantage of knowing several gentlemen who go with it and with whom I shall mess. We shall travel very slow on horseback and I am therefore provided with a suitable horse with Mexican saddle, accoutrements, blanket, etc., etc., quite *à la Spagnole*. All this used to be very pleasant, but I assure you there is no longer the least romance in it at all, and I would gladly turn my face tomorrow towards old unpretending Norwich rather than the finest city the world has to boast of, not excepting the far famed City of the Montezumas. Jalapa is said to be a beautiful town situated in a delightful valley surrounded by lofty mountains and I expect to find there an old acquaintance, Mr. Kennedy, formerly of New York, who came consigned to me when I lived at Lima. He is married to a native, has—I am told—a large family, and lives in very good style, being rich, quite rich—we shall see in a few days, and as I shall have leisure there for some days at least, you may expect perhaps something of more interest than I can give you from this business place. . . . *Affectionately and faithfully yours,*
D. W. Coit

1. Negotiations for peace had been going on intermittently for many months, with increasing intensity as General Scott approached the capital. The wily Santa Anna sparred for time until the last minute, though an armistice was finally signed on August 24, 1847. See Justin H. Smith, *The War with Mexico* (New York, 1919), Vol. II, pp. 120–139 and 233–252; George L. Rives, *The United States and Mexico, 1821–1848*, Vol. II, pp. 500–525; and Henry, *The Story of the Mexican War*, p. 345.
2. After Scott's successful penetration of Mexico, Santa Anna and the Mexican government adopted an official policy of harassment and guerrilla warfare. See Smith, *op. cit.*, especially Vol. II, pp. 168–172; Rives, *op. cit.*, Vol. II, pp. 202–204.

My dear Wife,   *Jalapa, March 15, 1848*

I have written you twice since I left home. The first letter I sent from Jamaica, giving some particulars of my voyage to that Island, and again on my arrival at Vera Cruz, though my letter was written principally at sea. Finding that there was not likely to be any train or escort direct through to Mexico for a very considerable time, and my business there being of an urgent character, requiring my presence at an early date, I thought best to avail myself of a government train coming to this place in the hope that an earlier opportunity would offer here for pursuing my journey than if I had waited at Vera Cruz. The result is likely to justify my expectations, for I find on arriving here that Col. Hughes, the governor at this place to whom I brought a letter of introduction,[1] is to proceed in four or five days with an escort, directly through to the Capital, offering me the best possible chance, so far as I can at present judge, of getting there.

As to my journey here, you will hardly be able to form an idea, even after I shall have used all the power of description which I have at command, of the annoyances and perplexities I have had to go through. I must begin by telling you that this government train with which

1. Colonel George W. Hughes (1806–1870), topographical engineer, was with General J. E. Wool in northern Mexico, and later became governor of Jalapa, after Scott's entry. He made a notable effort to keep order. Smith, *op. cit.*, Vol. II, pp. 224 and 230. In 1849 Hughes had charge of a survey to determine the best route for a railroad across the Isthmus of Panama for Aspinwall and Stephens.

I came was composed of about eighty wagons, conveying provisions, stores, etc., for the use of the troops at the various posts through which we had to pass. For the protection of these wagons, a force of some two hundred cavalry and infantry were sent, not so much to guard them from the attack of any regular Mexican troops as from that of the guerrillas, or outlawed bandits, who still exist in considerable numbers at certain points of the road.

Several merchants and sutlers (dealers in goods for the use of the army), together with a number of officers not having command, were availing themselves of this train to get forward to their destination, and it was to a party of these, consisting of some eight or nine, that I attached myself. They had provided provisions, bread, etc., for the route, and I was to come in as one of the mess, paying a proportion of the expense. The only mode of traveling was on horseback and I had to provide, therefore, my horse and equipment, together with a pair of good thick blankets and what change of clothes I could carry in a small valise, leaving my principal luggage to be sent forward by the regular train, to meet me at the City. The wagons, troops, etc., only got the first day about six miles from the City of Vera Cruz, but it was far enough to perceive the machinery of the whole affair and to give an insight as to what I had to expect for the future.

I must here tell you that the troops selected on these occasions are for the most part volunteers,[2] decidedly the least disciplined and the most dissolute, blasphemous class of our troops, not exceeded by any unless it be the wagoners and those having charge of the horses and mules, and of these recollect we had about a hundred men. Now just imagine all these lawless fellows at liberty after a day's march, some of them drunk, perhaps from liquor brought with them or, as sometimes happens, from liquor stolen from the wagons, and making fires along the roadside for half a mile to cook their suppers and afterwards to keep off the mosquitoes, while they stretched themselves on their dirty bit of blanket for the night. I say fancy these men, and the tenor of their blasphemy and obscenity, for you cannot get away from it, and you will have some idea of my company.

Now as to my immediate party: we first sought for the most desirable spot by the roadside for securing our horses and spreading our own blankets for the night, after we should have taken a lunch from our cold beef or ham or whatever it might be. I attached my horse to a sapling at a few yards from me and choosing a place under an overspreading bush, for the whole country where we were was thickly covered by underbrush, called here "chaparral," I placed my saddle for a pillow, spread out my blankets, and putting on a light cap with which I was fortunately supplied, introduced myself into this apology for a bed.

But what a miserable night I had of it! As to sleep, for hours it was entirely out of the question: the novelty of the situation in which I found myself in the open air in my hard bed; the vile wretches I have described cursing and swearing all about me; and at the same time assailed by mosquitoes, flies, ticks, and other equally noxious insects. Presently a guard came to place the sentinels for the night. They stopped to leave one perhaps eight or ten yards from where I lay. I heard the instructions distinctly—"You are to walk along this bank and keep a sharp lookout into the bushes. If you see anybody moving about there, call out three times 'Who's there?' and if no answer is given then fire." Then, in a whisper, the watchword "Taylor."

These sentinels were relieved through the night at intervals I supposed of about two hours, and in the intermediate time hailed one another with "All's well"—which passed along our

2. When war was declared on May 12, 1846, Congress authorized the president "to accept 50,000 volunteers" and appropriated $10,000,000 for the war. At that time, the regular army numbered fewer than 10,000 men. There was much criticism of this system. See, for example, Smith, *op. cit.*, Vol. II, 513.

line till the sounds were lost in the distance. After midnight the camp became tolerably still, only a distant sound of the howl of a wolf in the chaparral might be heard. Then, not far from this time, I was startled by the loud call of the sentinel, "Who's there?", twice quickly repeated, and then the crack of the musket. A deathlike stillness succeeded for a minute or two, when very soon the guard came in haste to know what had been the occasion of the shot; but after an explanation, which I could not understand, they again went away, giving the men a caution not to shoot a jackass again. I then supposed he had fired at a bush or a stump by mistake, as I had been told was not unfrequently the case, and again endeavored to compose myself to sleep, in which I at length partially succeeded, notwithstanding the multitude of drawbacks.

At least two hours before day the sound of the bugle called us to our feet again. The mules and horses had to be fed, harnessed, and attached to the wagons. The men had also to get their breakfast, and all this in the dark where all had to be guided by feeling rendered it pretty slow work. I went, too, to get my horse, when, judge of my surprise and chagrin, the poor animal had been shot through the head by the stupid ass of a soldier. What was to be done? It was not so much the value of the animal (some $40) as the disappointment in getting on my journey. Fortunately I found the wagon master had some extra lead animals and he very kindly offered [me one]. *[Unsigned and evidently incomplete]*

My very dear wife, *Mexico, April 1, 1848*

... I left Jalapa rather suddenly after all, a small train coming unexpectedly in from Vera Cruz for the City and hurrying through, encamping on the way about four miles from the town. With my best exertions I could not get under way till nearly dark, and then had to hire a little Indian to carry my carpetbag, he jogging along on foot while I was mounted on my mule by his side. I had scarce left the town before it became so dark I could not distinguish objects at half a dozen yards from me; and there I was on a road I never had seen before, in pursuit of a camp I hardly knew where, in a *guerrillero* country, and alone, or with only the poor Indian I have named. It was rather pokerish, I assure you, but I kept my six shooter in my hand, took courage, and pushed on as fast as my Indian could trot, which he did with a pretty heavy load on his back nearly all the way. After a while, an hour or more, we made out the lights ahead and I was soon among this lawless set of men of whom I have given you some idea in my former account of my journey to Jalapa.

I then sought out the Colonel (Emery)[1] and reported myself. He (to my discomfort on the journey, not much of a gentleman) received me rather cavalierly in his tent, told me I could put my carpet bag in the ambulance (a term given to a rather light wagon for taking the officers' baggage), and left me to shift for myself. I had done something of the sort before, so was not quite so much at a loss (though dark as pitch) as I might have been. I went first to get my pony quarters, that is, to tie him to some post on a pavement without straw, under a shed, could I find one unoccupied, otherwise, in the open weather; next I succeeded in buying for him a little maize (Indian corn), and having thus provided badly enough for his wants

1. William H. Emory (1811–1887), a lifetime soldier, became a first lieutenant in the Topographical Engineers in 1838, and later served at different military posts throughout most of the United States. During the Mexican war, he became a lieutenant-colonel of volunteers, after serving as chief engineer officer and acting assistant adjutant-general with Kearny's Army of the West. *DAB;* see also Dwight L. Clarke, *Stephen Watts Kearny, Soldier of the West* (Norman, 1961), *passim.*

(considering that he was my only dependence for conveyance for a very long journey), I set out to look for the softest spot on the pavement or ground where I might stretch myself for the night.

Every spot in and out doors seemed occupied, but looking about, by the help of a piece of tallow candle which I had succeeded in buying, I found a couple of young Frenchmen in a small stable sort of place, with a tiled or paved floor, who were very hospitable, offering me bread and whatever they had to eat and gave me permission to stretch my blanket by the side of theirs, where with my saddle for a pillow I got through the night till three o'clock in the morning as best I could. At this hour the bugle sounded and now all was soon in motion, fires lighted, soldiers and wagoners preparing breakfast in groups all about. Their horses being harnassed and attached to the wagons and the cavalry saddling and getting ready, when in about an hour or more, the bugle again sounded the advance, and we were all put in motion. Thus you see what my manner of life was with some shades of difference until I arrived here.

I shall not find time at present to say much of the face of the country through which we passed. A great part of the way, however, although at a height of some 6,000 or 7,000 feet above the level of the sea, was a perfect plain, of great extent, without fences, but occasional ditches, cultivated in Indian corn, barley, and wheat, the latter just now heading out. Of the aloes and the cactus tribe, in many situations, there was no limit to the extent and abundance, and scarcely any to the size. These plants with us requiring so great care and cultivation and withal puny things, are here of immense size, growing not unfrequently to the dimensions of the largest quince bushes, indeed much larger.

We frequently heard of guerrilleros and of their robberies on the road, but at present they only act in small parties and know better than to attack a train with 80 or 100 cavalry. At one place we passed the body of a poor soldier who had evidently been murdered a few days before and thrown a little on one side into the bushes, a straggler we supposed from some train, recently passed along the road. The sight was most revolting, as you may suppose, but after all it is only one case in at least ten thousand, of those who have suffered even more than this poor wretch, in privations, sickness, and finally death, in this country. On the way—I think it was at Perote—a soldier joined us, rather a good-looking young man, who after seven months' detention by illness had finally recovered almost by miracle and was going forward to join his regiment, or rather skeleton of a regiment, now in the neighborhood. This regiment, called the "Palmetto," is well known as having suffered immensely by battle but infinitely more by disease.[2] He told me that when they arrived first in the country they were 1,100 strong and they are at present reduced to less than 100. I find many, both officers and men, anxious to leave the country and get home again, and no wonder with such results staring them in the face. [*Unsigned and evidently incomplete*]

2. The Palmetto Regiment, of which Pierce Butler was colonel, came from South Carolina. This regiment suffered severely from disease at Vera Cruz while waiting to be sent inland, and later in battle at Churubusco, where Butler and other officers were killed, and many men killed or wounded. Henry, *The Story of the Mexican War*, pp. 340–342.

DIGGING FOR GOLD—WITHOUT A SHOVEL

My very dear Wife,   *Mexico, 7th April, 1848*

It is now just a week since my arrival here. I wrote you immediately afterwards, giving some few incidents of my journey from Vera Cruz. I am now prepared to say a few words regarding this far famed city.

You will perhaps be surprised when I tell you that any curiosity I may have had to see a place of so much notoriety and to draw the contrast between it and the other large cities of South America is already fully gratified, and that I would gladly turn my face homeward tomorrow had I only to consult my wishes. I find a vast difference in my feelings and views now from what existed when I formerly visited the different parts of South America and of Europe; there was a compensation, then, in being absent from one's country and family, but nothing whatever abroad can now make any tolerable amends for wife and children and home. But notwithstanding, my duty in regard to pecuniary considerations may still render it necessary for me to be yet some time absent.

Taking into view all the encomiums I had heard of the city, I expected to have found it very superior to Lima; it is larger and somewhat better built; there are more large and showy streets and houses, but neither the climate nor the location are, in my view, equal to those of Lima, and the morals and general character of the people are, I think, decidedly worse.

We arrived in the evening, and I had some difficulty in finding a place to stop, but at length with some entreaty succeeded in getting into what was said to be one of the best hotels in the place, called the "Grand Society"; this name applies to the two upper stories of the building, the lower part or basement being a separate concern and called the Astor House. Now this is a licensed gambling house, and licensed, too, by some one or other of our general officers. It is on a very large scale, with many rooms devoted to it, and a great variety of gambling tables spread out in all directions, heaped with piles of gold and silver—probably on the whole not less than $10,000 constantly in view. Here the officers of the Army of all grades up to the colonels (I have seen none of the generals) may be seen, I believe the whole 24 hours, mixed in with black legs and some of the worst description of the Mexican population.

This gambling, with horse racing, nightly masked balls, and fandangos of the lowest description, with excess of drinking, may be said to constitute the occupation of a very large proportion of our volunteer officers; there may be some exceptions but they are few; the officers of the regular Army may also to a great extent be covered in exceptions to these excesses. This state of things has been brought on in a great measure by the inactive idle life which the troops have mostly led for the six months past, and unless a change takes place by their being at least removed from the City to places of less exposure, there is no telling what the results may be. Already the most daring robberies are being committed and the officers of our Army are implicated in them. A short distance from the hotel where I have been is another, called the "Belle Union," a similar gambling establishment.[1]

I shall relieve your mind by telling you that I have removed to other lodgings and they are of a most agreeable description, too. Mr. Drusina, who transacts my business here, a most agreeable gentleman, has offered me apartments in his house, where I am delightfully situated, having all the quiet and security I could desire.[2]

I have seen General Scott but for a few moments. His whole time is engrossed by the trial of General Pillow now going on, on charges preferred against him by General Scott.[3] This

---

1. The Bella Union Hotel, managed by Matthew Daniels, advertised in *The American Star*, a newspaper published in Mexico City during its occupation by American troops.
2. In his later letters, Coit told more about Mr. Drusina and his family. Consult the Index.
3. Gideon J. Pillow (1806–1878), born in Tennessee, was a graduate of the University of Tennessee, 1827. Shrewd, but not particularly profound, he became a successful criminal lawyer in Columbia, Tennessee, with

General Pillow is a relative of Mr. Polk, or he never would have obtained the prominent rank in the Army he has and of which he is in no degree deserving. The evidence against him of endeavoring to arrogate to himself by underhanded means the credit of successes which belonged clearly to General Scott, General [Persifor F.] Smith, and others, will be established beyond all controversy.[4] His manner, too, in the courtroom is most exceptional, and in my opinion the court does not understand what belongs to its own dignity or it would not hesitate to put the mark of its disapprobation and reproof to conduct which disgusts every well-bred man who observes it. True, I have observed the court to call General Pillow to account for the coarseness of his manner towards witnesses, as well as his disrespect of them, reminding him that he was not before a civil tribunal where such things might be overlooked. I could not help thinking, however, that they might still further have maintained their dignity and the respect due them as a military court by requiring of the general that he should desist from cutting up the tables, as materials for the use of his penknife, while with his legs crossed on top of the tables he was addressing them. The dignity and gentlemanly deportment of General Scott was in striking contrast with this.

April 12

This letter was commenced, as you will perceive, some days ago. I again take pen in hand to add a few lines preparatory to the departure of the mail by which it will be sent to Vera Cruz tonight. . . .

I think you will like to know how my time passes here, how, in fact, I occupy myself. Well, I rise in the morning somewhere from seven to eight o'clock, and the greater part of an hour is occupied in shaving, ablutions, etc., etc. By this time the servant advises me that breakfast is ready in the dining-room adjoining my bedroom, a large room some thirty feet in length, with high ceilings, both that and the walls neatly painted in fresco. This, by the by, is in the third story, the kitchen being on the same floor in the rear. My breakfast consists of either coffee made very strong and weakened with very feeble milk, to which the cow in the middle of the yard I should suppose had contributed largely, or tea (green tea). With this they give me a couple of eggs, either boiled or fried, and as this is the constant dish, I make the variety as much as possible by taking them boiled and fried alternately. The bread is always the same, in cakes, made just about large enough for one's breakfast and tolerably good. As to butter, that is entirely out of the question. It is as rare and would be almost—not quite—as great a treat to me as one of your letters; I make a substitute for butter of the alligator pear, "aguacate," as the fruit is called here.[5] It is about the size of a large pear, has a thin skin with large stone, the pulp about the consistence of ice cream, with a sort of coconut flavor, to my taste very delicious. This, in lieu of butter, with a banana or so completes the déjeuner.

After breakfast I go below to the counting-room, learn the news, ask for letters, often dis-

---

James K. Polk as his partner. He held no civil office and took no prominent part in politics, but delighted in undercover political manipulations, in which he considered himself adept. He claimed major responsibility for Polk's nomination to the presidency.

Despite his lack of military training or experience, Polk appointed him a brigadier-general of volunteers in 1846, and subsequently advanced him to a major-generalship. His military career brought little honor to either himself or the army, although he took part in a number of important campaigns and was twice wounded. *DAB*; see also Eugene I. McCormac, *James K. Polk, a Political Biography* (Berkeley, 1922), p. 340 and *passim*.

4. Persifor F. Smith (1798–1858) of Philadelphia, lawyer by training, moved to New Orleans where he held various civil and judicial offices. When the Mexican war broke out, he was commissioned a colonel in the United States Army, took part in the capture of Vera Cruz and most of the battles that led to the capture of Mexico City. A man of magnetic personality, "gallant and judicious," he was highly regarded by officers and men alike. Smith, *The War with Mexico*, Vol. II, *passim*. Later, as Coit notes, he became military governor of California.

5. That is, the avocado.

The Great Plaza (Zócalo) and the Cathedral, Mexico City, 1848

INTERIOR OF THE CATHEDRAL, MEXICO CITY, 1848

Right: A TOWN RESIDENCE, MEXICO CITY, 1848

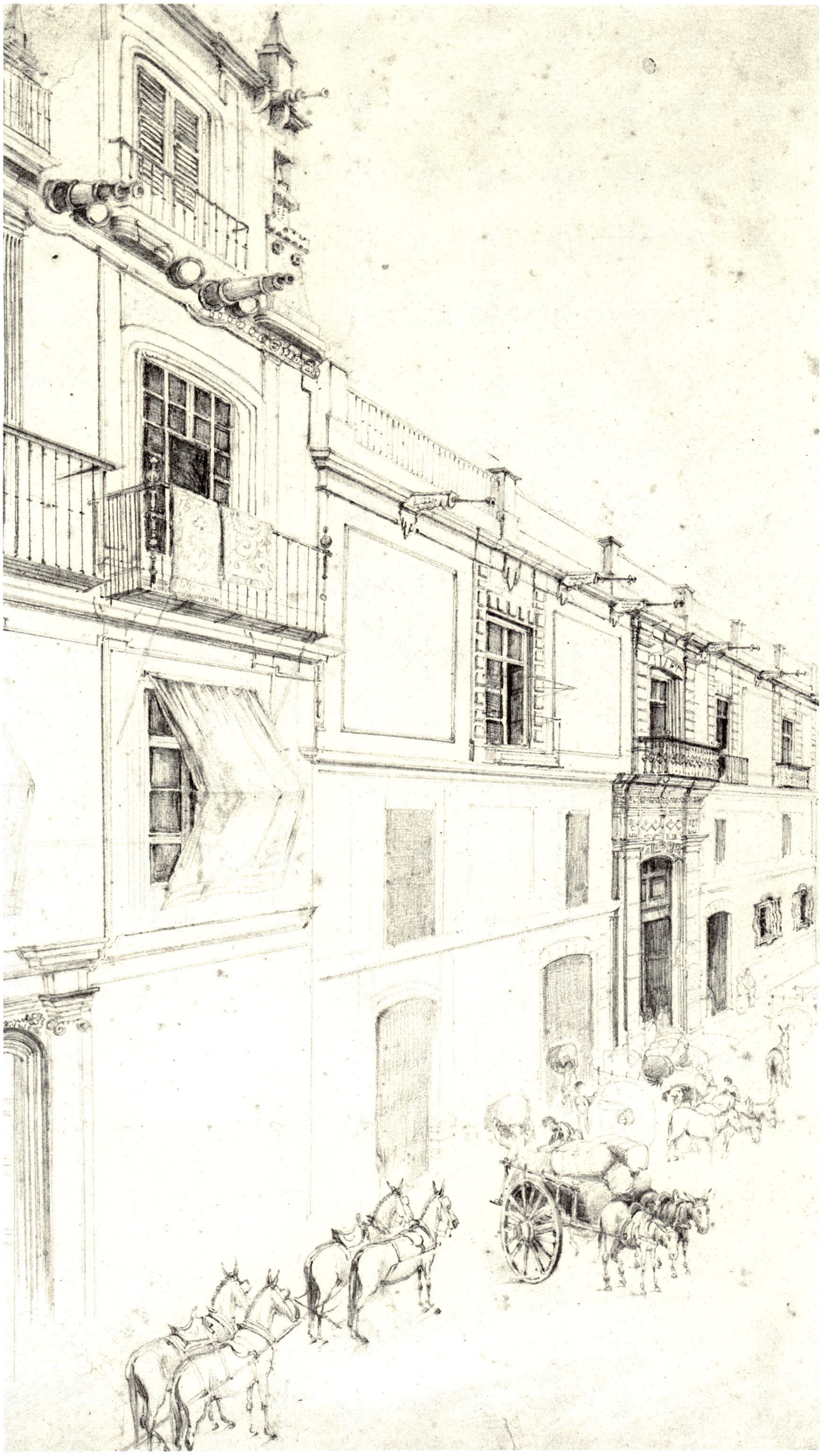

Street Scene, Mexico City, 1848

appointed in finding any from you, and then if any writing requires my attention proceed to it, in the counting-room where I have my desk, or (what I rather prefer) up to my quiet bedroom in front of the large glass door which looks out on the gallery, surrounding the open square round which the house is built. This gallery is filled with a splendid show of vases, geraniums, and other familiar plants.

Here I pass the morning, generally till dinner time, with my correspondence; at three o'clock, sally out for dinner. I generally get this, as the best place I can find, at a restaurant in the Hotel of the "Grand Society," the house I have already named as one I lived at on my first arrival. Here I dine from one of the small tables with which the room is filled, calling for such dishes as I know the house to furnish.

But I am losing sight of my day's occupation. If my writing engagements are not pressing, I take a short walk after dinner, taking care not to stray beyond the principal streets or particularly towards the suburbs where the streets are so disgustingly impure and the people that you meet so filthy, half-clothed, and miserable in appearance (almost entirely Indian) that you can think of nothing but contagion and disease and are glad to hurry your steps to a purer atmosphere and less disgusting objects.

Sometimes toward the evening I turn into the grand plaza or square [the Zócalo] to observe the parade of the troops. Many of the regiments are marched there from their barracks for drill. After this I sometimes drop into a coffee house and take a cup of coffee or chocolate, which, by the by, is good of its kind, and then turn towards home. There are two or three houses where I have freedom in visiting, to pass an hour or two in the evening, and where it is customary at eight or nine o'clock to take a cup of tea *a l'Anglaise*. One of these houses is immediately in front of where I live, occupied by a German gentleman, Mr. Kaufman, connected with Mr. Drusina's house. It is a very pleasant meeting of generally eight or ten well-bred people, where an hour or two is passed very sociably and reasonably. Mrs. Kaufman plays well and in this way aids in making the time pass agreeably. There is also one other house, occupied by a Mr. Hargous of New York and a Mr. Vos, to whom I had letters and where I have a general invitation.[6] There are no ladies here but one meets generally several of the most respectable of our Army officers. A cup of tea is always prepared and an hour or so here also passes agreeably, and thus ends the day.

I have now, my dear wife, filled my second sheet and may not have time to add to it. My thoughts are constantly with you and the dear children. Embrace them, one and all, for me. I trust that they are good children in my absence. Libby, I presume from your letter, may be with her Aunt Pink now. She ought to write me. Remember me, with kind regards, to all the dear friends who may inquire for me, particularly Aunt L., Cousin Mary and family, George Ripley, etc., etc.

Yours ever affectionately,
D. W. C.

6. See Note 1 to Letter of July 23, 1848. Mrs. Kaufman, it is said, was a favorite of Nicholas P. Trist, the American peace commissioner.

My dear Wife,   *Mexico, April 22d, 1848*

My last letter to you was about ten days ago, I think, under date of the 11th or 12th, and although I still remain without any of yours to reply to, I will not be deterred from addressing you a few lines to let you know that I am well, if no more.

Since my last, both the commissioners, Mr. Sevier[1] and Mr. Clifford,[2] have arrived and are awaiting the movements of the government, with a view to the conclusion of the treaty of peace which has been so long under discussion. This being Holy Week, little was expected to be done, but on the ensuing week it is expected that the Congress will be assembled at Querétaro (which, you know, is the present seat of government) and matters finally adjusted. It is said this morning that our commissioners are to leave today on their way to Querétaro, to have nothing wanting on their part. There are yet those who affect to believe that the treaty will not be ratified, and there are doubtless many in the country opposed to it who would prefer to see the war continued, but the probabilities are altogether the other way. A couple of weeks will probably determine the matter one way or the other.

General Pillow's trial (although it may, with almost as much propriety, be called General Scott's trial) was brought to a close yesterday—that is, so far as it could be carried in this country. It is to be adjourned, or rather was adjourned, to meet in the United States, probably in Washington, and the court will immediately remove there. I learn that General Scott leaves this morning for Vera Cruz, being exceedingly anxious to reach home with the least possible delay. I wish it had been in my power to have joined his escort, for I am tired enough of Mexico and indeed never was so near homesick in my life, but when this pleasure is to be mine, I mean that of turning my face homeward, is more than I can tell. The probabilities, I think, are that our friends may wish me to continue in Mexico through the year, and if they do my interest will be so much promoted by it that I shall feel it my duty to stay. . . .

                                                                    Yours ever affectionately,
                                                                               D. W. C.

---

1. Ambrose H. Sevier (1801–1848), born in Tennessee, was in politics all his life, becoming a representative and then senator from Arkansas. He held the latter office from 1836 until 1848. During the Mexican War, he was chairman of the Senate Committee on Foreign Relations, but resigned on President Polk's invitation to become minister to Mexico. Though he had suffered from ill health, he accepted. Following the war, Polk had intended to make him Boundary Commissioner. Instead, he named the ambitious John B. Weller, when Sevier died early in 1849.

2. Nathan Clifford (1803–1881), born in New Hampshire, moved to Maine and opened a legal practice there in 1823. In 1846, he entered the arena of national politics by becoming attorney general. Then, with the confidence of Secretary of State Buchanan, he and Senator Sevier were sent to Mexico to conduct the final negotiations for a treaty of peace. On the exchange of ratifications, Clifford remained in Mexico as minister of the United States, but with the defeat of the Democrats in 1848 and the election of General Zachary Taylor, a Whig, as president, Clifford was recalled. *DAB.* Taylor's participation in the Mexican War is told by Brainerd Dyer in his biographical study, *Zachary Taylor* (Baton Rouge, 1946).

My very dear Wife,   *Mexico, May 17th, 1848*

Having just finished my correspondence for the mail of this evening for Vera Cruz, I refer to letters to H. & A., I will endeavor to fill a sheet for you, although I wrote you at some length but about a week since. . . .

Mr. Drusina's family may, I suppose, be considered one of the fashionable ones of Mexico, not dashingly so, for there does not appear to be any aim to show, but an expensive one with a handsome establishment in town and country and a large retinue of servants. What think you of sixteen servants in a single household? Mr. Drusina enumerated their offices to me on one occasion, but I doubt if I could recollect much more than half. I do remember that each of the young children had its waiting maid, *viz.*, a little Indian body, and the young lady had, of course, her maid. Then there were two or three permanent seamstresses, and not less than three or four men connected with the horses and carriages, etc., etc.

After declining two or three invitations to pass the Sabbath in the country with Mr. Drusina, I at last accepted one to go on a Saturday afternoon and return the following Monday. We accordingly started about three o'clock in a handsome town carriage, I should call it, drawn by two pairs of fine black mules, a postilion to each pair. We had besides two outriders belonging to the family, well armed, as we were in the carriage, for on the road there had been several highway robberies, and Mr. Drusina, who passes on the road almost daily, always goes well prepared. Our way lay over the great plain which extends many miles from the City in every direction and had nothing of paramount interest in it or about it other than passing over one of the battlefields, Churubusco, through which, with infinite loss of life, our brave troops had to force their way to the City. The hacienda, or family estate, to which we were going, called San Antonio,[1] lays at about ten or twelve miles from the City and is one of the most celebrated for its beauty (so far as a perfectly flat country can be called beautiful), its high cultivation and its great extent, that can anywhere be seen in the country. Already when we were a league (or two and a half miles) from the dwelling, we were upon its grounds. Here was farming on a magnificent scale indeed. What think you of a farm requiring 400 yoke of oxen permanently to do the work, with as many young cattle coming on, constantly in training, and with 250 milch cows, half of which are generally in milking at once, the milk from which is sent to town? But the main product of the place is corn and wheat, of which immense quantities are raised, as you may judge from the number of oxen employed to till the ground principally with this object.

But let me get you to the house before my paper is consumed, for I shall be unable to give you more than a single sheet at this time. Our mules moved at a rapid pace and we soon approached a great mass of buildings resembling rather a small castle than a private residence, and were driven through a lofty gateway into a large court, on one side of which stand the ranges of building, including a chapel attached to the house, and at the extremities, on the other, the miserable low, black, hovel-looking dwellings of the Indians attached to the place (for all the work is done by this poor degraded class of beings), and the extensive granaries, thrashing floors and barns of the establishment. The interior of the building corresponded well in appearance with the exterior, an open court in the center, built entirely round with corridors, and the rooms opening from this, all with very lofty ceilings, and the floors universally tiled. An exceedingly lofty hall leads from this corridor (not less than 20 feet high) serving as a dining room (being lighted entirely from overhead). Towards the front of the house, looking out upon the road, here again was a long range of lofty and large apartments, drawing rooms, etc., extending the whole length of the house. But I have already used up my

1. San Antonio lay a little south of the Churubusco battlefield.

paper and you will hardly get an introduction to Mexican ladies, the inmates of the house, at this time, and it would certainly, after all the civilities and attentions received, not be very civil or treating them with proper attention to bring them forward at the fag end of my letter, so they must remain as a "corps de reserve" for a future occasion. The drawings progress tolerably. I have a new subject in hand, the court of a convent,[2] being the quarters of our troops, with abundance of figures, etc., etc.

My best love to all our friends, and accept an extra allowance for yourself and our dear little ones.
Yours ever affectionately,
D. W. C.

2. Probably the convent of San Francisco. See Coit's letter of October 12, 1848.

My very dear Wife,   *Mexico, May 25th, 1848*

I have written you twice at considerable length since the month commenced, on the 9th and again on the 17th. I thought before this time the question of my remaining in the country on the business of our friends, Howland & Aspinwall,[1] for the remainder of the year would have been decided, but it is not—at least, no advice has reached me on the subject. At the time of making my arrangement on the first suggestion of theirs for a stay of a couple of months here, or until the first of June, a conditional agreement was entered into that provided, should they desire it, I would remain until the 1st January next ensuing, or through the present year, and of this they were to give me seasonable advice and this I now expect with some anxiety.

It is now very much to be desired on my part that they determine on my remaining—the consideration being a very important one—for even supposing that they determine otherwise, that is, that they will not require my services, still circumstances are now such that I cannot leave the country for a considerable time. The sickly season has already arrived on the coast and I could not without too great exposure go to Vera Cruz to embark, so that my return before the month of October may be considered in any event entirely out of the question.

Our troops in the country are in a most unfortunate predicament. Peace being now all but concluded, it becomes necessary immediately on that event taking place to march them forthwith to the coast and embark them, and the time as to their exposure to disease will be the very worst in the whole season. True, there is a condition in the treaty that they may remain within fifty miles of the coast, encamped, until the sickly season be passed, but the commanding officers say that they cannot avail [themselves] of this condition. Many of the men are enlisted during the continuance of the war, and the moment peace be made their term of service expires and no discipline can be exerted over them under such circumstances. More than that, their exposure to sickness would be such, were they to remain, that it is thought that the mortality would be as great as if they take the risk of the *vomito* (yellow fever) by immediate embarkation. It is an unfortunate dilemma, in which the officers are equally involved with the men, for they cannot leave their commands, but must go with them for good or for evil. I feel much for them, for there are those amongst them for whom I feel a regard and respect and in whose welfare I take an interest.

May 27th. I began my letter, you will perceive, two days ago, but having since been considerably engaged with my letters to our New York friends, your letter has remained till the last. This delay, however, gives me the opportunity of giving you an important piece of news, which reached us last night, *viz.*, that peace is finally concluded, the Senate at Querétaro having passed the pending treaty on Thursday night [May 25], and our Commissioners from

1. See Introduction, p. 10.

home having arrived there about the same moment, doubtless exchanged the necessary ratification on the following day.[2] This will be the cause of much rejoicing in the United States, and strange as it may seem, even of more, I suspect, than here, where there are many opposed to the measure and who it is feared will raise the standard of revolt against the existing government the moment our troops are out of the way.

Your ever affectionate,
D. W. C.

2. After some delay, ratifications were exchanged on May 30. The city of Querétaro celebrated the return of peace with merry-making, fireworks, and music. Rives, *The United States and Mexico*, Vol. II, pp. 647–655.

Mexico, June 11th, 1848
My dear Wife, *Sunday afternoon*

I don't know how I can better employ the remaining hours of the day than by holding converse with you. I have generally been in the habit of attending an Episcopal service held in the palace twice on each Sabbath, the services by the Reverend Mr. McCarthy, but on going this morning at the usual hour all was desolate and deserted, and I went away with a heavy heart at the idea of this pleasant meeting being broken up, without any probability of my being able to unite with others in public worship for many months to come.

Very soon after my last letter of 27th May, the Army began to move in detachments for the coast, or rather the vicinity of it, where they wait until vessels are ready to convey them to the United States. The very last division under General Worth is to leave tomorrow morning, and of course it will be a momentous day which shall see the flag of our country, which has for so long a time waved over the palace of this proud City, lowered for the last time to give place to that of the Mexican. What will add not a little to the excitement of the natives and doubtless operate on their superstitious notions is that the day happens to be that of their patron saint, "Nuestra Señora de Guadalupe" (always a great feast day), who will doubtless have the credit of having, by her influence, produced them this peace.[1]

It is surprising to notice how the Americans, aside from those of the Army, have thinned off within the last fortnight, leaving with different divisions of the Army—and tomorrow will leave the City quite bare of them. Everyone who *could* go seems to have determined on that course, so that of those who remain there will indeed be very few. I have described to you in my former letters the Hotel of the "Gran Sociedad," where I have been accustomed to dine, as a place always thronged with Americans—a complete pandemonium. But how changed! As I go daily to my lonely dinner in the restaurant above stairs, I am struck with the entire change which has come over the place. The bars, the gambling rooms, all deserted; and from being one of the most dissipated and uproarious places in the whole City, or in the world (for I have never met anything to compare with it), it has become the most still and quiet.

Our Commissioners, Messrs. Sevier and Clifford, complete their final arrangements, as I understand, with the government today (the Sabbath notwithstanding) by paying over to them the indemnity of $3,000,000, which you know by the treaty they were to receive from our government, and then Mr. Sevier is ready to take his departure for the United States with the troops, leaving Mr. Clifford here, who is to remain till the autumn in the capacity of Minister, or Chargé—I don't know what title he takes to himself.

And now a word as to my own arrangements. I think I told you in my last that I had then no intelligence from our friends, Howland & Aspinwall, as to their intentions regarding my

1. Although December 12 is the traditional date of the festival of the Virgin of Guadalupe, the patron saint of Mexico, the occasion may be celebrated on the 12th of any month. Donald Attwater, *Catholic Encyclopaedic Dictionary* (New York, 1931), p. 234.

stay, which I was anxious for—as settling the matter of remuneration, which originally had been fixed upon—the more so as I should in any event have felt obliged to have remained till autumn from the sickly season on the coast having arrived and the impossibility of embarking for a long time unless in vessels filled with troops, at imminent risk. The letter to you had barely left when I received the wished-for communication desiring me to remain till the last of December—of course, just as I wished. The additional compensation is a liberal one, even more so than the first, seeing that it does not involve any new voyage or journey. That, however, I should have been obliged to make in any case.

I doubt not you will readily acquiesce in this new arrangement, for which you will have been in some measure prepared, as one altogether desirable, taking into view all the circumstances.

One thing more in regard to my stay which you at least will be glad to hear. You know I have had the good fortune to get under Mr. Drusina's roof while his family should remain in the country, but the season being at hand for their return, I anticipated that I should have to look for quarters elsewhere. Yesterday, however, my mind was put at rest by his telling me that I would only have to change my room to another part of the house, and that my remaining would not incommode them at all.

You perceive that I have not yet adopted the journal manner for my letters. I will therefore look back and call to mind some of the incidents which have occurred since my last. I don't know whether I have yet explained to you that this is a period of the year called the rainy season. It continues for four months, commencing with June. It is not at all like our easterly storms, but more like our thunder squalls in summer. The morning will be generally pleasant, but the afternoon and night a succession of thunderstorms, with much thunder and lightning and torrents of rain.[2] This is by way of prelude to an endeavor to give you some proper idea of one of these thunder gusts, and at the same time to describe an adventure I had in one of them.

In the afternoon I had been to call on a Spanish portrait painter, long a resident here, when, leaving to go home, I perceived a heavy cloud threatening immediate rain and quickened my steps, thinking that if I could reach the *portales*, or piazza, all would be well, as I could step into a coffee house and occupy the time until the rain should have passed. I barely succeeded in reaching the place when it began to pour in earnest, and this continued for about an hour without intermission; by this time, the whole city was inundated.

You must understand that the city stands in the midst of a very large and very flat plain, difficult to be drained and which never has been thoroughly so, and thus in the rainy season half the neighboring country has generally been under water, although the City, by a great outlay of money, has been an exception and been kept tolerably dry, yet since the Americans have been in possession the drains have been neglected and there is no proper outlet just now for the water, so that with the heavy rain I am speaking of, for but one hour, the City was literally inundated. Many of the streets had the water standing in them from two to three feet deep. I was at a distance of two squares from home, and in the streets leading there the water stood all the way up to the hubs of the carriage wheels.

The rain finally slackened and hacks began to move about, but it was impossible to get one. Hundreds were under the portales in the same predicament as myself and had a preference, being of the country. Those without clothing (and there are many such or with the merest apology for clothing) waded off home in their nakedness, not much incommoded. Others who

---

2. Cf. Frances Erskine (Inglis) Calderón de la Barca, *Life in Mexico, During a Residence of Two Years in that Country* (London, 1843), pp. 40–41, 141, 170, and 207. There were many later editions of this classic description of Mexico.

had some show of trousers and petticoats (for in these matters there is no distinction of sizes here) rolled and pulled them up, very much above the knees, and they too got off, but those who were blessed with stockings and shoes had to manage differently and everyone to look out for himself. In one direction, by going across the grand plaza, the water might be avoided, and I was given to understand that by taking that route and going round about to the head of the street I lived in, I should stand a good chance to get home. I made the attempt, but at the opposite side of the plaza I found a lake to be forded, but by calling an Indian to my assistance, I got over this onto tierra firma again and proceeded on, but the next crossing I came to I had the same difficulty to encounter, which was overcome as before. I was now at the head of my own street and here it was free of water, but I had not proceeded many yards toward home before I met it again and was forced to seek Indian aid again, by which I eventually reached the house and was landed on the stairway, the court being full of water. This is said to be an extreme case, but I think it likely to recur constantly through the summer unless the drains are opened.

Monday morn: I had written thus far when a call from an American gentleman, a Mr. Shaw, portrait painter from New Orleans, interrupted me and prevented my resuming my pen.[3] This morning at six o'clock the roar of cannon in the plaza aroused me and reminded me at the same time that the final ceremony, already referred to, of lowering our flag, delivering up the palace, and hoisting the Mexican flag, was taking place, accompanied by an exchange of salutes. Desirous of witnessing this last show of our troops in the Capital, I hastened to the plaza, where the sight was truly imposing. The infantry and cavalry, about 3,000 strong, were drawn up in a hollow square occupying the whole place. The artillery, consisting of six beautiful brass pieces, occupied the center; and the Mexicans were in the act of firing their salute of 30 guns (our artillery having fired theirs and given the others the use of their pieces, the Mexicans having none remaining of their own). General Worth and his suite at this moment came into the plaza and very soon after our troops were seen filing out of the plaza, taking the road leading to Vera Cruz.

I had an accidental meeting with Mr. Sevier, of whom I had previously taken leave. He, with his secretary, together with General Worth and his suite, will go on in advance of the troops, escorted by a troop of cavalry, and probably arrive in Vera Cruz in a week or so where a vessel will be in waiting to take Mr. Sevier direct to New Orleans. Whether General Worth will also go by the same opportunity, I am not informed. I have omitted mentioning General [William O.] Butler, who as Commander in Chief, will doubtless also proceed in advance with the escort. . . .[4] *[Last part of letter missing]*

3. What brought Stephen W. Shaw, a portrait painter from New Orleans, to Mexico in 1848 may perhaps be inferred. It was an exciting place, with many famous people, especially military heroes. Prior to this time, he had painted General Persifor F. Smith's portrait for the city of New Orleans for $1,000, and he had also done one of General Taylor.

The next year, 1849, he was attracted to San Francisco, which became his home, and he took part in an exploration of Humboldt Bay in 1850 and other adventurous episodes on the Pacific Coast. He was a prolific painter, with more than 200 portraits to his credit. Benjamin Parke Avery, "Art Beginnings on the Pacific," *Overland Monthly*, July, 1868.

4. William O. Butler (1791–1880), native Kentuckian, soldier, lawyer, and Congressman, had a remarkable career in several fields. He served with distinction under Andrew Jackson in the War of 1812, but resigned from the Army in 1817 to study law. After a term in the local legislature, and two in Congress, he declined to run again. When the Mexican War broke out, President Polk appointed him a major general of volunteers under General Taylor. At the battle of Monterrey, he was second in command. In 1848, recovered from wounds, he joined General Scott in Mexico. Shortly before the treaty was concluded, he succeeded to command of the American Army on Scott's removal from this post. *DAB*. See also M. M. Quaife, ed., *The Diary of James K. Polk during his Presidency, 1845 to 1849* (Chicago, 1910, in 4 vols.), Vol. III, pp. 269–280; Henry, *The Story of the Mexican War*, pp. 382–383.

My very dear Wife, *Mexico, July 1, 1848*

But a week has expired since I wrote you, as usual under cover to our friends, Howland & Aspinwall, but it was a short and hurried letter. I therefore give you this the sooner to make amends, though I have little in the way of news to interest you. We are getting on very quietly here in the City, the police of the national guard continuing very efficient, though on all the public roads there are a great many robbers and no one expects to move from one part of the country to the other without going through the ordeal of being robbed.

I think I have before mentioned to you a revolt (a *pronunciamento*, they call it here) which sometime ago took place at "Aguas Calientes" (Hot Waters—very properly named on this occasion), headed by General Paredes and Padre Jarauta, a celebrated character in these kinds of movements. The ostensible object of this revolution is opposition to the peace party, and I am sorry to say their leaders have got together a rather strong force—that is, strong in view of the weakness of the present government—and have recently strengthened themselves not a little by taking possession of Guanajuato, a town of some importance, as being the center of the richest mining district in Mexico.[1]

Many think that the government will not succeed in putting down this revolution and that before many weeks we shall have the revolutionists here taking possession of the City and government. General Paredes is well known here, but is not popular and is thought a very unfit man to govern the country. Among other things he is fond of his bottle and has heretofore (for it is not his first movement of this kind) shown strong partialities for a monarchical form of government. But this does not matter. It is force that governs here, military force generally, the people at large (the great mass poor miserable Indians) having little to say in the matter. If the people had the least resemblance in character to our people, they would, in the City alone, having a population of 150,000, raise and organize in a week a force sufficient to put down such a faction as this at once. Nor would they wait for it to come here but would look it up wherever it might be.

But how differently these people do things! Here is the legitimate government of the country and in these circumstances, resting as quietly as if nothing was the matter, and I doubt if they will make any serious effort for resistance until Paredes with his 2,000 troops or so is at their gates. True, they have a remnant of their army remaining—I mean the government have—of perhaps also 2,000 men, but they cannot depend on them, and although they are sent against Paredes headed by some of their best officers, those most to be relied on, yet they are as likely to go over to the other side, indeed more like so, than otherwise. I refer to the men and subordinate officers as likely to go over, not the general officers. Will you believe that they have in the country about 10,000 officers to about 2,000 or 3,000 rank and file?—so strangely do they manage their affairs, these Mexicans.

Although the city has formed within a month or two past a very efficient body of troops termed a national guard of about 4,000 men, yet the object of this has been especially the protection of the City, a police to keep order, and a very good effect it has had; everything has been perfectly quiet since the Americans left; but it was never calculated that these troops would be called to do the duty of the regular army, nor is it probable that if Paredes comes here, they will turn out to oppose him. Probably he will enter and take possession without

1. In the troubled political situation after departure of the American troops, this revolution in Aguas Calientes was one of the more serious. The movement had the support of the governor of the state, Don J. Miguel Cosío, and the guerrilla leader, Padre Cenobio Jarauta, as well as of General Mariano Paredes, but it collapsed. Paredes was defeated and fled to Europe, while the bandit, Jarauta, who plundered friend and foe alike, was caught and shot. Bancroft, *Mexico*, Vol. V, pp. 548–550; Niceto de Zamacois, *Historia de Mejico* (Barcelona and Mexico, 1877–1882), Vol. XIII, p. 319 *et seq.*

opposition; no doubt of this, I should say, if the troops sent against him all go over to his party.

There is one good thing about Paredes, I am told: that he looks sharply to the security and safety of the public roads and will, no doubt, if he carries his point of possessing himself of the country, put down with a strong arm the numerous bands of robbers by which they are infested—and so far he shall have my hearty concurrence.

Paredes, I must tell you, is an acquaintance of Mr. Drusina's, and so much of one, too, that he has formerly been invited to his dinner table, one of a large number of guests, and since the return of the family to town Mrs. Drusina has called on Mrs. Paredes, who they represent to be a superior woman. It is always politic, you know, to have friends at court, particularly in a country like this, where the old adage of "kissing goes by favor" is particularly applicable. If you meet with alarming accounts in the newspapers of matters and things in this quarter (I don't know that you will, but nothing is more likely, seeing the state of the country and the kind of people), don't be alarmed on my account if there should be serious troubles. I shall keep close till they get quiet, having no occasion whatever to go abroad. Besides, the houses are very strong and secure, almost castles as to strength.

I have been a little indisposed two or three times since I have been here which I attribute mainly to eating fruit freely and shall now be more on my guard. Indeed, prudence in eating here is thought to be very necessary, particularly for such as are not accustomed to the climate and who do not take much exercise. The climate is peculiar, if the extreme rarity of the atmosphere alone be considered. Consider that we are 7,000 or 8,000 feet above the level of the sea. The least extra exertion, particularly going up a flight of steps quickly, causes you to breathe with difficulty; even turning in bed causes something of this feeling, which I also remember formerly to have experienced in South America on some of the great heights there....

With much love to the dear children, your father and mother, and remembrances to other friends, *Affectionately and faithfully yours,*
D. W. Coit

My very dear Wife,   *City of Mexico, July 7th, 1848*
Although I have written you very recently (on the 24 June), yet as I am writing brother Joshua[1] by the mail of this evening I will not lose so good an opportunity of having a few moments intercourse with you. I regret that I have none of your favors to acknowledge, the last one from you being now nearly two months old, 11th May. One from brother J. dated 31 May I received yesterday. He says, "There are no incidents of interest in our family, unless I mention that Mrs. L. L. Howland returned a few days since from the south in much the same state of health in which she left and too feeble to see her friends." This is melancholy news and I fear we are soon to have another breach in our family circle.

As Howland & Aspinwall forwarded this letter of brother J.'s, I take it for granted, if they had had another of yours, it would have accompanied it. . . .

---

1. Joshua, Daniel's younger brother (born August 25, 1800), was the youngest of the six children of Daniel Lathrop Coit and Lydia Lathrop Coit. He graduated from Yale in 1819, studied law, and practiced for many years in New York City. He never married. Chapman, *The Coit Family*, pp. 54–58. Joshua wrote a brief "Sketch" of Daniel which was printed as a part of the latter's *Autobiography*, pp. 57–63.

Daniel, the oldest child in the Coit family, was born November 24, 1787; then came Lydia, b. August 25, 1789; she married Professor James L. Kingsley; Henry H., b. June 17, 1791, who married Mary Breed; Maria, b. June 13, 1793, who married Peletiah Perit of New York; Eliza, b. August 23, 1796; she married Wm. C. Gilman of Norwich, often referred to in the letters as Brother Gilman. And then Joshua. Chapman, *loc. cit.*

The city continues in a perfectly quiet state, though it may not be always so. I have mentioned to you the revolt by General Paredes. By the last accounts from Guanajuato (pronounce the *j* as if it where *wh—Guanawhato*), the government troops were close upon him and an action likely to take place. On this the fate of the country turns. If the government troops are true, they ought to come off victorious, for they are superior in numbers and probably in discipline. We look with great anxiety to the result and my next will probably communicate it to you.

Were it not for books and the pencil, my time would hang very heavily on my hands, as you will believe when I tell you that my proper business does not occupy a tithe of it, and that I frequently pass twenty hours out of the twenty-four in my bedroom.

In relation to the Havana business, don't open your lips about it to anyone. At present it is [nothing] more than an idea of my own—nor do I know [how] Edward may receive the proposition which it [Ms torn] I may make him in a few weeks.

I, for the most part, dine at the old place which I heretofore mentioned to you, restaurants in the Gran Sociedad, though sometimes I have an invitation to stop at home and dine with Mr. Drusina. They live first rate, as Jones would say. The dinner is something after this order: Mr. and Mrs. D.—he sitting at the head of the table and serving, while she sits next on his left hand—then Miss . There are besides, on ordinary occasions, a couple of the younger children and one of the clerks. . . .

With much love to the darlings, and believe me as ever *Yours affectionately*,
D. W. Coit

My dear Wife,   City of Mexico, July 22d, 1848

Having disposed of the laborious part of my correspondence for the present post, I turn with pleasure to the agreeable part of it, that of holding a little intercourse with you, and first to thank you for your very gratifying letters of 27th May and 27th June, both of which came by one post. . . .

And now before anything else I must hasten to tell you of the great event here. Yesterday we received the most important and at the same time unlooked for intelligence: that General Bustamante, commanding the government troops, has been completely successful in a general attack upon the revolutionists under General Paredes at Guanajuato, who were repulsed at all points and the famous Padre Jarauta taken prisoner. Paredes himself, with the troops which remained to him, were surrounded by much superior forces, and there appeared no doubt that they must either surrender at discretion or at least be dispersed, without the least probability of being able to continue their revolutionary enterprise.

The general opinion here is that Paredes will clear out and endeavor to save himself by flight as best he may, leaving his troops to take care of themselves, well knowing that if he falls into the hands of the victors his life is forfeited and that he, as a very unpopular disturber of the peace and a rebel, cannot count on clemency.

What may bring his own perilous situation home to him the more is the tragic end of his companion, the Padre, who was shot within two or three hours after he became prisoner. His fate (though a brave man) excites little commiseration even among this people, for he was a dangerous, bloodthirsty disorganizer, and all connected with our Army will rejoice at his end, for he was very daring and successful in his warfare with them, many an American having fallen by his hand in his various encounters with them between this City and Vera Cruz.

Now, will you believe that the newspapers here, referring to his speedy execution, speak of his confession and dying like a "true Christian." . . . I cannot express to you how much I am delighted with this news, the more acceptable as little expected. We were anticipating nothing short of the overthrow of the legitimate government, which might have been attended with much bloodshed, anarchy, and confusion, and the consequent interruption of the mining operations and all commercial transactions. Having large quantities of goods under my direction belonging to our friends Howland & Aspinwall, and also debts due them, I felt much anxiety and solicitude at the alarming state of things, from which I am in a great measure relieved, and now think there is a fair prospect that I may bring their affairs under my charge to a satisfactory conclusion and leave the country before such another conjuncture may arrive, and you will, I know, rejoice with me in this prospect. . . .

Much love to all who inquire after me, and believe me as ever faithfully and affectionately yours,

D. W. Coit

My dear Wife, *City of Mexico, Sunday, July 23rd, 1848*

I have taken pen in hand at length with the resolution to redeem the promise I half made you sometime ago of keeping a daily note of occurrences here—a journal, if you please to call it so.

My own life is certainly just now very monotonous, being passed for the most part in my room, except that I go abroad occasionally for an hour or two for exercise and sometimes to take a sketch. My evenings, however, are not infrequently passed at an American house, that of Messrs. Hargous & Vos, where I meet an intelligent and agreeable circle and generally pick up the news of the day. While our Army was here, this evening party was large, composed of many of the superior officers, some of whom are very well-bred, interesting men. Of those more particularly distinguished and with many of whom I became to a considerable degree intimate, I wish to retain a list, as otherwise some of their names will pass out of my memory, and I will give it here.

At the head of this note I think I should place General Percifor F. Smith of New Orleans, a gentleman distinguished as an officer as well for his sound judgment and discretion as for his bravery, of which he gave many proofs during the war, while in point of education and moral character he had few if any superiors; General Scott, General Worth, General [Robert] Patterson, Major Stewart of the Commissary Department, Captain [Charles] Naylor, a gentleman of superior attainments, a writer and formerly member of Congress from Philadelphia; Captain [Francis?] Taylor of the Artillery (who I invariably met at the Sabbath services at the palaces), Captains [Arthur B.] Lansing, Merkle (aide of General Patterson), Henry, and [Robert E.] Lee, this last being of the Engineers and certainly one of the superior men of the Army—a topographical map he has made of the country for a circuit of some miles about the City is one of the most minute and beautifully executed things as a work of art that I have ever seen; it was intended for our government and will undoubtedly be published.

But to return to the evening meeting at Mr. Hargous'. It is now reduced to a very small number of private gentlemen, hardly of less interest to me than ever, being composed of men who have passed a greater part of their lives in the country, have been through the numerous revolutions which have taken place, been acquainted with Santa Anna and all the prominent men of his time, understand well their characters and the duplicity, selfishness, and rapacity of their acts, by which this unhappy country has been for a long series of years worse governed and more plundered and abused than any other that ever existed, until with all her natural advantages and internal wealth, which are unbounded, she is reduced to the last extremity, and really unable to govern herself.

Among the gentlemen I refer to is a Mr. Miller, an Englishman, who has been upwards of twenty years in different parts of the country and many years engaged in business in this City. He is well educated and intelligent and has a most intimate knowledge of all passing events during that period. Then Mr. du Coin, also a merchant here for some twenty years; and the Messrs. Hargous & Vos have been here little short of that time and their mercantile operations have been very great. They have made a great deal of money, some hundreds of thousands, it is said, by the advantages derived from the war, owing to their being the oldest and most substantial American house and having had the preference in contracts and exchange negotiations through intimacy with the Commissary officers and others. True, *this* government is owing them very large sums of money, but this they now expect to get very shortly reimbursed through our government by the terms of the treaty.[1]

At the time of the declaration of war, Mr. Hargous conducted the branch of the house at Vera Cruz. He became suspected by the government, was seized, and after a sort of trial ordered to leave the country. He returned when our Army took possession of Vera Cruz, volunteered as aide to General Worth, which of course gave him a no less active than exposed situation in some of the most important battles of the war. He has a fund of anecdotes and information on all these interesting topics. Mr. Hargous, though at present here (formerly a permanent resident, being married to a Mexican lady), makes New York his home, where he has resided for the last six or seven years. His wife is the sister of a Señora Trigaros, a distinguished lady, her husband having formerly been one of Santa Anna's ministers (no great recommendation, you will say) and superior to the mass of his countrymen. He, too, makes occasionally a pleasant addition to our circle.

But I have wandered entirely from the object I had in view when I took my pen, which was to give you some account of a stroll I took this morning, during which I was led to notice some of the peculiarities of this people as connected with the religious observances, which may serve to afford you a moment's gratification. This, to me, is one of the principal objects of interest here. I never weary of entering the multitude of rich churches, with which this City abounds,

---

1. The Hargous brothers carried on business under the name of Hargous & Co. at 33 South Street, New York. The firm is listed in the city's directories from 1842 to 1873. Peter A. Hargous, the president, was first given in 1835 at 10 Old Slip, and at 33 South Street beginning in 1838. On his death in 1864, an obituary notice in the New York *Evening Post* states that he was an outstanding shipping and commission merchant. He was born in Philadelphia, of French descent.

Louis Eugene Hargous first appeared in the New York directory in 1842 as "Mexican consul," stationed in Mexico City, and then simply as "consul," 33 South Street, through 1846. From 1847 on, his occupation is given as commission merchant. He was in Mexico City during 1848, representing the company in its very extensive operations with the American government for supplying the troops. During the war, as the Mexicans pursued a scorched-earth policy in the path of the invading forces, the American Subsistence and Quartermaster's departments were hampered by lack of funds. In July, 1847, the Commissary owed more than $200,000, and the troops' pay was more than four months in arrears. Borrowing money was most difficult, and required a substantial premium. Under these circumstances, the firm of Hargous & Co. was able to render important aid. "Without the services of Louis S. Hargous, an American merchant at Vera Cruz who acted as General Scott's financial agent," says one writer, "the Army would have been even worse off for funds." At Vera Cruz, his firm took $90,000 of the Quartermaster's drafts, "when there were no funds there to redeem them, and at Puebla he was the only resource of both the Quartermaster's and Subsistence departments after the funds borrowed from the Pay Department had been exhausted." Erna Risch, *Quartermaster Support of the Army; a History of the Corps, 1775–1939* (Washington, 1962), pp. 294–295.

Coit mentions also a Stanislaus Hargous, who had charge of the office in Vera Cruz. He is not listed in the New York City directories. Coit often went to the home of Louis E. Hargous in Mexico City for a social hour. See his letter of August 12, 1848; and also Paul N. Garber, *The Gadsden Treaty* (Philadelphia, 1923), p. 45.

and noticing their magnitude, their architecture, and the rich gilding and ornament with which their interior abounds and to which much additional effect is given by the gorgeous imposing ceremonies, the form of worship, as well as the picturesque exteriors and groups of the monks and worshipers.

Taking a different route this morning from my accustomed one to the grand "plaza" and cathedral, I observed the balconies and windows of the street I was in, decorated with pictures, draperies, and such like ornament, indicating that some Catholic ceremony was coming off in the church just by. I accordingly entered, and making my way through the kneeling crowd (the utmost liberty of locomotion being permitted to all in going in and out and where they please, even during the services, if it be done with decorum), approached the grand altar and took a seat in one of a row of rather inviting seats of many armchairs with a very old and threadbare Brussels carpet spread out before them.

On making my observations, I came to the conclusion that I had not come at the proper moment for the ceremonies intended, which were indicated by the extra decoration of the altars to the Virgin and our Savior, with draperies and gold fringes, and the greatest profusion of gay flowers in masses and the invariable accompaniment of lighted wax candles. But still the floor was covered with numerous worshipers at their prayers, and here one is always struck with (what we consider) this incongruity of persons and things.

You see the well-attired formal group of women and children kneeling side by side with the most disgusting, filthy beggar, with hardly rags to cover his nakedness; or by the Indian, no less repulsive in appearance, with his market basket or pack by his side; or it may be the idle, vagrant *lépero*[2] who only lives by plunder with an occasional murder when it becomes necessary and who, notwithstanding, may be very punctual and apparently devout in attention to his religious duties—the Mass, daily prayers to the Virgin or some saint, and other like mummery. Just behind me were seated four musicians, three with guitars and one with flute, playing the most fantastic airs that can be imagined and carrying them through innumerable variations. An old Mexican near me wishing, as it appeared to me, something of his own choice beckoned one of the players to him and whispered something to him, whereon, resuming his place, something very like an Italian air was commenced and kept up with much spirit.

Now the hour has come for sending my letters to the post. I did intend to have sent you two or three sheets, but have not had time to prepare them. I wished to have said something about a revolution we came near having here in the City, but which was discovered and put down in time and we are now all quiet again. Particulars you will hear in my next. I wrote you fully a day or two since, with an enclosure for Jones,[3] which I hope you received.

Much love to all, and believe me as ever truly and affectionately, your husband, *D.W.C.*

2. By this colloquial term, Coit meant the dregs of society, cutthroats and the like.
3. Jones was Coit's hired hand, who managed the garden for Mrs. Coit during her husband's long absence.

My very dear Wife, *City of Mexico, August 12th, 1848*

... In my letter already referred to of the 23d ult., I mentioned the signal success which the government troops had had in defeating the insurgents under General Paredes and Padre Jarauta, the latter of whom, having been taken prisoner, was immediately executed.[1] General Paredes made his escape, and his army dispersed, except a considerable number taken prisoners, some of whom, report says, were shot. I, at the same time, expressed a strong conviction that this revolution having been so effectually put down, the country would now remain, for a considerable time at least, quiet under the legitimate government which exists, but the results since have shown my ignorance of political matters here and how little correct opinion can be formed of the times to come.[2]

At the very moment I was writing, a new pronunciamiento, with different views from the other, was just on the point of exploding here in our midst in the City. To give you the particulars of this in the order of their occurrence I must go back to my journal, commencing on the 23d July. In the evening I called at the house of the Messrs. Hargous. These gentlemen (three brothers) have been for many years engaged in the trade with this country, two of them residing in New York, one in Vera Cruz, and a partner, Mr. Vos, managing the business here. At present one of the New York partners, Louis, together with the Vera Cruz partner, Stanislaus, were here, having large claims against the Mexican government which, through means of the treaty, they now expect to recover. Their position as the oldest and most influential American house in Mexico, at the time hostilities commenced, have rendered them very prominent, and besides have thrown commercial advantages in their way in the negotiation of large amounts of bills, in contracts, etc., by which they are believed to have realized a large fortune.[3]

I have in my former letter mentioned that at this house of the Messrs. Hargous there was regularly every evening a large assemblage of the leading and most distinguished officers of the Army. Here was always a capital cup of black tea, a very cordial meeting, and frequently most interesting conversation on the various interesting topics of the war, and that of the treaty of peace, which was for several months pending. On this recent evening referred to, I had not been long seated before Mr. Clifford, our Minister, came in. He was in a great bustle for the theater, his private box was at our service, and his carriage at the door. Mr. Hargous must go and I, too, must go. "What!" exclaimed an American gentleman sitting near, playing at cards, "Do you expect *Mr. Coit* to go to the *theater* on Sunday evening?" I simply replied, "Mr. Coit endeavors to be consistent and to do here nothing that he would not do at home." In that Mr. Clifford seemed to feel my remark, and how could it be otherwise? A gentleman who has lived all his life in Maine until within a short time, when his talent as a lawyer and at the same time as a warm politician brought him into notice and procured him a post in the cabinet at Washington as Attorney General. I say he seemed to feel it, for he sheltered himself behind the old adage that "when he was in Rome he must do as the Romans did."

In the course of conversation, I found to my regret that the gentlemen of experience here did not agree with me as to the probabilities of peace and quiet now that Paredes was put down. They think that this country, and even the City here, is full of material ripe for revolution. There exists an immense army of officers who are not paid in time of peace and whom nothing short of this can satisfy, and the desire is, looking exclusively to their own interest, to have Santa Anna back again. No doubt he has many friends here who keep him well advised of all that is going on and who are watching the opportunity to create disturbance and throw obstacles in the way of the existing government with the view to pave the way for his return.

1. Bancroft, *History of Mexico*, Vol. V, pp. 548–550.
2. This troubled period of Mexican history is discussed at length by Bancroft in *ibid.*, Vol. V, pp. 82–236.
3. See letter of July 23, 1848.

24th. I did not go abroad till my dinner hour, three o'clock, occupying the morning with reading and writing, when, having taken my solitary meal at the Gran Sociedad, I looked in at Mr. Hargous' where, to my astonishment, I heard that the past night we had been on the very brink of another revolution which had come to the knowledge of the government only just in time to prevent it. It must be premised that they have in their pay a body of American soldiers, deserters, who they retained about them at Querétaro and who, after our Army left, were brought here. These deserters, a disorganized, reckless body of men, have been petted and made much of, far better paid, too, than the Mexican troops. At their head was the notorious Captain Riley, who deserted from our ranks early in the war, before the commencement of hostilities, and fought in many battles against us. He was finally, with many other deserters, taken at Chapultepec, tried, condemned, branded on the cheek (he could not, under the circumstances, be executed), and expelled from the Army.[4]

This Captain Riley has been promoted in the Mexican service to the rank of colonel and commanded these renegade Americans, about 200 in number, under the name of the San Patricio division. Well, this body of men, joined to others disaffected, were to surprise the heads of government, make them prisoners, attack the different quarters of the national guards and other defenses of the City, and make themselves masters of it, which could of course only have been effected with much bloodshed. Fortunately, as I have said, the government discovered the plot in time, immediately seized upon Riley and other prominent leaders, and put them in close and solitary confinement, there to await their trial. Today further precautionary measures have been taken by sending the rank and file of these dangerous and refractory men to Guadalupe, a village at a league's distance from the city, where it is thought they cannot make further trouble and will be quiet.

25th. Evening. Fresh troubles have burst upon us this afternoon. The San Patricio troops, which for security were sent to Guadalupe yesterday, have made a pronunciamiento, having been joined, it is said, by some of the disaffected Mexican officers from the City. The government has sent a force of two or three hundred men of the national guard, with three pieces of artillery, against them, but doubts are entertained of their being able to subdue them. On the contrary, it is feared that they may be beaten and lose their cannon, which would give much additional strength to the revolt. All must remain this night in suspense and anxiety. The national guards are under arms; large patrols, one of which I hear just passing under my window, are being marched through the streets.

Another awkward circumstance has occurred, unfortunately, at this time, to add to the embarrassment of the government. A notorious guerrillero, robber, and murderer by the name of Roque Miranda was lately surprised and taken by a party of the national guards. He was tried and condemned to death on the charge of murder, under the clearest proof of his guilt. The law requires, however, a review of the sentence by a second and higher tribunal, and here, to the astonishment and indignation of everyone, the sentence has been revoked or modified to ten years' imprisonment (which, from the many facilities of escape, is considered next

---

4. This was Sergeant John Riley, or Reilly, or O'Reily, Company K, Fifth United States Infantry, later a lieutenant. He had formerly been a sergeant in the 66th Regiment of the British Army, stationed in Canada, from which he had also deserted. In May, 1846, before the declaration of war, while serving under General Taylor in Texas, he crossed the Río Grande into Mexico on the pretext of going to mass, deserted the U.S. forces, and was given a commission as lieutenant by the Mexicans. Joined by other renegades, he formed the "San Patricio Battalion." He has been described as energetic, fearless, daring, and a good leader. His group fought with great bravery against General Scott's forces, especially at Churubusco.

The total number of deserters during the war is generally given as between 7,000 and 9,000. See Sister Blanche Marie McEniry, *American Catholics in the War with Mexico* (Washington, 1937), pp. 73–95; and Edward S. Wallace, "Deserters in the Mexican War," *Hispanic American Historical Review*, Vol. XV (1935), pp. 374–383.

to a pardon), and this result has been effected, it is said, by bribery of the judges. From the circumstance of the man's having some hundreds of doubloons at his command and the well understood venality of all public officers in the country, not excepting those holding the highest and most important trusts, the theory seems altogether probable. The national guard are so indignant at this that they threaten to resign, at least such part of them as are most to be relied on, and hence another difficulty.

26th. The threatening appearances of yesterday have passed off much better than was apprehended. The San Patricio division at Guadalupe, finding a considerable force with artillery coming against them and being without their leader, separated, a part going off into the interior and the remainder making no resistance, so that they were at once made prisoners. They stated that they had no desire to revolt against the government, but that they were dissatisfied at Riley's being taken and imprisoned, and such like excuses. It appears now most fortunate that Riley's treason and treachery to the government was discovered as it was, for it is ascertained that the plan was to have assassinated President Herrera and the ministers, and then to have possessed himself by force of the City.

I called on Mr. Clifford and we talked these occurrences over. He thinks that the government, with whom he has had an interview this morning, having now got at the bottom of the conspiracy and taken their precautions, will be able to prevent any further outbreak. There are, however, known to be here not a few designing men, friends to Santa Anna, who, too great cowards to act themselves, are constantly seeking to instigate any ill-disposed or mischievous spirits like Riley to make a row, and if possible overthrow the government when their favorite may have an opportunity to return and they be enabled to share in the plunders of the public purse, which is sure to follow such an event. The present government is too honest for them. They are moderate, well-intentioned men, particularly Herrera, disposed as far as possible to correct the gross abuses under which the country has so long suffered during the administration of Santa Anna and others as unprincipled as he, and hence the opposition they meet with. . . .

Affectionately,
D. W. C.

My very dear Wife,   *City of Mexico, August 21st, 1848*

A most unexpected opportunity presents itself of writing to you, which I embrace the more gladly as we are deprived of any sure conveyance since our troops left, oftener than once a month, as my last letter will have explained to you. Lieutenant Beals of the Navy arrived here express from San Blas yesterday on his way to the United States as bearer of important dispatches from Commodore Jones to our government.[1] These dispatches doubtless have reference to the highly important discoveries of gold mines of the most extensive and richest description in California.

The accounts which this gentleman brings in regard to these discoveries are truly marvelous and one would think if they are in any considerable degree to be credited that we may soon

---

1. This was Lieutenant Edward F. Beale of the United States Navy (Coit's spelling is phonetic), who had come to California in 1846. On this trip he carried dispatches from Thomas O. Larkin to Secretary of State Buchanan and from Commodore Jones to the Secretary of the Navy. Beale traveled by forced marches. The news he brought was later embodied in President Polk's message to Congress on December 5, which made the discovery of gold official. See Bancroft, *History of California*, Vol. VI, ch. 7; Stephen Bonsal, *Edward Fitzgerald Beale, A Pioneer in the Path of Empire* (New York, 1912), pp. 42–63; and Ralph P. Bieber, *Southern Trails to California in 1849* (Glendale, 1937), p. 22.

View from Drusina's Hacienda, San Antonio, 1848

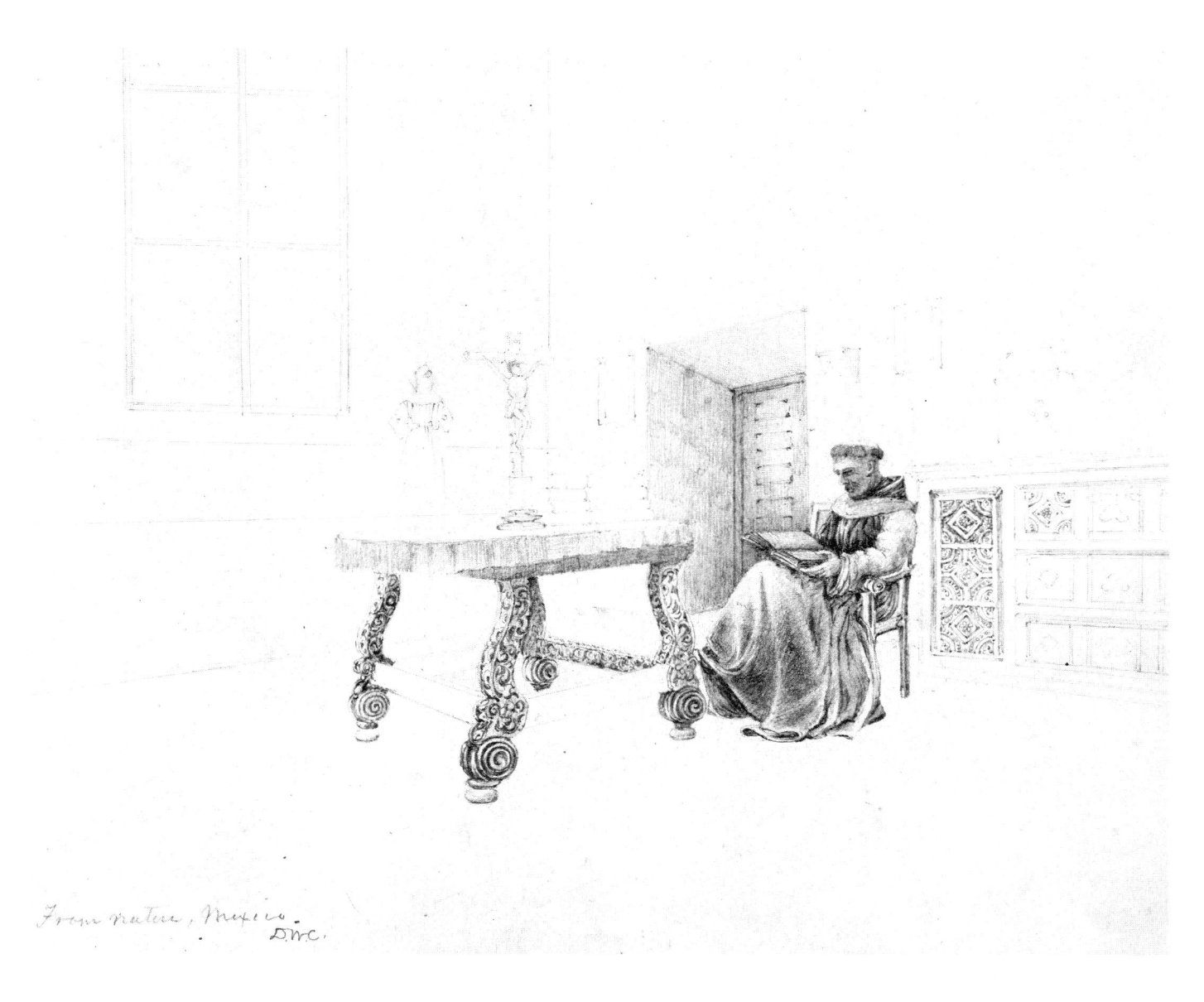

PRIEST READING IN CONVENT OF SAN FRANCISCO, MEXICO CITY, 1848

LOAFERS EATING IN MARKET PLACE, MEXICO CITY, 1848

TWO SKETCHES: BURRO AND CHARRO ON PONY, 1848

have gold in such abundance as to be overstocked with it. These mines are principally or wholly on the American fork or branch of the Sacramento, which empties into the Pacific at the Bay of San Francisco. The gold is of that description called by the Mexicans "Oro placel," or gold from sand.[2] It is in small flat particles and is obtained by washing the sand or soil of the bed of the river, which is found to be so rich in them that a common laboring man in a very rude manner of working readily obtains an ounce of pure gold per day, and such as have greater facilities, twice as much.

The extent of the mine is very great. It is found to exceed a hundred miles in length (they are actually working it at eighty miles apart) and it is free for the present to everybody, and the whole operation of acquiring wealth so very simple that a child, it may be said, has the power of coining gold, it is not surprising that every soul in the country capable of the least exertion should be engaged in it, and so it would seem they are. Every other occupation is deserted for this. Whole villages are depopulated, and even the government troops are said to have deserted, in mass, to become miners.[3]

One great difficulty in this rush of the whole population to a new business, entirely unforeseen, is that they have not tools for working; a pickaxe and a shovel or a spade are indispensable, and so great is the scarcity of them that two or three ounces of gold, or thirty or forty dollars, is paid for such an implement. These extraordinary prices for articles of the first necessity, in their operations in California, remind one of similar occurrences at former periods in working the mines of this country, where steel has been known to be so scarce, and at the same time so indispensable, that it has been paid for in its own weight of silver—the steel put in one side of the balance and the "plata piña" in the other.[4]

In a particular case, before the independence of the country, iron being at a very low price, a merchant here bought on speculation a very large quantity, many tons weight, at $7 per hundredweight. He at first determined not to sell until it should have doubled its value, but the revolution coming on, and supplies from abroad being cut off, and this being an article of indispensable necessity, it rose to $60 per cwt., at which the entire parcel was sold, thus giving its proprietor a large fortune.

But to return to California. As all this golden region is the property of our government, it is altogether probable that they will immediately take measures for its preservation to the country, and this I anticipate to be an undertaking of no very easy performance. A considerable army would hardly be sufficient for the purpose. The very character of the mine is such— a soil saturated with gold for upwards of a hundred miles in extent—as to render it almost an impossibility to protect it effectually from depredation, particularly if we consider the population already in possession, and feeling a sort of right in the property; one, besides, not overscrupulous as to the means, and resolved each for himself to possess a share, right or wrong.

Lieutenant Beale found the road between San Blas and this City much infested by robbers, and narrowly escaped being plundered, if nothing more. Before arriving at Guadalajara, learning that two Mexican officers had been murdered on the road and a company of government troops sent forward to act against the robbers, he hastened his speed to overtake them for his protection, when he came to a place which showed evidently that a sanguinary conflict had very recently taken place there. The ground was covered with blood, with bits of clothing scattered about. Fortunately the combatants had retired, but he learned afterwards that the

2. Or more commonly, *placer*, meaning sand bank.
3. In addition to Bancroft's *History of California*, see such books as John W. Caughey, ed., *Rushing for Gold* (Berkeley and Los Angeles, 1949); also his *Gold is the Cornerstone* (Berkeley an Los Angeles, 1948); and Rodman, W. Paul, *California Gold* (Cambridge, 1947).
4. "Plata piña," *i.e.*, virgin silver treated with mercury.

robbers were in such force that they had attacked the troops and completely defeated them, killing ten of their number and wounding many more. A day or two after this he was menaced by three robbers, who were deterred by his resolute manner from doing him any injury, and again escaped. Few men could perform the journey he has just done in the same period of time; he told me (traveling post) that he rode 350 miles in three days and a half—never getting sleep other than in the intervals required for changing horses (from 15 to 20 minutes at a time), during which he threw himself on the ground wherever it might be (often in the mud) and slept soundly. He leaves here again in an hour or two and expects to reach Vera Cruz (270 miles) in two days, also on horseback.[5]

The various revolutions which have been attempted, both here and in other parts of the country, since our troops took their departure have, one and all, failed, and we are at present in quiet, though how long we are to remain so it is exceedingly difficult to foretell. The decision shown by the government in making examples of some of the revolutionists, both in Guanajuato and Mazatlán, in both of which places several officers implicated were promptly shot, has evidently had the effect of intimidating the disaffected and keeping them quiet. . . .

With much love to all our friends and particularly to my darlings, I remain, etc., affectionately and faithfully yours,

D. W. C.

5. The unsafe condition of the roads and the constant danger to which travelers were exposed is well described by Madame Calderón de la Barca, who wrote of her experiences in Mexico from 1839 to 1842. See her *Life in Mexico, op. cit., passim.*

My very dear Wife,   *City of Mexico, October 12th, 1848*

The time approaches for the monthly departure of the packet from Vera Cruz and I therefore seasonably take pen in hand that you may not at the last moment "be put off with a few lines," as you term it. I confess I had not supposed that my frequent and generally lengthy communications had rendered me liable to what, if I took it literally, might be considered an imputation of neglect. I know you did not mean this, so I will not be offended, and we will have, at any rate this time, a good long chat together.

I must begin by telling you that I have been for a very long period of time deprived of any of your letters or of any tidings from you whatever, your last being under date 22d July. I do not accuse you of neglect in writing, not doubting that your usual course of two letters in the month has been persevered in, and consequently that not a few of your letters are now on the way to me. The difficulty has been in a most provoking irregularity in the communications between New Orleans and Vera Cruz. So long ago as when our troops left the country, I anticipated there would be this difficulty and I therefore urged it upon Howland & Aspinwall that they should avail themselves, to a certain extent at least, of the route via Havana for their letters. If they had done so, I should not only have had *their* letters for August and September, of which I am also deprived, but yours likewise.

As to myself, my life is one of so much uniformity, I might say monotony, that a few lines will explain it as faithfully as a volume could do. Did I not ever give you the routine of a day? I think so, and if I did I cannot add much to it now.

The room I have at Mr. Drusina's suits me even better than the first I had, principally from being quite retired, that is, separated from the other apartments so that I am not at all in the way; indeed, I do not see the family or they me except in going out or into the house. It is in what is called the *entre sol*, or story between the ground floor (entirely occupied by store, offices, and counting room), and the third story, which is where the family reside. My room is large and airy, being about 30 feet in length by 20 in breadth, with two windows looking out on the street. It is plainly furnished, as I prefer; the stone, or large coarse tile floor, covered with oil cloth; a brass bedstead-sofa, covered with yellow worsted damask; and plain old mahogany chairs, table, and washstand. There may be seen at present (but this is only temporary) two or three parcels of large pictures leaning against the walls, with a large roll of the same in the corner, but of these anon. As to my intercourse with the family, it is extremely limited. Madam is reserved, not a very approachable person, particularly by one sensible of not speaking the language very well, and I do not visit unless occasionally at dinner, by particular invitation.

Perhaps I may as well give you here some attempt at description of the family, as you ask it. Mr. Drusina is a German by birth, though for some time a resident in England in early life; about 46 or 48 years of age, of medium size, about my height, light complexion with rather small bluish eyes (wears glasses), and small features, with an abundance of light-brown hair, curling just sufficiently to make it becoming; his manners are easy and gentlemanly, with enough of enthusiasm, which shows itself in his countenance by a peculiar animation, and slightly nervous affection when much engaged in any important conversation. He speaks English, French, German, and Spanish with equal correctness and is one of the most intelligent, well-bred, gentlemanly men I have met there.

Mrs. Drusina, in appearance and in disposition, is the entire opposite of her husband. She is of one of the prominent families of Mexico. I should judge about ten years younger than he, rather above the ordinary height, quite thin, with black hair and large prominent black eyes, complexion dark and sallow, with but little animation or conversation. I have been informed that she was at one time affected by religious gloom, even to temporary derangement. She dresses a good deal, and having an extensive family connection, as well as acquaintance, with carriages and coachman and footman at her beck, she is abroad almost every day. They have six children, the eldest a young lady of about fifteen, now just entering society. There are then two boys, one about eleven and the other two or three years younger, the remainder (the youngest about a year old) girls. The children all resemble the father much more than the mother, having his light complexion and rather small features; they appear perfectly well-bred and well-managed, remarkably so for this country. A simple intimation of a wish is sufficient to command their instant obedience. The boys when they come into the presence of their father approach him with the greatest gentleness and affection and kiss his hand—indeed, more perfectly respectful children in their deportment to their parents I have never seen.

As to myself and my daily occupations, I generally rise about seven, sometimes an hour earlier, which gives a little time for reading or writing before breakfast, which is regularly brought to my room at eight o'clock and always consists of the same thing—tea, black but indifferent, two boiled eggs and a cake of bread. I was a long time without butter, but Mrs. Kaufman, wife of the gentleman before mentioned to you as the confidential clerk of the house, offered to procure me some and through her kindness a half pound of fresh butter has been sent me every Saturday, which carries me through the week, at the cost of 50¢ or $1 per lb.—and what you would call very poor, too.

After breakfast I engage in any writing or business I may have in hand. If there is nothing urgent of this kind, I take my drawing board and pencil, and having some object previously selected, perpetrate a sketch. In doing this I have frequently been led to ask permission to enter private houses or courts or perhaps a church or convent, and have only in one or two instances been refused Indeed, I have generally met with civility and even attention. At the convent of San Francisco, I have made friends with the sacristan and two or three of the padres, who have even sat for me to sketch them, and they have also taken me to their rooms, and to the more secret and secluded parts of the interior, furnishing me with table and chair and permitting me to sketch where I pleased. I have consequently made no less than four sketches in different parts of this immense establishment, one of the exterior court surrounded by the picturesque buildings, one of an interior square surrounded by colonnades, another of the sacristan, with a friar reading, and another of the *cementerio*, or burying place, formerly a court, planted with trees and shrubbery peculiar to the climate, and in the time of the Spaniards kept in beautiful order but now little better than a ruin—none the worse, however, for a picture.

The morning being passed in some such manner as I have described, about three o'clock I go to my restaurateur, where I get a very simple—I cannot say a very good—dinner, but such as it is it answers the purpose: a thin pottage or soup, a small beefsteak or mutton chop or wing of fowl or duck. This would be very well if the meats and poultry were good of their kind, but they are in such places almost invariably poor and insipid, and sometimes it requires a very good appetite to get through them.

Dinner over, I generally stop in at the café on the ground floor of the same building (formerly the pandemonium I before described to you, but now a quiet, decent resort). Here I read the newspaper of the day, get a very good cup of coffee, and then turn my face homewards only two or three squares distant. I now read or write or work upon my sketches till night, and as a general rule go 'round to Mr. Hargous' at seven or eight o'clock where there is, as I have before told you, a good cup of black tea and conversation till ten o'clock, when—as regularly as your churchbell rings for nine—we break up and go to our homes.

Any variation from this routine for months has been so seldom that I can, in a moment, recount the instances. I have once in a week or two taken a family dinner with Messrs. Vos and Hargous. Once I dined with the Minister, Mr. Clifford, to meet a party; once dined with Mr. Drusina under the same circumstances; and once with Mr. Davidson, the agent of Messrs. Rothschild,[1] where I have also been one evening at a musical party. Mrs. Kaufman, who is an excellent musician, gives a small soirée and musical party every Saturday evening, where I have a general invitation and have gone once only. I have further been to a single concert at the theater. And there you have the whole length and breadth of my dissipation in the gay City of Mexico after a six-months' residence! Mr. Kaufman has gone off rather suddenly to Europe on the business of the house, taking his wife with him, and proposes to be absent a twelve-month. They have no children. They are well-bred, agreeable people, have been very civil to me, live only next door, and with my limited acquaintance I shall feel their loss.

Mr. Clifford returns to the United States on the 1st November. I wish I was ready to go down to Vera Cruz with him, as it will be a safe and agreeable opportunity. He will go in the diligence with an escort furnished by the government and go through rapidly in four days. He proposes to return again in a couple of months, bringing his family. It is an honorable and distinguished station, that of Minister, and besides I think may here be lucrative if he is willing to economize—but I, at least, do not envy him his situation. Mr. Hargous, he of New York, will also probably be of Mr. Clifford's party, both going and returning, and he, too, thinks of bringing his wife, a Mexican lady, to visit her friends.

[*Remainder of letter missing*]

1. There were two Davidson brothers, Benjamin and Lionel. Later, in 1851, Lionel remained in Mexico City and Benjamin went to San Francisco, where he also represented Drusina & Co. and N. M. Rothschild & Sons. Letter of William de Drusina & Co., Mexico, July 16, 1851, in Coit Collection, Bancroft Library.

My very dear Wife,   *City of Mexico, October 31st, 1848*

My last letter to you was under date 12th inst., since which I regret exceedingly to say I continue to be deprived of any tidings whatever from you, your last letter being of July (no date). From Howland & Aspinwall my dates are only to the 30th August, but I was then advised of other letters which had been sent (private letters of William, probably enclosing others from you), which have never reached me. It is some satisfaction, however, to believe that my letters reach you with more regularity.

At this moment I have an excellent opportunity of writing you by my friend, Mr. [Louis] Hargous, who leaves tomorrow in company with our Minister, Mr. Clifford, direct for New York. A vessel of war being in waiting in Vera Cruz for them, they will meet with the least possible delay. With what pleasure should I join this party! The Mexican Minister to the United States makes one of it. They take the entire diligence to themselves, have a cavalry escort on the whole route provided by the government, and thus go through pleasantly (so far as pleasure is connected with any travel in this country) in four days. But I must bide my time. I have still two long months to look forward to, long in prospective, reminding me of Young's graphic description of time, who "in advance behind him hides his wings and seems to creep, decrepit with his age"; but I shall soon, I trust, have occasion to finish the sentence, "behold him when passed by: what then is seen but his broad pinions swifter than the wind."

To tell you the truth, however, my time does not pass either unprofitably or disagreeably, and, with the exception of separation from you, which to be sure is a sad drawback, I may say rather pleasantly. I have the satisfaction of reflecting that I am accomplishing something substantial for your benefit at very little cost of labor, while my leisure moments are usefully occupied with the pencil in illustrating this celebrated City and its neighborhood in a manner which, so far as I know, has not been before attempted, and which may result in considerable pecuniary advantage. I have already taken nearly thirty views and have, moreover, written by the last packet to England to my old acquaintance, T. S. Cooper, to know if he would like to undertake the publication in London, offering him the benefit of publishing these if, as an equivalent, he would furnish me the same on lithograph stones to publish in the United States.[1] It is very doubtful, with the constant demand on his time, whether he will accede to this, though if he should I should consider it at least equal to $2,000 or $3,000, and possibly more. Should I get an unfavorable answer from Cooper, it may even be worth my while to go to London or Paris, perhaps both, to see to this publication myself. But this is a matter for future consideration, and in the meantime I mean to be very industrious in accomplishing as many interesting sketches as possible.

I have within a few days, through the introduction of Mr. Davidson of London, acting as [blank] consul, made the acquaintance of the Marquis de Radepont,[2] living just across the

---

1. Thomas Sidney Cooper (1803–1902), celebrated English painter, early showed strong artistic inclinations, which he had no opportunity to develop. He managed to gain admittance to the Royal Academy, however, and then went back to his birthplace, Canterbury, where he made a livelihood by selling sketches and drawings. The first exhibit of his work, shown at the Royal Academy in 1833, proved to be the beginning of a long and distinguished career. His reminiscences, *My Life*, were published in 1890. Various portfolios of his works were issued by Ackermann and others.

The relationship between Cooper and Coit was very close. Many of Coit's sketches were accepted by him, given dramatic, finishing touches, and then issued under Cooper's signature. On his own behalf, Coit introduced Cooper to a part of society hitherto closed to him. Joshua Coit in *Autobiography*, pp. 60–61.

2. Justin H. Smith wrote about him: "The Marquis de Radepont, who accompanied Scott's army to observe its operations, was particularly astonished that the General had so little control over the volunteers, a state of things that more than once endangered all, he said." *The War with Mexico*, Vol. II, p. 513.

way from me with the Conde de Cortina (who by the way is a great connoisseur of pictures).[3] This gentleman was sent out by the French government during the occupation of the country by our troops to notice their movements and operations. He is by profession an engineer and sketches very prettily, having taken many views on the whole route from Vera Cruz to this City, which I regret to say I neglected to do as I ought to have done. True, the mode of traveling would have prevented my doing much. I had, at least, an opportunity in Jalapa. Possibly circumstances on my return may enable me to make up for this. This gentleman called yesterday to see the sketches I had taken and professed to be highly pleased with them, and we, at the same time, arranged for visiting in company several places in the neighborhood of the City offering good subjects for the pencil.

The Conde de Cortina is one of the educated, as well as one of the rich, men of the country. He has at Tacubaya a beautiful residence, offering from its top one of the most charming panoramic views of the Valley of Mexico and the battlegrounds in the vicinity that can be seen. He has had the politeness to give me an invitation to visit him for the purpose of seeing his collection of pictures, one of the largest private collections in the country, and at the same time invited me to breakfast, which it must be understood is more like dinner than breakfast with us and nearly at as late an hour as our early dinners, being from eleven to twelve and the dinner hour seven. I shall avail myself of this opportunity for a few sketches and you shall hear more about it hereafter.

I have been in the habit lately of taking press copies of my letters to you, and as my last had some reference to business which I should not like to have neglected, I determined to send the copy lest the original should have miscarried. This will preclude the necessity of referring to those business subjects in this letter.

Captain Starbuck, who I think I mentioned to you as in the employ of Howland & Aspinwall and who was on his way from the West Coast to the United States (to take the command of one of their steam vessels about to sail for the Pacific) in the early part of summer, and who, by the fall of his horse at Guadalajara, broke his leg badly, arrived here a few days since. His anxiety to get on induced him to start on his journey before his leg was sufficiently healed, and although he hired a comfortable carriage with two friends to accompany him, yet he suffered very much on the way. He is now recruiting very fast and will, I doubt not, be in good condition to proceed to Vera Cruz in about a week, preparatory to taking the English packet to Cat Island on the 16th of the month—which, of course, will afford me another good opportunity of writing you. The weather here now is most delightful. With the month of September, the rainy season passed away and we have now a season corresponding with your first autumn days, though with more uniformity of temperature, taking a whole month together.

November 1

Our Minister, Mr. Clifford, took his departure at four o'clock this morning for Vera Cruz, where a government vessel waits to convey him to the United States, accompanied by the Consul, Mr. [blank], temporarily appointed by himself here; by Mr. Louis Hargous and others, filling the coach with his own party, nine persons. As the roads have been for a long

3. The Conde de Cortina was a distinguished Mexican (1799–1860). Author of a large volume of writings, he was honored with membership in numerous learned societies, and the Mexican government bestowed many offices on him. In 1835–1836, for example, he was first deputy of the Federal District, twice its governor thereafter, minister of hacienda in 1838, president of the junta de hacienda in 1841, a member of the ministry of war in 1844, and won other offices and innumerable honors. Conservative in his views, he fought for law and order, and in politics supported General Santa Anna. On the death of his mother, he returned to Spain to inherit the family title, Conde de Cortina, on March 14, 1848. José Guadalupe Romero, *Biografia del Exmo. Sr. D. Jose Justo Gomez de la Cortina, Conde de Cortina* (Mexico, 1860).

time much infested by robbers and are known still to be so, every individual was well armed and the government has furnished an escort for the whole distance: four soldiers riding on top of the coach, while the remainder are mounted men stationed along the road at such intervals as to enable them to keep up with the carriage, which travels rapidly, considering the rough state of the roads, going through to Vera Cruz in four days, passing the first night in Puebla, the second in Perote, the third in Jalapa, and making a short day from there to Vera Cruz.

The roads continue in a most deplorable state as regards robbers. The government having had advice that there was a very large body of these brigands organized for the purpose of attacking, the last *conducta* from hence to Vera Cruz, which went under protection of a considerable force, ordered out a reinforcement of 200 men for its additional safety. It remains to be seen whether even this number was sufficient for the purpose. Another smaller *conducta*, going from some of the mines of the interior to one of the mints, only last week was attacked by thirty robbers, who succeeded in dispersing the guard, wounding several of them, and carried off $30,000 in specie. . . .

After breakfast I received a very agreeable call from my kind friend, Mr. Vos. "Come," said he, "the carriage is at the door and if you are disposed for a ride to Tacubaya you have not a moment to lose." At this place Mr. Vos has one of the prettiest summer retreats that I have yet met in this country. The whole affair does not occupy more than an acre of ground, but yet that acre is managed with so much art and skill, so judiciously laid out and filled with trees and creepers and shrubbery of all kinds, that there is nothing left to desire, even though everything be in miniature.

But before we enter the house we will describe the drive from the City all the way to the battleground which, although I have passed it frequently, does not lose any part of its original interest. First, on leaving the City and at its suburb, driving through The Alameda (a public park adorned with fine old trees, with fountains and public walks), we come upon the *paseo*, or public drive.[4] Passing the length of this some half mile, we arrive at the *garita* or Gate of Belén, where the Mexicans had a stray battery which annoyed our troops exceedingly in their approach to the City. From this point, a broad level road, perfectly straight, extends to Chapultepec, divided in the middle by an aqueduct built on arches for the whole distance. Upon this road our troops had to march up to the different batteries planted along its sides without other protection than such as the arches of the aqueduct temporarily afforded, and carry one after the other until they made their way into the City.

Leaving Chapultepec at the right, this same broad road extends across this marshy plain to Tacubaya, broad dikes, surmounted with strong hedges of the maguey plant, confining it on either side. We now arrive at the village situated on rising ground and commanding a view over the valley and road to Mexico. The cottage we visit has the characteristics of most of the country houses of the better class: a strong, very high wall of masonry surrounds all the grounds. The front of the house differs little from this except that two or three large and lofty doors, conducting through the wall into the interior that, communicating with the main part of the house, opens upon a beautiful little paved court with a stone fountain in its center and crowded with just as many orange, lemon, and pomegranate trees as can be accommodated within its limited extent.

[*Remainder of letter missing*]

4. This famous park, familiar to all visitors to Mexico, is still so named.

City of Mexico, November 8th, 1848

The most extraordinary accounts continue to be received of the wonderful riches of the gold mines in California and so well authenticated are they that there can no longer be any doubts entertained on the subject. I have just been shown a letter from Mazatlán of no less than four entire sheets of letter paper exclusively on this subject, giving many most interesting details, some of which I will proceed to give you.

The writer of that letter had become a purchaser of some of the parcels of gold dust which had found the way to the Mexican coast. One large lot of the value of $30,000 he had purchased from an American gentleman who had obtained it under the following circumstances: He, with another American, had been some time in the country engaged in farming operations. Hearing the extraordinary reports of the gold mines, they determined (he and his partner) to take the Indians whom they had in their employ, some thirty in number, and proceed with them to the gold district to try their hand at the business. So great is the value of labor, owing to the facility with which every man can collect gold for himself, that they agreed to find their Indians and pay them besides $2 per day. The result of the undertaking was that these two Americans, at the expiration of only six weeks' time, divided $60,000!! as the result of the labor of their party for that time. Being asked how he could make up his mind to leave the gold district while he was amassing wealth so rapidly, he replied that various considerations contributed to it. First, the Indians they had employed became dissatisfied and refused to work any longer under their contract, and again the two months which were to succeed were known to be extremely sickly. Then they were greatly in want of provisions, tools, and clothing, particularly of woolen clothing, the weather being exceedingly cold, and still further, by bringing his gold to a Mexican port, he could realize 50% more for it in coin than it was worth in California, or could exchange it very advantageously for the necessaries he was in need of.[1]

One great difficulty, however, in leaving the country was the means of conveyance. There was an abundance of vessels, but no crews to navigate them. Not only the sailors but the officers themselves in not a few instances had deserted them to become miners. In this category are a number of whalers who, having gone into port for the purpose of supplies, have been entirely abandoned by officers and crew. An American brig arrived in the port of San Francisco recently for the purpose of disposing of some remains of her outward cargo. Her anchor was scarcely down when the officer of the port came on board and the all-engrossing topic of mining and its results was alluded to and among other things he stated that almost any description of ordinary labor was at $80 to $100 per month on shore. This was either overheard by the crew or it came directly to their ears, for as the result they one and all determined on leaving the vessel forthwith, which was only partially prevented by the Captain's immediately slipping his anchor and proceeding to sea. I say partially prevented; three of the crew actually leaped overboard to swim to shore.

In the case I am referring to, our adventurer succeeded at length in procuring a crew by paying to the common sailors $80 per month. So great has been the proportion of gold dust collected already, as compared with that of coin, that the former—which is nearly of standard quality and consequently of the intrinsic value of $16 per ounce—had been sold in large quantities at $8 only per ounce. This low price will not exist long, however. Mexico is full of

---

1. These stories are characteristic of the fantastic tales told everywhere of the riches to be had in the California gold fields. See, for example, Caughey's *Gold is the Cornerstone*, especially chapter 2; *Three Years in California, William Perkins' Journal of Life at Sonora, 1849–1852* (Berkeley and Los Angeles, 1964), edited by Dale L. Morgan and James R. Scobie; Bancroft's *History of California*, Vol. VI, p. 67 *et seq.*; and Bayard Taylor, *Eldorado, or adventures in the Path of Empire* (New York, 1949), especially chapters 6 and 9. This popular book was first issued in 1850. It has been reprinted a number of times.

gold and silver coins and large sums are already being shipped from the west coast to California for the purchase of the gold dust, which will soon raise the price there to its proper value, leaving only a fair exchange between the two countries. But this must, of course, increase the already enormous profits of the mining interest.[2]

The continuous extent of this mining district is upwards of 100 miles, so far as has yet been discovered, and nothing more has heretofore been necessary than to take the surface soil for washing; even the width and depth of the treasure has not yet been ascertained. Sufficient, however, is known to justify the estimates that there exists a stock sufficient for ten years' consumption, even though many more hands are employed than at present.

November 9th. Since writing the foregoing, I have received a letter from an intelligent gentleman residing on the West Coast, confirming to a considerable extent the foregoing and adding some further interesting particulars. He says Governor Mason, well known in the United States, has traversed the whole of the gold region and says that about $35,000 in value (estimating the gold at $16 per ounce) is collected daily, or at the rate of upwards of $10,000,-000 per annum.[3] Further, in working this gold mine, other rich mines of quicksilver, etc., have been discovered. And much platinum is also found in the gold washings which heretofore, from ignorance of the miners, has been thrown away as useless. The gold already brought to the West Coast has been sold at only $14 per ounce, a very low price, offering a far better remittance to Europe or the States than coin. Various parcels have been assayed at the mints and are found to be nearly of the standard of Mexican doubloons. [*Unsigned*]

2. The shortage of coins was acute. See Antonio Franco Coronel's dictation, "Cosas de California," made in 1877 for H. H. Bancroft, a part of which is quoted by Morgan and Scobie, *op. cit.*, pp. 21–25; and *The Annals*, pp. 214–215.

3. The most authoritative descriptions of the gold discovery were made by Thomas O. Larkin, United States consul, and Colonel R. B. Mason, military governor of California. Larkin's first report to Secretary of State Buchanan on this subject was made June 1, 1848, followed by more detailed accounts as the evidence of gold increased. These are dated June 28 and November 16, 1848. Mason's report was dated August 17, 1848. Both men wrote on the basis of personal observation. Their accounts formed the basis of President Polk's message to Congress on December 5, 1848, which made the great discovery official. Hammond, *The Larkin Papers*, Vol. VII, pp. 285–287, 301–305; and Vol. VIII, pp. 37–39. Mason's report is printed in 30th Congress, 2d Session, *House Executive Document 1* (Serial 537), pp. 56–64. Both Mason's and Larkin's reports on the gold discovery are printed in Joseph Warren Revere, *A Tour of Duty in California* (New York, 1849), reprinted as *Naval Duty in California* (1947) by Biobooks of Oakland, pp. 184–201.

My very dear Wife,   *City of Mexico, November 12th, 1848*

I have still the same unfavorable report to make in regard to my letters from New York. Another packet has arrived at Vera Cruz without bringing me a single line from anyone. This entire suspension of letters gives me, of course, a good deal of uneasiness, but fretting about it will not mend the matter, and so I endeavor to take it philosophically. . . .

I am now, my dear wife, about to break a new subject to you which I fear will be the occasion of renewed anxiety and pain, as it refers to a longer separation between us than has ever before been contemplated. I have the prospect of going to California, the "El Dorado" of the present times, on business which promises great pecuniary advantages and which, I think, it would be wrong for me to decline. After hearing all the "pros and cons" in the case, I think you will entirely agree with me.

The object in view is the purchase of gold dust, which has become so abundant in that country, owing to its easy acquisition, that the price, as compared with dollars or coin of any kind, is exceedingly low. I have said that I have the prospect of going on this business; there is quite a considerable degree of uncertainty attached to it. The matter as yet is only understood between Mr. Drusina and myself and has to be submitted to Howland & Aspinwall, whose concurrence is very important. I wrote by this opportunity a very full, private letter to William on the subject, offering my services, if he will engage them, and on his determination the whole affair will hinge.

I suppose you will be glad to have some further particulars as to the nature of the business and the remuneration to be derived from it, and on the condition of entire secrecy I will communicate it to you. The plan is to embark $200,000 in silver from the West Coast (of Mexico) for the purchase of gold dust in California at the port of San Francisco. This gold is intended to be disposed of in Mazatlán or other ports on the Coast to those who wish to make remittances to England or the United States, and receiving dollars for it (which make a bad remittance), renew the operation, which probably may be done four or five times in the year. I am to remain permanently in San Francisco to make the purchases there, Mr. Drusina here, and Mr. Bissell, Howland & Aspinwall's agent on the coast, managing the business in this country.[1]

It is proposed by Mr. Drusina to allow me 5% on all purchases, so that on the first purchase of $200,000—which would probably be completed in two months after my leaving this city, I should realize $10,000. If this operation should be renewed once, twice, thrice, or more times in the course of the year, it is easy for you to make the calculation what it would come to. It is true there is uncertainty in all things, and it does not do to overestimate, but a safer or more simple or feasible business seems hardly possible, and no person has the advantages which Howland & Aspinwall possess for undertaking it: their steamers running every month between San Francisco and the Mexican ports; Mr. Bissell, with an assistant, being on the Coast to do the needful there; Mr. Drusina here to make the exchanges; and myself in California—the capital on the spot and forthcoming at a word. Here is all the machinery in a nutshell and it only requires one word from William to set it in motion. It appears to me that he can hardly decline an operation offering such advantages, but still it may be.

Now as to the journey and voyage from this City to San Francisco—of this you will desire information, and I am glad on this point also that I can make so favorable a report. I would say at a word that it may be considered more pleasant and desirable than the journey to Vera Cruz and voyage from there to New York. The journey from this City to Mazatlán is a very long and tedious one, but to Acapulco, where the steamers first touch on their voyage from

---

1. Probably George W. P. Bissell, the United States consul at San Blas.

Panama to California, it is not much more than half the distance and is easily accomplished on horseback in seven or eight days. Then the weather at the season when I would go is delightful in the Pacific, too calm generally for any other than steam vessels; and the voyage to San Francisco, I presume by steamer, some fifteen days. Arrived at San Francisco, the climate is pleasant and healthy, and you will bear in mind, under our own government and laws. I should probably arrange so to leave matters here as to render it unnecessary to return, but take passage by steamer all the way to New York, via the Isthmus. As to the precise time I may remain in California, it will depend entirely on circumstances. I think at present a twelve-month will so far accomplish my objects as to enable me to do so, and how soon this period of time flies away!

Now, what say you? Has my determination been right or otherwise? If our separation is a sacrifice and trial to you in your own home, with all your children and friends about you, what must it be to me away from all these endearments, in a strange land, deprived of all religious privileges and with a people, repugnant in very many respects to my feelings?

I intended to say that in the journey to Acapulco I expect to be accompanied by several gentlemen of my acquaintance who are desirous also of visiting California and will go all the way through with me. This will make it almost a trip of pleasure rather than otherwise. Certainly it would have been so at one period of my life, though it is true that my desire for novelties of this kind has amazingly cooled down of late years.

Nothing can be determined on before I get William's answer to the present, and this in all probability will not reach me before the 8th or 9th January, when we should receive the packet letters of that month. I request Howland & Aspinwall to send their letters to avail themselves of that opportunity, and for that purpose they should leave New York for Havana by the 10th or 12th of December. The last of that month the packet leaves there for Vera Cruz, and as above remarked, eight or ten days afterwards, about the 8th January, the letters are received here. I wish you to write me then, say about the end of the first week in December, sending your letter under cover to Howland & Aspinwall, requesting them to *enclose it in the letters they may be sending me via Havana to meet the English steamer there at the last of the month.* Just use, in your letter to them, that form of words, and in your letter—that is, to me—communicate, that is recapitulate, *all the events of interest* that your letters have contained since that of July. It is now exceedingly doubtful whether I receive any of the letters you may have written since that period. They have probably been remitted by Howland & Aspinwall via New Orleans, on which route a strange and unaccountable fatality has attended them. The last date I have of theirs is 30 August. Mention is made in that of a private letter of William's, written about the same time (and which I have always thought might have contained one or more of yours) which has never come to hand.

I have a sheet of the marvelous written for your amusement, which has come here in letters from the West Coast where they are constantly receiving very direct information from California and the gold region. You may correct this and give it to Mr. Sykes, if you choose, for publication, calling it "Extract from the letter of an American gentleman, now in the City of Mexico."

This letter will, at Vera Cruz (where for safety it will be sent by courier), be delivered with my letters to Howland & Aspinwall to Captain Starbuck, the gentleman who, coming here from the West Coast, broke his leg in Guadalajara and has been consequently detained in his journey a long time. He stopped here to recruit some time and finally left in the diligence for Vera Cruz, where I sincerely hope he may arrive in safety. He has been for nine years in the employment of Howland & Aspinwall in the Pacific without visiting the United States, made many voyages to Canton, and made a great deal of money for them and I doubt not is very well off himself. His broken leg will have cost him, in one way or another, some $1,500. Among other things, he paid the expenses of two men all the way here and now over to the United States to take care of him. His doctor's bill for setting the leg and afterwards looking at it a few times was $250, which it seemed to him was not a very cheap job, but on inquiry he was informed it was not out of the way—in fact, quite reasonable. Now don't tell our good doctor about this or he will be running off here with that sweet wife of his to make his fortune. The charges of professional men here are enormous. I know of one, a lawyer, who is conducting a suit of so much importance (involving valuable mining property) that he is to receive, if successful, $300,000. This is to make sure of the man, to prevent the possibility of his being bribed and selling his client.

In regard to my intended movements, do not at present lisp a syllable to anyone, [not even] the best friend you have. Possibly nothing will take place and if it should, it will be sufficient to say that I have been obliged to delay my return a little. I do not wish anyone, not even in the family, to be informed of what my prospects are.

And now my best love to my dear children, who I pray you to embrace one and all for me, and when you write tell me particularly if the boys have been good and obedient to you. Remember me with kind regards to all our friends, and believe me as ever faithfully and affectionately yours,
D. W. Coit

November 13

Your letters of 20th September and 11th October have this moment come, and what sad intelligence they contain. I grieve for you, dearest, more than for myself. May God comfort you in your heavy bereavement, though I can add He gave and He has taken away. Blessed be His holy name. I think I shall nevertheless prosecute my plans. I have duties to perform to you and our remaining children, even though it be at much personal sacrifice and inconvenience, and I know you will acquiesce in what I think to be duty. The sad particulars must have been impressed by telling, which I shall not now review—and I am sorry to pain you by repetition.
In haste, ever affectionately,
D. W. C.

DIGGING FOR GOLD — WITHOUT A SHOVEL

My very dear Wife,   *City of Mexico, January 4th, 1849*

... I have been gratified to make the acquaintance here within the past few days of a Mr. Atherton, very recently from San Francisco.[1] He is a native of Boston, but has been living a good many years in Chile and Peru and for the past two years in California. He is on his way to the United States for the purchase of goods, meaning to return to San Francisco either by this route or by the Isthmus, in a couple of months, sending the cargo he means to get away, I presume, 'round Cape Horn.

Knowing that it could not be otherwise than gratifying to you to see one that had been so recently with me, I have got his promise to call on you and I promise you a treat in his accounts of the "El Dorado" he has just left. I have purposely paid him a good deal of attention here and he seems grateful for it. His knowledge of California, the people, and trade there is such that he can be of great use to me on his return, and he is under no engagement there to prevent his making an arrangement with me for going to the placer, or mines, while I remain at San Francisco. I have felt the need of just such a person as he appears to be, which will be almost indispensable to me in carrying out the important business I expect soon to have on my hands. The circumstances under which he goes to the United States, entrusted with an important commission by one of the first houses in California, speaks of itself strongly in his favor. He takes with him very strong letters to Mr. Comstock, Alsop & Co., and others.

I am yet ignorant whether Howland & Aspinwall will listen to the proposals I have made them. If they do not, I can only tell them they will miss it greatly. Fortunately, I can carry out my plans without them, though certainly not in so satisfactory a manner. I much prefer to have my interest united with theirs in the business. Within the week the matter will no doubt be decided. By the next packet, which should by this time be in Vera Cruz or nearly so, I ought to have their definitive answer. If they decline, I shall immediately conclude an arrangement with Mr. Drusina and probably be ready to leave here for Acapulco to embark in the steamer of that month for San Francisco. A number of friends—Mr. Vos and others—mean to go at the same time, which will make it very pleasant and at the same time safe, I mean the journey from here to the Coast.

After I get my letters above referred to, I will write you again per this opportunity, which is the packet of the 16th, and perhaps can say something more definite. The present is only a few lines I write to give in charge of Mr. Atherton to secure his calling on you. He takes the diligence for Vera Cruz tomorrow morning and will remain there till the packet sails. You must not fail to draw out of him some of the marvelous stories of gold-finding and the hardly less so accounts of the prices of necessary provisions and goods at the placer, such as the Indians (who get as much gold as anybody) buying coined silver with its weight in gold dust

---

1. This was Robert Atherton, brother of Faxon Dean Atherton, a businessman who had been in Chile for many years. See the letters of the latter to Larkin in *The Larkin Papers*, Vol. VIII, pp. 42–43, and throughout the series. Robert had been on the Pacific Coast for about ten years—the last two in San Francisco—where he had come on December 13, 1846, bringing a letter of recommendation from his brother in Valparaiso. M. G. Vallejo, *Documentos*, Vol. XII, No. 255.

Robert had left San Francisco on December 10, 1848, in the brig *Laura Ann*, debarking in Mazatlán to travel by horseback across Mexico by way of Guadalajara, Mexico City, and Vera Cruz. He reached New York on Sunday, February 11, 1848. Both the New York *Herald* and the *Weekly Tribune* carried extensive accounts of an interview with him in which he confirmed the extent and richness of the gold discovery. His reports were a full month later than any others from California and hence were considered of first importance. The gold-bearing region, said Atherton, was 1,000 miles in length and 300 in width. The labor of mining gold was hard, he admitted, and not all were successful, but his readers must have been excited to learn that he had seen one gold chunk of seven pounds, and a friend had seen one of twenty-one pounds. He brought "bills of lading of gold to the value of $200,000, shipped on an English account. . . ." New York *Herald*, February 12, 1849; New York *Weekly Tribune*, February 17, 1849.

and who have a way, further, in bringing their blankets and other necessaries, of spreading their gold dust out, and then dividing it into little heaps of an inch square or so with the finger drawn across the mass, counting these heaps as dollars and then paying $50 or $60 for a coarse blanket—but enough for the present.

I go out directly with Mr. Atherton to dine at Mr. Hargous.' He keeps house with our Minister, Mr. Clifford, but you know he is about in the United States at present and Mr. Walsh takes his place as Chargé. This gentleman, most unfortunately, fell from his horse on the 1st January on a ride on the paseo and broke his arm, badly; of course he is on his back in bed, but doing as well as can be expected. Mr. Drusina gives a dinner party on Saturday, on the occasion of Mr. Davidson's leaving to go to England, also on the next packet. I think I have before told you that this gentleman is the agent of the Rothschild's; he returns again shortly. You see how dissipated I am becoming.

By the bye, Madame Drusina has been ill, very ill, since I wrote you, and it has been the occasion of many hopes destroyed.

Adieu, dearest, for the present. I trust you will get another letter of a later date simultaneously with this.
Ever affectionately and faithfully yours,
D. W. Coit

My very dear Wife, City of Mexico, January 30th, 1849

I have already written you twice in the present month, one of the letters given in charge to a Mr. Atherton, whom I hope you will have seen, as he promised me to call on you at your father's. . . .

I presume your thoughts are not unfrequently turned towards California since I wrote you of the prospects of my going there. I am vexed with Howland & Aspinwall for so much neglecting my communications to them, although it won't do to tell them so. I have been expecting an answer to a letter of much importance (*to me*) written in November, and to this time am disappointed. Until I get their answer, I cannot make arrangements with others on the subject of which I heretofore wrote to you.

How people are beside themselves in the United States on this California gold business! I doubt not that many will be ruined by it and many others lose their lives. We learn that this was already the case at the Isthmus, where great suffering and mortality were said already to exist among the thousands waiting to get passage from Panama to San Francisco. I think that those who may have no passage engaged on the steamers, if they do not wish to lay their bones there, had better go home again with all speed, if indeed they can now get a passage back to the United States—which is somewhat doubtful.

It is quite uncertain as to the time of my leaving, certainly not now until some time in March. The recent accounts from San Francisco which I have received from the West Coast a day or two since represents the winter in the interior at the placer to have been very severe. Many who had the temerity to remain there for the purpose of working when they could, badly supplied with food and clothing and shelter, are said to have died from exposure and hunger. My letter states that the sailors were deserting by dozens from our ships of war, and of course the merchant vessels are nearly all deserted. What the immense number of expeditions will do which are coming out from the United States, no one can tell. I fancy a large fleet laying at anchor in the bay without a sailor on board and of course without the possibility of getting away, and I further fancy goods, many articles at least as cheap as in New York. Men are continually arriving here in parties of six, eight, or ten from Vera Cruz on their way to Mazatlán or San Blas to embark, uncertain whether they will find an opportunity even on merchant vessels. The steamers are, of course, out of the question. The miners in the interior of this country are also leaving with the same destination. A party of ten of them have just come into town on their way to the Coast to embark. . . .

Mr. Clifford, our Minister, arrived here last evening by the diligence, bringing his wife and two of his children with him. They met with no accident on the road; I think for my part that women and children are better left at home, so I won't propose to you to come to me.

The country continues very quiet. We don't now hear the word revolution uttered once a month. All idea of it seems to have died away. Heretofore the army was at the bottom of these outbreaks, but as there can hardly be said to be any such thing at present, at least near the Capital, all danger from that source has ceased.

You have no idea what a delightful winter climate this is. No such thing as frost, at least in the City; no fires in the houses; and the roses, geraniums, and oranges all in bloom. . . .

Ever faithfully and affectionately
D. W. C.

P.S. By looking among the ship advertisements in the newspaper you shall see for yourself when vessels may be sailing for Vera Cruz.

My dear Wife,   *City of Mexico, February 9th, 1849*

. . . In the absence of the business letters which I ought long since to have received, I am kept in doubt and uncertainty as to my future movements and general proceedings, nor can I under the circumstances add to what I have heretofore said on the subject. I still expect to go to California, but as to the precise time I am entirely unable to say when. Parties are now arriving almost daily in the City on their way from Vera Cruz to the West Coast, hoping there to find shipping which will take them to San Francisco. By shipping I mean merchant vessels, the steamers, I take it, being entirely out of the question.

I met at Mr. Clifford's yesterday a young gentleman of the name of Bolton who seems to be quite alone here, waiting to join some party who may be going to the Coast. He is quite a young chap and altogether too effeminate—delicate, and I should say inexperienced—for the life he will have to encounter in California. A party of four young men left here for Mazatlán about a fortnight since and when some fifteen or twenty leagues on their way, were overhauled by a party of thirteen robbers who, taking them off from the road into a bye place, there tied them and then stripped them of all they had, including their horses, leaving them to foot it back here as best they might. They did not leave here in the first instance very flush, but they returned, as you may suppose, in much worse plight. Fortunately, they found friends who assisted them with a new outfit and they started again yesterday with a larger party.

The *Eugenia*, to which I have referred as having arrived in Vera Cruz, brings, I learn, 130 new candidates for the gold region who may now be expected her in a week or two. One of the party, I understand, is addressed to me or has letters to me. I don't know from whom or with what object, probably for information simply.

My health has been perfectly good throughout the winter, and in so delightful a winter climate with little to do but take care of myself, it would be an exception to a general rule if it were otherwise. Through the attention and kindness of Mr. Vos, I get a drive occasionally in the country to one or another of the villages in the neighborhood. These villages are of quite a different order to country villages with us. They originated in the time of the Spaniards as resorts for the rich families of Mexico, and great wealth was bestowed on them in large churches and convents, with extensive gardens and orchards, enclosed by massive walls almost as high as the buildings themselves.

The houses are also built of corresponding size and architecture, enclosing one or more courts which are generally filled with orange, lemon, and various other ornamental trees and shrubbery, with a fountain almost invariably in the center. One of my last sketches was a court of this kind belonging to Mr. Vos's house at Tacubaya. It is one of the smallest of its kind, but every foot of it is occupied with suitable objects of interest, and a perfect little gem in itself. It has been a laborious thing to sketch and much more to fill up afterwards with so much of detail, but as it is quite different from anything we have, or indeed anything that I recollect to have seen published, I think it will please, and pay for the trouble. An orange and a lemon tree are on either hand in the foreground, loaded with the fruit, now just ripe, of which my portraits are said to be very striking.

I shall probably send you home these sketches ere I leave for the West Coast, together with some other curiosities which I have succeeded in obtaining, the most curious of which are a set of rich tapestry hangings, originally sent out by the King of Spain to a rich Mexican as a return for a large amount in bars of silver he had sent the King. The subjects are very humorous, representing the most amusing passages in the life of Don Quixote. There are seven of these hangings, quite large (the largest measuring some 18 feet long by 9 or 10 feet in height), sufficient to cover the walls of a large room. They came into my possession in a curious way, as you shall hear some day. . . .

My best love to the dear children and to your father and mother. I think the *Eugenia* by which this will go will probably return very shortly to Vera Cruz and by her I beg you will write. If you enclose your letter to the care of Mr. Lewis Hargous at his country room, he will give it course. *Ever faithfully and affectionately yours,*
D. W. Coit

P.S. My last was under date 30th January.

My dearest Wife, *City of Mexico, February 12th, 1849*
I have had the very great pleasure, on the arrival of the packet letters for the month, to receive your missing letters, *viz.*, of November 30th, December 4th, and January 9th, bringing the very best of all news, *viz.*, that you and the children were well. I regret exceedingly to learn of the distressing illness of your dear mother, but as she was on the mend at the date of your last, I trust she will be, ere this reaches you, perfectly restored. . . .

In relation to my future plans, the letter of Howland & Aspinwall and another from William were indeed a damper. I mean their letters, declining my propositions as to California, or indeed any new business transactions whatever, giving me permission to return. I have heretofore told you that even though they did decline, I might still go under Mr. Drusina's auspices, but I had no reason to think that by himself he would go to the extent desirable, and further his opinion was liable to change, the more liable as he had been somewhat annoyed, waiting an unreasonable time for the answer of Howland & Aspinwall and also from some unfortunate business with them. When, therefore, I got my discouraging letters from the house, all my plans and bright prospects appeared for the moment blasted and I had, I assure you, the most gloomy day that I have experienced since I have been in Mexico; but what short-sighted beings we are! We never can see much beyond the length of our noses, and often when appearances are most unfavorable, they are working round for our ultimate good.

I passed, as I said, a very dull day, not caring to see Drusina or at least to speak to him on business, knowing that he had a whole mail of letters to read and digest. But the following morning I called and advised him of the course the business had taken with Howland & Aspinwall and that there was nothing to expect from them. Perhaps he saw that I looked more sober than usual on this occasion, for he said, "Mr. Coit, if you still encourage the inclination to go to California, don't be uneasy. I think there will be no difficulty in the matter. Since we talked this matter over, certain parties in Europe with whom you know I have extensive operations (naming one of the first houses known but whom it is better that I should not at present name)[1] have just placed $100,000 at my disposal for such a transaction, and in some respects it offers better advantages than what was anticipated from your friends." Again, "I think several of my friends here will like to join in the undertaking, thus making it an object of more importance to you. You know I am very busy and until I get off my packet letters I can say nothing more, but just write Mrs. Coit in general terms that you will still be able to carry out your views, with no loss to your prospects."

Was not this noble? And is there not besides a pleasant reflection in it, aside from any pecuniary consideration; *viz.*, that the moment almost that I leave my humble retirement and without any means and thrown among strangers, I am able to form friendships and inspire confidence such as the foregoing indicates? You know my most important relations with Messrs. Huth & Co. were formed much in the same way.[2] Still, my dear wife, I have learned to look with distrust upon all brilliant prospects, and even now in this matter which puts on so bright an appearance, I may from some unexpected cause meet disappointment. It would appear clearly the leading of a kind providence, so it should be met and acted upon; but if a change comes over my prospects, I trust you will not find me cast down and disheartened. As to making a secret of my going to California, that, of course, is now out of the question, as you say, but as to the circumstances under which I go, that may be kept in your own breast, and I must enjoin that it be so. I shall not make this communication to anyone else.

I can say nothing definitive as to when I may leave for the Coast, perhaps in three or four weeks. You shall know reasonably soon. In the meantime, address letters to me *by every steamer* bound to Chagres; the regular mail for San Francisco will leave every month by that route. I shall now particularly want the clothing I sent for and hope Gilman[3] will be able to send these and also the gold scales and weights ordered, by the Isthmus, recommending them to the care of Messrs. Howland & Aspinwall's agent there, to whom he can mention as a reason for asking his particular attention to them that I have been the agent here in procuring for the steamers the important privileges they are to enjoy in entering the Mexican ports.

Much love to my dear children and to your father and mother and accept a large share on your own account from *Your ever affectionate and faithful husband,*
D. W. C.

1. This was the Rothschild firm, already distinguished as an eminent banking organization. Coit, *A Memoir*, p. 140.
2. Frederick Huth & Co., a German firm with extensive operations elsewhere in Europe and America, had employed Coit as their representative in South America in 1822. Coit, *A Memoir*, p. 63 ff.
3. This was William Charles Gilman of Norwich, who married Eliza Coit, the younger sister of Daniel Wadsworth Coit. See, for example, the letters of February 15 and April 29, 1849, and others. For genealogy, consult Frederick W. Chapman, *The Coit Family; or the Descendants of John Coit* (Hartford, 1874), pp. 58 and 111.

My dear wife   *Mexico, February 15th, 1849*

... In the letter referred to I mentioned that although Howland & Aspinwall had declined acceding to the propositions I made them for some business in California, yet the probabilities were that I should still go under equally favorable auspices. An event, however, has occurred within a day or two which again throws some doubts in the way. We learn that a pronunciamento (which may be translated revolt) has taken place amongst the troops in the neighborhood of Guanajuato, that they had declared in favor of General Santa Anna (who you know has been for some time in exile in the island of Jamaica), and that they were about marching towards Tampico to put themselves in intercourse with a party he is known to have in that part of the country, and eventually to favor his return to Mexico. What all this may lead to it is difficult to foresee—to no good certainly, as it embarrasses the present government and alarms all who are engaged in commercial operations. I cannot yet foresee what effect it may have on my prospects, certainly nothing favorable, and it may be very unfavorable; a few days must determine ...

I am not quite certain, in the last letter which I wrote Brother Gilman, whether I requested him to send me regularly by mail once a month the weekly papers of the *Courier* and *Enquirer* and *Herald*. This of course implies that he shall subscribe for them by the year. I think you and he determined right on the whole in not executing my general note of things for California but only that part which related to clothing, gold scales, double-barrel gun, and a few necessaries, as detailed in my last letter to him.

In ordering the variety of things I did, if the expedition had been sent for account of Drusina & Co. as was possible, I should not have had to pay freight, and this was much of a consideration.

I hope Gilman will be able to send the things (I mean of the limited order) by the Isthmus so as to meet the last or third steamer there, which as she will not leave New York till about this time, can hardly leave Panama before the first of May next.

You are doubtless aware that there is or is to be a regular mail once a month between New York and San Francisco by which we can communicate with great regularity; as you will rely on hearing from me by every one of these opportunities, so you on your part will not fail to write by every one. As Howland & Aspinwall may not wish the trouble of our correspondence going through their hands, I think you had better send your letters when you get to Norwich to the care of Brother Gilman, sending them a few days before the steamer of each month leaves New York for Chagres or the Isthmus.

I write this without any certain conveyance for it after it arrives at Vera Cruz.

Yours always faithfully and affectionately,
D. W. Coit

My very dear Wife,   *Guadalajara March 15th, 1849*

I left Mexico at so short notice and with so much to do at the last moment that I did not write you as I intended. It gives me pleasure now to acquaint you of my arrival here three days ago, without accident. Our party consists of 18 persons, besides muleteers and servants, all perfectly well armed. True, we have encountered some inconveniences on the road, such as sleeping on the ground in the open air, and on pavement, under cover scarcely any better, but you know I am not a novice in these matters and stand them for aught I see as well as others. The extreme heat from 12 o'clock till 3 or 4, riding on horseback, is to me the most trying thing. It is certainly a delightful winter climate, always mild and pleasant; it has not rained here since October last! We expect to leave tomorrow for Tepic, a journey of five days, when I shall be within a day's journey of San Blas, where I hope to embark for San Francisco. Mr. Meredith, a cousin of Louisa Howland, is the captain of our party and a Mr. Lawton, of New Rochelle, our lieutenant.

I write this in haste, almost in the dark and in a crowded room, so that you will excuse my saying more till I get to Tepic. I never realized my age more than on this journey. I seem to be considered the father of the party and am treated with all the attention and respect from everyone that I could possibly desire. My best love to my dear children—and accept for yourself, my dear wife, a very large share. I presume this will find you returned to Norwich—write me every month and in good season for the packet from New York.

Yours very affectionately and faithfully,
D. W. Coit

My very dear Wife,   *San Francisco, April 11th, 1849*

You will be rejoiced, I am sure, to hear of my safe arrival at this place on Sunday, the 1st inst., in the short and agreeable passage of one week only from San Blas. I will, before saying anything of this place, go back to Mexico and give you some general account of my leaving there and journey across the country.

I think I stated to you in one of my former letters the probability of my proceeding to Acapulco to embark as being the nearest to the city; fortunately, a party of the many adventurers who are crossing from Vera Cruz to the West Coast arrived in [Mexico] City, among whom were a number from the City of New York, with whom I became acquainted. Mr. Meredith, a cousin of Louisa Howland, had been appointed captain of this party and urged me to join them and go to San Blas to embark, instead of Acapulco. I hesitated on account of the short time I had to make preparation and on account of the much greater distance of the journey. At length, considering the great security from robbery which the opportunity afforded, there being twenty persons—determined young men and well armed—I made up my mind to join them and forthwith provided myself with a suitable Mexican horse, and an extra mule, and our party was soon on the road.

You would have laughed to see our motley group, for the luggage which, including various washing machines for the "placers," sieves, tin pans and other such apparatus, required two wagons, awkward rickety affairs, which were drawn by three lean, lank mules, with dreadfully raw backs and shoulders—I mean each one was drawn by three mules abreast. The drivers—Mexican Indians—corresponded in appearance, their heads bound with a handkerchief when they had anything on them, and each with his wife or woman who accompanied him all the journey, sometimes on foot and sometimes mounted on top of the luggage.

Our gentlemen themselves were hardly less grotesque in their dress and appearance; each had arranged his costume according to his fancy, and it might be imagined that that of the savage and frightful had prevailed. I don't know but this had as much to do in keeping off robbers as the sight of rifles and revolvers—and lacking coats and trousers, somewhat the worse for wear and the perils they had already gone through on the journey between Vera Cruz and Mexico, sometimes the trousers without the coat and sometimes the coat without the trousers, I was going to say, but I am mistaken—these last were never removed the whole journey of 20 days. Then such odd-shaped hats, of all colors. In the morning their broad brims would be triced up and, in the middle of the day, slouched or tied under the chin to keep the intense rays of the sun off.

At this period of the day nearly all were in their shirts, which were generally red, some blue, but none white. If any had been ever thus, they had long forfeited any pretentions of the kind. Now add to this costume a rifle, slung at the back, a pair of large revolvers (in holsters), a pair of smaller ditto in a belt at the waist, and fancy a superabundant growth of whisker, mustache, etc., with a nearly total abstinence from the toilet, and you may form some idea of the figure we cut. No wonder that the entire population came out to stare at us whenever we entered a town or village, and that the big children caught up the little ones and ran indoors to save them from our clutches.

We generally made a very early start in the morning, getting up before daylight, which after all was no great hardship, considering the accommodations—I will not say which we enjoyed, but which we had—a blanket spread on a stone pavement or floor, with a saddle for a pillow; or dressing, by an inch or two of candle, with a newfashioned Mexican candlestick, made by melting and dropping the tallow of the candle on the floor, and then fixing the candle in it. We then sallied out to find our horses at the corral, or stable, where they were all turned in loose; these were then to be watered, perhaps at some stream or river at a considerable distance from the house, and then saddled, and the blankets and loose articles used during the night, tied on behind, or otherwise put in the wagons.

A colored man, an American, had been engaged as cook for the party. He was provided with a large traveling chest in which were kept the tin cups, plates, forks, spoons, and other necessaries connected with our meals. He was generally the first up, made his fire, and by the time our arrangements were made for the road, had a cup of coffee for us, and we generally had a piece of dry and indifferent bread to eat with it. This was our breakfast, and unless we could buy bread, eggs, and some such things on the road, we went without any regular meal till night.

A league or two before arriving at the town or village or rancho (common house) where we were to stop, the captain would elect some three or four of the party to ride forward and make provision such as the place afforded, of rooms, stabling for the horses, meat, eggs, bread, and other necessaries for our dinner. Tired, hungry, and covered with dust, we arrived at these resting places, having some days been in the saddle, almost without dismounting, for 10 or 11 hours, for neither mules, horses, or men, as a general rule, stop to feed and rest during the day, as with us, but keep on, at a slow pace, generally a walk, of perhaps three miles an hour, until the day's work is done. Our cook now went to work to prepare our dinner, a very simple meal, generally of fried beef, called beefsteak, boiled eggs, and occasionally pancakes. This was devoured with great gusto, and then the guards being appointed to watch the luggage for the night, two men at a time serving two hours, we turned in, or rather laid down in our clothes and slept most soundly.

I should state that my own particular case was somewhat an exception to the foregoing in two or three things, viz., my friend, Mr. Drusina, on leaving Mexico made me a present of a small, portable, jointed iron bedstead, folding up in a trunk, with a pillow; this proved a great luxury, not only on the road, but on the deck of the vessel in coming here, and now while here, it is still quite useful. Again, the party would never permit me to be on guard, and they were one and all ready to do me at any time during the journey any kind office in their power. I was very glad to have it in my power on arrival at San Blas to repay some of these attentions ten fold. I succeeded in procuring passage for Mr. Meredith and another gentleman in the steamer to this place[1], and two others also obtained passage indirectly through me.

But I find that I have used up all my paper without saying a word of this place, as I intended, and I have no time by this opportunity to fill another sheet. Another steamer of Howland & Aspinwall's line leaves here within a week for Panama, by which I will write again. Suffice it at present to say that I do not regret coming here. I have been fortunate in getting *temporary* lodgings with a gentleman, a Mr. Probst in Howland & Aspinwall's employ, while every nook and corner of the small place is crowded to excess, many rsepectable people living in tents.

With my best love to my darlings, to you most of all, I am, dearest,

Affectionately and truly yours,
D. W. Coit.

1. See the Introduction, p. 14.

My very dear Wife: *San Francisco, April 29th, 1849*

I wrote you on my arrival here, it being just four weeks today, though I did not come on shore until the following day. Since that time no tidings have reached me from you; neither have I had opportunity of writing, the sailing of the steamer, *California*, having been from week to week and from day to day delayed. There is now a prospect that she will get away day after tomorrow, and I am glad to avail myself of the kind offer of a Mr. Johnson, who returns a passenger, to take charge of my letters. This gentleman is a connection of the Bray family of New Jersey, and consequently of our good Dr. Coit's wife, and claims, moreover, to be acquainted with you, and said he would call on you at your father's, but I fear you will be disappointed in seeing him, as I fancy you, ere this, returned to your own home at Norwich. Would that the time were come to show my face in the dear old place again, but the time for that seems yet remote, and I do not suffer myself to think too much about it.

The first thing which I think you will desire to know from me is, how I like the place and whether I regret having come here. I can without hesitation give a favorable answer to these queries. The situation of the town, together with the noble bay, and the hilly or mountainous country by which it is surrounded, is infinitely more picturesque and beautiful than I had been led to suppose. You will, I trust, have a more vivid idea of it at some future day from my pencil than it would be in my power to give you by the pen. Suffice it to say on this point that I have already made three sketches from the surrounding heights which are very much admired, if I may judge by the expressions of praise which have been bestowed upon them. You will not be pleased that I add that two of them have been begged of me from a source where I could not give a denial. General Smith,[1] who is the commander in chief here, and whose

1. General Persifor F. Smith arrived in the steamer *California* on February 26, 1849. As commander of the military division of California, he superseded Colonel R. B. Mason. Bancroft, *History of California*, Vol. VI, p. 272 ff.

friendship is not to be slighted, asked one for himself and one for his wife, and perhaps, instead of regretting their loss (though, true, they can easily be replaced), I ought to be glad of an opportunity of doing him this favor. A Mr. Pendegrass, an English artist,[2] is taking some sketches also of the place, but in my opinion they are neither truthful nor executed with artistic skill, and yet he gets $25 for his *pencil* sketches which may occupy him a day or two at most. So you see, if worst comes to worst, I can earn my bed and board at least.

But to return to the queries with which I started. Having answered the first, as to whether I like the place, in the affirmative (though there is the objection of climate, which on account of the almost daily blowing March winds the year through, and the entire absence of rain through the summer, is very disagreeable), I proceed to the second, as to whether I regret having come. My sole object in this being a pecuniary one, it is not to be expected that I could accomplish much in so short a time, but so far as I can judge I have done right in coming.

My principal inducement was the exchange business proposed to me by Messrs. Drusina & Co. Owing to the much higher price of gold dust than was anticipated here, the profits to them will not be so great as was supposed, and it remains to be seen whether they will, in view of present appearances, carry out their original plan. If they do, I shall reap much benefit by it, as I am to have a certain commission which accrues to me whether the business be good or bad. I brought only a small sum with me for them, about $8,000.00, which I have already invested and sent forward to London on their account. The quality of this dust was very fine and I think the result will induce them to go on, though some four or five months will be required to learn it, as after it is ascertained, it will have to be communicated from London to Mexico.

In the meantime, until I hear from Mexico, which will probably be by the next steamer, I must remain in much uncertainty. I hope they will not wait (I mean Drusina & Co.) to get the returns from London, but that they will send me a good round sum for investment by the next steamer, which to me you will perceive is of no small importance. Should they, contrary to my expectations, decline entirely the operations in gold, I have still the promise of some commission business and can besides turn the small capital of my own which I have acquired to good account, so that the year which I propose to remain here will not, I trust, be otherwise than profitably employed. By the next steamer, which I think can hardly be delayed over three or four weeks,[3] I may be able to give you some more definite information as to the main point of interest to me, referred to above. I look with much anxiety for the arrival of this steamer as likely to bring me letters from you via the Isthmus. It seems a long time and is so, indeed, since I had this pleasure; possibly the clothes and other necessaries for which I wrote Brother Gilman in January last may also be received. I want them exceedingly.

In my last I gave you some account of the circumstances under which I left Mexico, joining a party who were coming through from Vera Cruz to Mazatlán to embark there for this place. I endeavored also to give you some slight idea of our outfit and appearance while in march, not very much unlike a gang of highwaymen. A considerable part of our journey was monotonous, over widely extended arid plains, mostly destitute of vegetation and trees, the appearance of which will be readily conceived when it is added that no rain has fallen here for five or six months. Here and there in some valley a little lower than the general level, where there might be a river, or smaller stream, so as irrigation could be effected, there might be seen

2. John Prendergast, described as an "amateur painter of California scenes, active between 1848 and 1851. He was an Englishman who came to San Francisco from Hawaii in July, 1848." New York Historical Society's *Dictionary of Artists in America, 1584–1860* (New Haven, 1957).

3. This was the *Panama*, which reached San Francisco on June 4, 1849. Bancroft, *History of California*, Vol. VI, pp. 137–138.

fields of grass, and in some instances of grain, just ripe for the sickle; in such places, a few fruit and other trees were also collected. As we descended into some of the lower valleys, several of the more gigantic species of cactus of the most extraordinary growth were observed, in the smaller towns and villages, wood (even fuel) being exceedingly scarce. Thus, cactus were used as fences to the yards and home lots, forming a most impenetrable hedge and even burying the houses in the luxuriance of its vegetation, the species called "órganos" sending up shafts into the air often 30 or 40 feet in height.

The first large town we arrived at after several days' journey from the capital was Querétaro, distinguished by a showy and lofty aqueduct conveying the water across a deep valley for the use of the town, but still more distinguished now as having been the seat of the Mexican government during their flight from Mexico—and the place where the treaty with our commissioners was concluded for peace. This is an old Spanish city and distinguished, as their large towns always are, by an abundance of convents and churches, with their lofty domes and steeples of elaborate and curious architecture. I would gladly have committed some of them to paper had time been allowed. Other towns of lesser note we passed through, and finally in about a fortnight arrived at Guadalajara, justly celebrated as one of the handsomest towns in Mexico, as it is one of the largest, after the capital. Here our contract for the carretas, or carts, ceased, and they were paid off, at a cost for the two, with six mules and three men, of about 250 dollars, they having paid all their own expenses. Our own private expenses, aside from the luggage, did not exceed 40 cents per day, for man and beast. True, economy was strictly studied. Every man was his own servant, even to the care of his animal. We had only one individual in that light—a colored man who served as cook, his expenses being paid as his sole remuneration.

We arrived at Guadalajara pretty well jaded out, and the two or three days required for obtaining pack mules to prosecute our journey was very acceptable for resting and recruiting. As to accommodations, however, we did not fare much better here than on the road. These Spanish or Mexican towns (except in the capital) have miserable *posadas*, or inns, worse bedrooms, and no beds at all. They give you a dirty room with a stone or tile floor, no furniture, and on this you are expected to extend your own *catre* (bedstead), or spread your own blanket, as the case may be.

These were the accommodations, if it be not an abuse of the term, which our party had to submit to in this fine city, myself being the only exception, inasmuch as I had a nice, portable, jointed iron bedstead, with sacking bottom, which folded up in a trunk. This proved a great luxury to me not only on the whole of this long tedious journey, but afterwards on the deck of the crowded steamer, and now in this equally crowded town, thanks to the forethought and generosity of my good friend, Mr. Drusina.

Guadalajara was the termination of our journey for wheels. From there to Tepic, or the coast, the face of the country is more broken with hills and ravines, and in many places simply a narrow mule path, so animals of burthen can alone be used for the transportation of merchandise or luggage. In passing these hills and ravines, we had more variety in the scenery than on the other side of Guadalajara. Several views were very striking and beautiful, but I had no time to take them. Only at Guadalajara I did get rather a striking sketch of the public or principal square, embracing the palace, cathedral, fountain, with orange trees, etc.

On our road to Tepic, which occupied six days, we met with no incident of importance, but a sad accident happened to a party of our countrymen who were a day or two behind us under the direction of Captain Hutton, entirely, however, through their own folly and imprudence. They had stopped at a town for the night where we had also been a day or two before (I forget the name), when, at starting in the morning, the main body of the party had moved on, leaving some seven or eight individuals behind; one of these men, on settling accounts, got into a dispute with a Mexican (I believe the innkeeper), about the bill, the whole difference being but a shilling or sixpence. Some hard words passed, when the American threw the money, which he contended was right, on the ground and was, with his companions, about to go, when the Alcalde interfered and ordered the man to dismount and pick up the money. This he indignantly refused to do. Then the Alcalde, being also, as appears, a colonel with soldiers at hand, ordered them to fire on the offending party, by which a young man who had had no part in the dispute was shot through the head and killed on the spot. The remainder of the party, with the exception of one who made his escape, were knocked or pulled from their horses and made prisoners. The man who escaped soon came up with the main party and gave the sad news. The result was that a parley took place between Captain Hutton and the Colonel, when the latter, finding probably on reflection that he had committed a serious outrage and that the affair would be laid before the government by our minister, came down from his high tone, offered to release the men in confinement, and to escort them out of the town, lest the populace, as he said, being excited, should rise upon and injure them.

This is the only accident of consequence which has come to my knowledge as respects these emigrating parties in crossing Mexico. With the exercise of common sense on the part of our countrymen, this would not have happened. In no instance where parties of ten or a dozen, well armed, have traveled together have I known of any attempt at robbery. It is now some six or eight months since a lonely part of the road between Guadalajara and Tepic was so much infested by these gentry as to become a serious matter and finally to attract the attention of the government. A company of troops was ordered to the neighborhood for its protection, and to disperse these marauders, but they were in larger numbers than was supposed and, calling all their force together, they attacked the soldiers and entirely defeated them, killing some 10 or 12 of their number. Although the robbers were successful on this occasion, they were soon afterwards overpowered and numbers of them taken and executed. On the very spot where they were successful over the troops, we saw as we passed, by the roadside, the captain and two of his gang hanging on a lofty gallows, with this inscription, "This is the punishment that the government awards to assassins and robbers." These criminals have been hanging here for a number of months, and no robbery, it is said, has been attempted in the meantime.

Long before reaching Tepic we had descended greatly from the high plains on which Mexico stands, 8,000 feet above the level of the sea, and of course we had to encounter a much warmer climate. Though this is far from being the hottest season, yet the sun, from 11 to 3 or 4 o'clock, sometimes without air, and riding all this time without dismounting, was almost insupportable, and we hailed with pleasure the sight of Tepic, some ten or twelve miles distant, as we descended some mountains into the broad and beautiful valley in which it lays. This, however, as before remarked, is not the season of vegetation and beauty in this country. That waits for the rainy season, which is now nearly at hand. It must be added that as this rainy season progresses into the middle and latter part of summer, the storms are accompanied by the most appalling thunder and lightning. This is peculiar to the whole coast, I mean this part of the Mexican coast—here in San Francisco, thunder and lightning are hardly known.

I was exceedingly fortunate to find Mr. [George W. P.] Bissell, the American Consul—and Howland & Aspinwall's agent, with whom I had been in active correspondence the past year, at Tepic. This is his home but, expecting the second steamer, the *Oregon*, to arrive daily at San Blas, he had been there to await her coming when, learning from my letters from Mexico that I was to be at Tepic and fearing that I might take the route through to Mazatlán without his seeing me, he had come 50 miles all the way for this purpose. It was gratifying to make his personal acquaintance, to meet his cordial reception, and to avail of the kind hospitality so heartily tendered me—a comfortable well-furnished house, good servants, a capital table and a nice fresh bed; only think of all this luxury after the provocations and fatigue I had so long undergone, the more to be appreciated as they were in a great measure unexpected.

I had only the evening, however, for conversation. Putting me in full possession of his house, he left the following morning before daylight for San Blas, promising to give me early information of the arrival of the steamer [*Oregon*] for my government, as I proposed to take passage in her. The following morning, before I was up, I had put into my hand a letter sent express from San Blas by Mr. Bissell to say that the steamer had arrived and that I must be there by 7 o'clock in the evening if I expected to secure my passage in her. Not a moment's time was to be lost. Through the aid of Mr. Forbes of Barron, Forbes & Co.,[4] I had "arrieros" and pack mules provided for Mr. Meredith and myself, and at half past nine we started. It is a tedious journey at best, and unfortunately our muleteer took the longest possible route, making the distance 54 miles when it might have been done in 8 miles or more less, arriving not till half past nine in the evening after being 12 hours in the saddle, almost without dismounting. Luckily, the steamer was detained until the following night, which gave me an opportunity of writing you via Mexico, which letter I trust you will ere this have received.

As before advised you, we had a very pleasant trip up here of 7 days and I was so fortunate as to get into pretty good quarters with Mr. Probst, who came here last December on business of Howland & Aspinwall, where I still am. As he retains his present home but 10 days longer, I have then, or before then, to look out for a new home. Expenses here are very heavy, the regular board of very crowded houses being $17 per week, and that with an indifferent table. It requires a good business to pay such expenses.

Quite a number of the passengers who came in the *Oregon*, thinking, I believe, almost to get gold by picking it up in the streets, after having visited the mines, determine to give up their brilliant prospects and return home in the *California*. Your papers will be full of their views of the country and of the mining business. For particulars I refer to them, for I have not time myself to go into these details. If I were simply confined to working at the placer with my own hands, I think I should be going home, too. The accounts from the placer are certainly, for the most, rather discouraging; the melting of the snows in the mountains has caused the rivers to swell and overflow to an unusual degree so that all the best diggings are under water; besides there are not a few persons sick there from exposure. The water they work in is cold, while the sun and heat are overpowering through the day; at night, cold enough to require two or three blankets. Many return under these circumstances, discouraged. By far the greater part, however, remain, and in the face of difficulties, even at the expense of health, gold will be obtained, and much of it, too, before the year is over. One other difficulty: at the mill above Sutter's, serious difficulties have arisen between the Americans, mostly the Oregon people, and the Indians; a good many have been killed on both sides and the most serious consequences are apprehended.[5]

I am glad to add in conclusion that there is a regular Congregational service in the little church, or school house, here twice on each Sabbath, with a lecture on Wednesday evening,

4. An English business firm at Tepic, Mexico. Alexander Forbes was British vice-consul at Tepic from 1847–1849. H. I. Priestley in *California, a History of Upper and Lower California*, by Alexander Forbes (San Francisco, 1937), p. xiii.
5. Bancroft states that half of Oregon's population "was emptied into California," attracted by the golden harvest they hoped to obtain. See his *History of California*, Vol. VI, p. 112.

the congregation regular in attendance and of a very respectable character. A Mr. [Albert] Williams, a Presbyterian clergyman who came out in the *Oregon* and who preaches occasionally, has established a school in the same building.[6]

My best love to my dear Libby and the boys. I trust your next letters will give me gratifying accounts of them. With much love to all those who enquire after me, I remain, dearest,

Yours faithfully and affectionately,

D. W. Coit

6. See the Introduction, p. 17.

[*first part missing*]   [San Francisco, May-June] *1849*

... House rent and servants' wages are the dearest of all commodities and are so like to continue. A very simple tenement, indeed, barely sufficient to keep you from the weather and give room to turn round, rents, as you will see, for $100 or even $150 *per month*, and, where the situations are the most desirable for business, for double those prices. Servants' wages are, for men, $140 to $150 per month—I don't know that women servants could be hired at all. Their labor gets paid for in the same proportion, $6 per dozen for washing (shirts alone, $8 per dozen). I have not yet had any washing done, and shall not until it becomes a matter of absolute necessity. I hope the clothing I ordered in January last has been sent on, particularly the shirts, which I very much want.

You will now desire to hear something about mining operations, and perhaps will be surprised after all the flattering statements that have been broadcast through the United States of wealth to be acquired here, almost without labor or trouble, to learn that almost without an exception, those who have arrived here and gone into the interior and viewed affairs there by the guidance of their own proper eyes and senses, have been egregiously disappointed, and many have already returned to the United States in entire disgust. It so happens, the present season, that the rivers in which gold most abounds are at an unusual height, owing to the melting of the snows, so that all the best diggings are under water, and will probably so continue for a month or more. This has too much discouraged those who went to the placers with expectations of immediate work, which would bring them in two or three ounces of gold daily, whereas they found that at present, instead of two or three ounces daily, they could not earn with certainty more than as many dollars—at least, such has been the case in a great many instances. Instead of waiting, then, for a more favorable state of the country, they have come away in disgust; some went back in the last steamer to Panama and others now wait here to avail themselves of the next steamer, satisfied to abandon all hopes of becoming rich by mining.

You will naturally inquire whether all those fine stories of single persons having extracted their $6, $8, or $10.00 the past year were false, and only circulated to mislead. I answer no, not a few persons were thus successful, but it was by no means a general thing. The great proportion of those who labored the past year got only a comparatively small sum or sums, and here was the great error in the statements at home, making it appear that great success would attend the labor of *every* one who chose to be industrious, but it was not so; neither will it be in the future. *Great* success will be rare, and a good deal accidental—somewhat like drawing the highest prize in the lottery.

Still, I doubt not that after the waters shall have subsided, a great deal of gold will be extracted in the aggregate the ensuing autumn and winter by the immense population who will be engaged in the extraction, and no doubt besides that many will be so fortunate as to hit on rich deposits, as they did last year, and obtain several thousand dollars worth, in as many months. One circumstance at least will be much more favorable to the miners this year than the last—they will obtain provisions and other necessaries at infinitely less prices than they paid last year. The class of persons who will, after all, be the greatest sufferers are those in the United States who have made large shipments of goods here in utter ignorance, as one would think, of the quantities or kinds of merchandise required. Already the harbor is full of vessels with many kinds of goods entirely unsalable, and which can only be disposed of at immense loss, and as yet the shipments from the United States in December, January, and February last, a part of which your letter from New York dated in January refers to, have hardly begun to arrive. I fear that many persons, who have shipped thus heedlessly and imprudently from the United States, will be great sufferers and many failures will be no doubt the result.[1]

June 17th. You will perceive that the foregoing has been a long time written in anticipation of some suitable opportunity, which has not presented itself. On the 4th, the third of Howland & Aspinwall's steamers, the *Panama*, arrived, bringing a full load of passengers, some 300 in all, with an immense quantity of letters—several cartlaods, requiring the united exertions of half a dozen people a whole day to sort them. I was kept a good while in suspense as to whether I should find any, but was at length gratified in the receipt of quite a number, yours of 16th and 17th April and my dear Libby's of the 16th, together with a letter from Brother Joshua and Brother Gilman, and a few lines from Wm. Aspinwall. After so long an interval without any intelligence from home, these letters have afforded me a high degree of satisfaction, assuring me as they do that you were all well.

On the 13th the *Oregon* arrived, bringing an equal complement of passengers with the *Panama*, but no new mail from the United States. She brought, however, a Mexican mail from San Blas and by this I had the pleasure to receive your letter of 20th March. By this steamer I also received the package of clothing, etc., which Wm. Aspinwall had the goodness to give in charge to Captain Budd and it is, I assure you, most acceptable. I only regret that it had not occurred to you to send me the particulars of cost of the various items, instead of naming the total cost in a lump. Some of the articles do not fit me, as the boots and shoes, and others I have no occasion for, such as the India rubber bed, blankets, coffee, pillows, etc., and in putting prices on them it would be desirable to know what they cost. Although all these things have fallen in price prodigiously, still, being of rather a nice description, they may be disposed of without loss. The shirts, sheets, towels, clothes from Worthington, etc., etc., will answer admirably, and above all I am gratified with the daguerrotypes, which are truly excellent and will be a great source of comfort to me. I thank dear Cousin Betsey for her kind remembrance and am glad that she so abundantly enjoys those divine supports which are so great a solace in affliction. Make my best love acceptable to her when you may have opportunity....

[*Last part of letter missing*]

1. In the early gold-rush days, before sufficient time had elapsed for goods to arrive from a distance, money was plentiful and prices high, as merchants sought to outwit competitors. Charles L. Ross and Howard & Mellus, at first the two chief rivals, kept a lookout for vessels entering the Golden Gate, and when one was sighted they would race to shipside to strike a bargain for purchase of the entire cargo. Later, as businessman Coit points out, the market could be quite capricious, high one day and glutted the next, with auction prices at a ruinous level. Even so, due to lack of adequate warehousing facilities, it was considered best to sell at once, rather than to hold a cargo in the uncertain hope of making a better sale later. Cf. Bancroft, *California Inter Pocula* (San Francisco, 1888), pp. 346–347, 350–351, and 358–359. See also Coit's letter of April 14, 1851, in which he writes that goods could be bought at auction in San Francisco so cheaply that they could be sent back to New York, and sold at a profit—to the San Francisco buyer.

San Francisco, July 15th, 1849

My very dear wife, *Sunday evening*

After an hour's communing with my daguerrotype family, and reading your last letters over for the twentieth time, I take my pen to hold a little chat with my dearest, best friend, and to be in some degree prepared for the next steamer, which, to our great disappointment, does not yet show herself, though some time due.

This day is particularly suited to more than usual intercourse with you, a day of rest and meditation, as it is, and I not infrequently begin and follow your footsteps through the whole of it. I rise with you in the morning, which at this season is at about six or seven o'clock, as I presume, and soon descend into the back parlor, where the family shortly assemble for your morning devotions, and where I trust the good health of your father and mother will always enable them to join you. Next comes the well-spread breakfast table, and I think, with more than usual pleasure in my own utter deprivation of any such luxuries, of your nice fresh butter and strawberries and raspberries, etc. Next comes the preparation for church, and the day being fine, and the children in their appropriate attire, I fancy the group winding their way thitherward, you without the wonted arm for your support. I look at every house, and corner, and tree, and face, on the way.

How unchanged all, and how different in this respect from the daily changing scene I am here in the midst of. In church, too, I recognize all the well-known faces—the Huntingtons, the Spaldings, the Arms, and numerous others. Here and there some one must be wanting, some one whom I had well known and respected, and shall now see no more; this is the inevitable result of every year. After one of Mr. Arms' best sermons and the service ended, my thoughts turn to the Sunday School and to my old scholars, probably now instructors themselves, as a number were very capable of being. I listen to the friendly greetings you meet in leaving church and on your way home, and to an inquiry now and then made after your absent husband. Your simple lunch comes next, and then the routine of the morning is repeated. At home again, you read a while, and then the children go through their exercises, catechism, etc. Now comes the social tea gathering, and the delicious fruit again. Do not be surprised that I expatiate on this—one who has tasted no vegetable substance for weeks, no, not even a potato, may well be allowed to speak with rather more than ordinary interest on such a topic. You now probably attend the monthly concert, or evening lecture, and thus concludes the day. When shall I have the happiness thus to pass the day with you again?

An abundance of vessels have poured in from the United States since I last wrote, of those which left in December and January, and in one or other of these have come several of our neighbors, who have, I believe, all found me out and given me much local news. Our neighbor Smith's son Henry has called several times. He has made an engagement to remain with Mr. Beach, Mr. Goddard's former partner, where he will be well paid. Tell the family this, and that I think it a better place than going to the mines.

Perit Huntington also arrived well and has proceeded to the mines about a week since. Mr. John Lathrop also called several times. He has now gone to the mines. Tell his wife from me that I never saw him looking better. I am afraid to say how many pounds of flesh he had gained, though quite as many as his clothes would compass. Our good friend, Dr. Coit, does not yet arrive, though this is not strange, very many vessels being yet behind. I am sorry, to tell you the truth, that he comes at all. This is no place for him, I mean this town, which is an extremely healthy place, and more physicians already here than can get a living—and besides, a most expensive place, unless with some such management as I told you in my last I had resorted to.

We have had a week of really warm weather, at least in the middle of the day, and for the most part without those most disagreeable winds I have heretofore spoken of, though the warmest nights invariably call for a couple of thick blankets. Finding the heat somewhat oppressive, I was induced for a day or two to put on a thin coat, and the result has been a pretty severe cold, which for a day or so, attended as it was by a slight diarrhea, made me half sick, but with a hot foot bath, and dieting for a day, all came right again, except a slight cough, which will not long remain. Diarrheas have been very prevalent, with which, whether right or not I can't say, the water stands charged.

The news from the mines is rather more encouraging. The waters are now falling fast, and in a very few days access will be had to the rich deposits in the beds of the rivers which are counted on for a large extraction of gold dust. Many individuals who came here when the waters were at the highest and went to the mines or placers with too inflated ideas of immediate success were so disappointed and disheartened that they returned here forthwith and took the first opportunity which offered for home again, several by the very steamer in which they came. These persons, I doubt not, on their return, to justify their own course, will give a most unfavorable report of mining operations, and I am prepared to learn by the next accounts from home that the reaction in public opinion on the subject will be very great.

My own opinion is, however, that the statements which you have heretofore had of the wealth of the country in its mines, and particularly in its gold mines, are substantially correct. True, every man who works at the placers will not be successful in the degree he may have anticipated, but a few indeed, comparatively, will hit upon the richest deposits (which are like prizes in a lottery, only here and there) and make themselves rich in a single year. The most persons who are industrious, are accustomed to hard work, and who will be persevering, can hardly fail to acquire some thousands in a few months—vastly more than the same class of persons would be likely to earn in any other mode of employment. When it is considered that there will be engaged in this business for the balance of the year some 40,000 or 50,000 persons, it may well be supposed that a very large amount of gold dust will be extracted in the aggregate, not less, I am inclined to think, than $15,000,000 or $20,000,000.

Up to the present time, owing in a great measure to the reasons I have given, not any very large quantities of dust have come forward here for sale, and there being much competition in the purchase, the price has been kept up very high—too high, indeed, for me to do much in it, or to hold out encouragement to my Mexican friends to extend their operations. The probabilities are that when the mines shall become more productive, as I have shown you will now very soon be the case, and the dust consequently shall flow in here more freely, I may then be enabled to purchase at lower prices, and thus the plan be carried into effect which was my inducement to come here.

July 22nd, Sunday evening. We have had a week of much interest since the foregoing was penned. On Monday morning the steamer was announced and everyone was on the "qui vive" for letters and news. So large were the mails, however, that the whole day was required with the aid of half a dozen persons to sort them, and none were delivered until the following day, Tuesday, unless a few by favor, amongst which I was happy to count my own. Your letter of 14th May was of more than ordinary interest, advising me, as it does, of your return to Norwich, of the outpouring of God's spirit in our dear church, and above all that our dear Libby is a participant in this greatest of all blessings....

I have spoken of the past week as having been one of unusual excitement. A principal cause of this has been the trial of a gang of fellows calling themselves Hounds and Regulators, who have been going about the town for some time past in the most public manner, drinking and carousing through the day, and at night committing the most unheard of outrages upon unoffending citizens, maiming and otherwise ill-treating them and robbing their property. After parading last Sabbath through the streets with drum and fife, visiting sundry restaurants and taverns, helping themselves and not paying, and thus passing the day, when the night had set in they proceeded to the outskirts of the town to a place called The Point, where they attacked a number of Chilean families, living in tents, in the most brutal manner.[1] Guns and pistols were used, and no less than six of these poor inoffensive people were badly wounded; all their stock of goods, together with a considerable amount of money, some $5,000 in all, was taken, and their tents torn down and destroyed.[2]

Heretofore there had been a criminal supineness and neglect on the part of the inhabitants (in the absence of a regular police) with regard to the consistent outrages of this body of depredators, but the matter was now becoming too serious in its character for any longer hesitation. A meeting was called by the Alcalde [Dr. Thaddeus M. Leavenworth], in the public square, of those disposed to promote order, and to put a stop to these scandalous proceedings. He made a report of his examination into the outrages of the preceding night and suggested that it was high time that the citizens should take measures to prevent any further occurrence of such scenes. Nearly a thousand persons, indeed, it seemed that nearly all the respectable part of the population, forthwith collected. A Mr. [W. D. M.] Howard, one of the principal merchants, was appointed chairman. Spirited addresses were made by Mr. [Samuel] Brannan, Mr. [Frank] Ward, Captain Smith, and others and the enthusiasm and determination of a few to act spread like wildfire to the many. It was determined on the instant to swear in special constables, to organize and arm, and send parties in every direction to seize on these Hounds and all others known to have been concerned in the affair in question, and to bring them before a court, which was organized to determine on their participation in the recent riot, and commit them for trial.

Now succeeded a scene of much excitement; armed parties were seen crossing the public square in all directions, some going in pursuit of, and others bringing in, the criminals; the poor abused Chileans, men, women, and children, coming as witnesses to give their evidence, some of them wounded as they were. In fine, about twenty of the prominent actors of these Hounds, including two or three of their officers, were soon made prisoners, and there being abundant testimony against them, they were sent off on board a man-of-war, there to await their trial before a jury so soon as circumstances would admit.

Sunday, July 29. I heard a sermon from Mr. Hunt[3] this morning on the subject of gambling, and certainly, if anywhere, there is occasion here for such a discourse, there being no law to prevent it and great numbers of idlers with their pockets full of gold, with scores of professional gamblers, who it would appear have been attracted here in greater proportion than

1. Evidently not only Chileans, but other Latins, who lived on the Southwest slope of Telegraph hill, up Vallejo and Broadway, in the vicinity of Dupont (Grant) and Kearny streets. The settlement of Sydney Town lay to the east of them. Bancroft, *History of California*, Vol. VI, pp. 169, 183–185.
2. The "Hounds," later called the "Regulators," were a company of desperadoes who terrorized the city in the summer of 1849. They were composed of rowdies of the New York Volunteers who had flocked to the mines on being discharged. "Drifting back to San Francisco," says Mary Floyd Williams, "they formed the nucleus of a criminal 'gang,' which adopted a semblance of military discipline, formulated rules, elected officers, and established so-called headquarters in a large tent known as Tammany Hall. They often paraded the streets with music and banners, and their commissary was provisioned by raids upon stores and restaurants, which were forced to supply their demands and 'charge it to the Hounds,' as the marauders marched away with insolent laughter. . . ." See her *History of the San Francisco Committee of Vigilance of 1851* (Berkeley, 1921), pp. 105–106. Bancroft gives an excellent and colorful description of these lawless times. See his *Popular Tribunals* (San Francisco, 1887), Vol. I, pp. 76–102. Another good account is given in *The Annals*, pp. 555–561.
3. See the Introduction, p. 17. On January 14, 1850, Coit had more to say about the Reverend Mr. Hunt.

other professions. All this leads to its being carried on to an alarming extent; indeed, there is no attempt at concealment. One-half the buildings around the public square,[4] including the largest hotel in the place, also on the square, are gambling houses, publicly open from morning till night and from night till morning, the Sabbath itself forming no exception to the rule. At this moment while I write, these houses may one and all be seen thronged by a mixed and motley crowd, drinking, gambling, swearing—the three universally going together. The gang called "Hounds" having had their trial before a jury (all except myself from our house having been called upon to serve) and pronounced guilty, with one or two exceptions only, were yesterday sentenced by the court to be sent home (I mean to the Atlantic states), a part of the number to be confined there for ten, and a part for five years. A most righteous decision, in my opinion. The effect here in preserving order for the time to come cannot be too highly appreciated.

The steamer is now expected to leave for Panama in a day or two, and as I have yet much to write for that occasion, may not find it convenient to add, unless something of importance should turn up. Remember me affectionately to my darlings, as also to your father and mother, with best regards to other inquiring friends and believe me, dearest,

Ever faithfully and affectionately yours,
D. W. Coit

4. The first hotel in the city deserving of the name was the "City Hotel," erected in 1846 at the southwest corner of Clay and Kearny Streets; *The Annals*, pp. 647–652. There were others, notably the "Parker House," erected in 1849 by Robert A. Parker, from lumber brought out from the East, ready framed, for the purpose. It stood on Kearny Street and faced Portsmouth Square. Indicative of the inflated prices of the day, it paid $120,000 a year in rents, one-half of which was paid by gamblers, who occupied the second floor. *Ibid.*, pp. 250–254; and Morgan & Scobie, *Three Years in California*, op. cit., pp. 87, 150, 337, and 340.

My dear wife   *San Francisco, August 19th, 1849*

The arrival of the steamer [*Panama*] is just announced, and we wait with much anxiety the delivery of the letters which, from the numbers always brought, and the long time required to sort them at the post office, we can hardly receive before tomorrow or the next day. In the meantime, I will commence my monthly letter to you, which the day being the Sabbath the more invites me to.

There is no abatement in the arrivals from the Atlantic states, and the consequent influx of passengers which pour in like a March flood. Some go off to the mines, but many stay permanently here, so many that, although buildings spring up daily on all sides with mushroom rapidity, still the demand for house room continues unabated, and rents are at awful prices. This steamer just arrived adds 350 persons to the crowd. A very great number of physicians, I learn, are on board, some 60 or 70, it is said. What they are all to do, although medical men are paid very high for their services, is more than I can tell. This reminds me that our friend Dr. Coit[1] has arrived, now about a week since. He has been perplexed, as almost every newcomer at first is, to know what to do, but I believe has pretty much determined to remain at this place and follow his profession. He tells me he came very near bringing a building for a hospital, and it is a great pity he did not, for whether he might have required it for that pur-

1. Dr. Benjamin B. Coit, born in Norwich, Connecticut, April 10, 1801, graduated at Yale College in 1822, earned his medical degree in 1826, and then was attracted to California, as we see, in 1849. There he remained until his death in April, 1867, a respected member of his profession. Frederick W. Chapman, *The Coit Family*, p. 200; The San Francisco *Bulletin*, April 17, 1867.

pose or not, it would have paid him a good round sum which in his situation would, I am sure, have been very convenient.

Another Norwich party has also arrived—Falkner the editor,[2] and Colonel Devotion, with a number of others whom I did not know. They, too, were in a great stew (to use a homely phrase) for a day or two. They had brought buildings, it is true, but they had not the most distant conception of the value of lots in suitable situations for their erection. Most fortunately for them, the plan of Falkner to establish a newspaper fell in with the views and wishes of a number of the leading men of the place, who came very opportunely, as well as unexpectedly, to his aid, proffering him all the money he required—some thousands of dollars. Again, the famous Steinberger, well known in the south as a great speculator (he has failed two or three times at least), and who is operating here in real estate to a great extent, furnished him a nice lot on very accommodating terms. This was all that was wanting, already the building is up, and so far completed as to receive the presses and printing apparatus, as well as some of the tenants, and all this has been the work of a week only, so you will perceive with what rapidity things move here.

Churches and congregations are also increasing somewhat, though where the affairs of this world are so prominently before the minds of men, it is very apt to be to the exclusion, in a great measure, of those of another world. I have before told you of a Congregational Church under the charge of the Reverend Mr. Hunt,[3] and a Presbyterian organized recently under the charge of the Reverend Mr. Williams.[4] They—the latter—worship as yet in a spacious tent, but they have secured a fine lot, and will shortly build. I have been to two services there today. Notice was given of a Seaman's Friend Society to be organized this week for preaching afloat. There is, besides, a Baptist Church already erected, and the Methodists have also their meetings. Last of all, the Mormons have their preaching, and to my great mortification I got caught within its precincts and had to sit out a very long and tedious sermon, when I expected to have heard Mr. Hunt. This was a week ago. The burthen of the discourse was the necessity for, and reason of, the "new revelation."

[August] 21st. After waiting two entire days and making sundry useless efforts to get through the throng pressing about the post office for letters, I have at length succeeded in getting mine, and am happy to find among them one from you of the 25th June, giving me the best of all news, that you were well. . . . By the bye, Beach has been very fortunate in his business since he came here. He had at an early period a number of consignments which he took with him to the mines and sold to much advantage, but the important hit he made was the purchase of a pretty large building lot on his first arrival for $4,000. I suppose he must have bought it on credit, for he had at the time no means available and doubtless was led to it from the circumstances of having a house coming out. Well, the result has been that his lot in this short period of time has risen to the value of $10,000, and having now received his house and put that on but a small part of the lot, it makes it a very valuable property. He occupies it himself for business purposes, but if he chose to rent it, he could without any doubt get $8,000 or $10,000 per year for it. Rents, however, are so exorbitantly dear that it is impossible for them to continue for any great length of time at anything like present rates. If I had had the courage to have entered into real estate speculations when I came here, I might now have

2. Possibly William Faulkner of Norwich, Conn., where he published a Democratic paper. He came to California with printing press, types, paper, and a two-story house in 1849. In August, he and Warren Leland started the *Pacific Press*, which was very successful for a time. See Helen Harding Bretnor, *A History of California Newspapers, 1846–1858* (Los Gatos, California, 1962), pp. 99–100, 340.
3. Introduction, p. 17.
4. *Loc. cit.*

San Francisco in 1849: North Bay and the Golden Gate

San Francisco in 1849: Portsmouth Square above Yerba Buena Cove

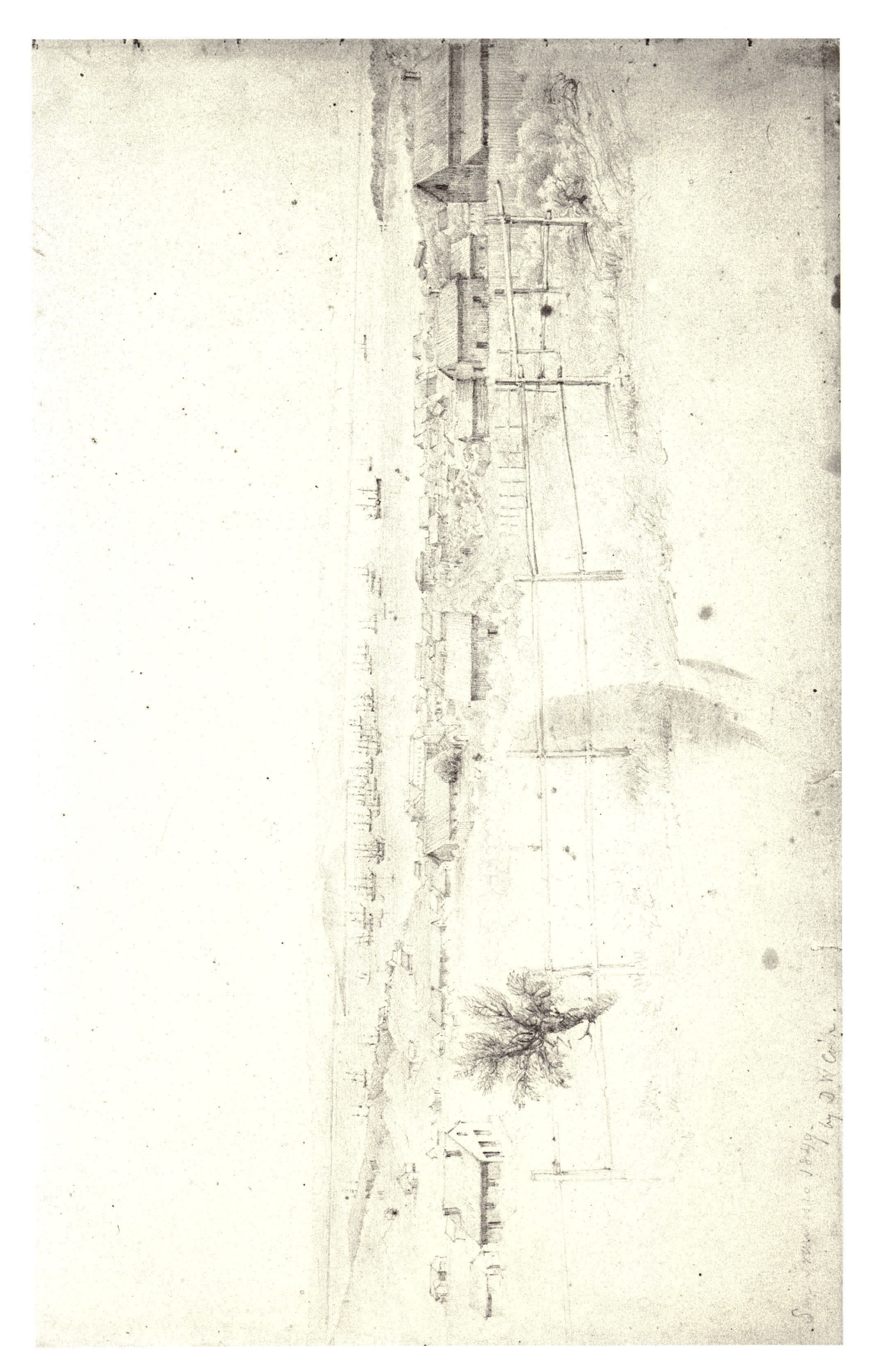

SAN FRANCISCO IN 1849: YERBA BUENA COVE FROM UPPER CLAY STREET

San Francisco in 1849: Yerba Buena Cove and Mission Bay from Telegraph Hill been a rich man, but I had different objects in view (which thus far have not been realized, except to a very limited extent) and, besides, I did not incline to incur risks.

I consider the risk alone of fire here exceedingly great.[5] The town is but one great tinder box, and a fire once commenced at the windward side would be certain to burn the whole of it to ashes, and this I predict will sooner or later be its fate. The material is all of combustibles, very dry pine, with a large proportion of canvas roofs; no engines, I mean fire engines; no hooks or ladders; and in fact no water (except in very deep wells) available where it might be most required. Many people have their all at stake under these circumstances. Is it not enough to make a prudent man tremble? Insurance I take to be entirely out of the question; no office would take such hazardous risks.
[*Remainder of letter missing*]

5. The fires that ravaged San Francisco have been described by many. See *The Annals*, pp. 241–242, 274–276, 290, 329–333, and 344–347; Morgan & Scobie, *op. cit.*, pp. 149–151, 353.

My dearest wife   *San Francisco, September 20th, 1849*
The last steamer which arrived from Panama on the 18th instant brought no mail from the Atlantic states and I, in common with many others, have to mourn over the gap which is thus made in our domestic correspondence. Passengers, however, have come who left New York as lately as 24 July and there are both newspapers and private letters to that date. Mr. Beach has been so fortunate as to get a letter from his wife dated in the latter part of July, but I do not learn that it contained anything of interest to me. He, poor man, has been very sick indeed, dangerously so, having had a brain fever or something approaching to it, but I am glad to say he is better, though still complaining much of his head and incapacitated from attending to business.

There are many cases of sickness amongst us, but they have mostly originated abroad, either on the rivers in the interior, which are always unhealthy at this season of the year, or at sea on board of crowded vessels for many months, with poor accommodations and oftentimes with indifferent food for sometime before getting here. Some of the passengers from Panama by merchant vessels have suffered very much and many have died on the voyage.

This place is, I think, generally a healthy one, notwithstanding one of the most disagreeable [climates] (to me at least) that I have ever been in. The whole summer has been so cold as to require winter clothing, even to flannels throughout, and at night two or three blankets, and yet we get along without fire except for cooking purposes. Some few houses have fireplaces in their parlors, but by far the greater proportion have none. The mornings are generally passable, occasionally very pleasant, but after noon a strong wind springs up from the northwest, coming in from the sea, and blows a perfect gale till night and oftentimes through the night. This, however, is not all; the air is filled with sand and dust, there having been no rain of consequence for six months past and the whole rear of the town (the quarter from which the winds blow) being composed of immense sand hills. You may judge then how disagreeable these winds must be, carrying the sand and dust into every crevice and seam of your clothing and into every pore of the skin. Clothing, of course, soon becomes soiled and, indeed, spoiled, and this is felt the more annoying and burthensome so far as undergarments are concerned, where washing, and that none of the best, costs you $5 to $6 pr. dozen.

The price of labor continues much as it has been and, I presume, will not vary much while gold can be so easily acquired. Carpenters, and mechanics generally, can earn $10, $12, and $14 per day, and a common laborer, at shoveling or digging, $5 or $6. I think that female labor is even paid at a higher rate in proportion. I had occasion not long since to have some common sheeting cotton sewed in strips of five or six yards with a view to make the ceiling of a room (such a thing as plaster being entirely unknown, or at least out of the question). The sewing was of the most simple, easy, and expeditious description, just running several stitches on the needle at once, I suppose about 6 or 8 to the inch.

Well, with some difficulty, I at length found a woman living in the outskirts of the town who would do it "to oblige me," and what do you think the charge was? 25 cents per yard!! And when I asked if she could not do it for 20 cents per yard if I had more to do, she said No, she could not *afford* to do it for less than 25 cents. She had abundance of work that would enable her to earn $8 or $10 per day. I asked her what rent they paid (she was married to a carpenter who was also getting his $12 per day). "Oh," said she, "we own the house. We've been here some time. My husband bought a little spot first and put up this house, and afterwards when he had earned a little more money he bought the rest of the lot" (a lot being 138 feet square). "Why," said I, "this must be a little fortune to you now." "Yes," said she, with a drawl and nasal twang which made it quite amusing, "my husband says if any one comes along that wants it more than he does, and will just give him $20,000 for it, why he may have it and we'll pack up and go home."

After this manner, numbers who, in the ordinary course of events, would never have been worth $500 in their lives have suddenly and in the most unexpected manner become possessed of great wealth. I know not a few of those ranking as tradesmen and merchants who were, not a year and a half ago, worth $5,000, who now count their $100,000 and from that to half a million, solely by the rise of real estate.[1]

But, to return to the subject of labor, I heard of another woman who, I was told, would do my work cheaper, and of her I went in pursuit. She, too, lived quite out of town where were, only here and there, small scattered houses. To get into her humble tenement I had to ascend on the outside of the house a small flight of steps which took me to a garret sort of room covered overhead by the roof and on one side only about four feet high and sloping up to 7 or 8 feet on the opposite side, perhaps 12 feet square. This was a more ladylike sort of body than my other acquaintance, a little lone widow with two tidy-looking children; she had never known what it was to work before she lost her husband. She was from the lower Mississippi and had come all this long way, poor and helpless as she was, to better her fortunes. She had found, she told me, real friends in some of the most respectable people of the place who had assisted her by furnishing work and giving her their countenance, but still she had to be very industrious and work hard to pay her expenses. "And what may you pay a month," I asked, "for this little bit of room?" (which being so far out of the way I thought might be very moderate). To my surprise she told me $40 per month, or $480 per year.

While on this topic of the high price of rents and the unexpected accumulation of property by very humble individuals, I am reminded of the family where I am accustomed to get milk. The husband, also a carpenter, has been at the mines for the past five months or so. Since I first arrived, shortly before he went, he bought a small lot and put a pretty well-built one-story house on it. Doing the work himself, I daresay the whole concern did not cost him over $2,000, and when he left to go to the mines he could not probably have got over $50 per

---

1. The writer in *The Annals of San Francisco* (1854), obviously speaking from personal observation, grew almost delirious in describing this period of the city's history. He concluded one paragraph with this statement, "*And every body made money, and was suddenly growing rich.*" Pp. 215–217.

month rent, there being but two very moderate-sized rooms without even an entry way or garret. On going for my milk as usual two days ago, the wife said to me that she was going to move into a smaller and more retired house back from the town, as she could not afford to live at a rent of $300 per month, a price which she has actually rented her house for. This is even better than selling milk at 6s. per quart (75 cents), the regular price it now brings, and this is the way things go in this strangest of all strange places.

The house which we took for six months, as I formerly told you, at a rent of $125 per month (between three of us), I doubt not would now rent for $300 or more per month. What I am to do when the time expires in November I know not, though in the meantime we rent out ourselves enough to more than cover all our cost, thus living rent-free thus far.

[Unsigned]

October [?] 30, 1849[1]

... I frequently stumble unexpectedly on old acquaintances and friends. I met recently our cousin, Tracey Bill, but only saw him once. He must have gone to the mines. I also met a young Mr. Fitch, from Fitchville, a nephew of our friend Asa, also a son of Mr. Lester of New Rochelle. I think I told you of my meeting Pell, the Mormon whom we knew at the latter place. He has stumbled on property too, I should think as much as $8,000 or $10,000.

As to my own prospects in business, which, as I told you before, had not come up to my expectations, they are now looking somewhat better, my last letters from my friend Drusina giving me encouragement that he would ship me considerable sums of coin for investment in gold dust. Indeed, the last steamer brought me $26,000, being a larger sum than any one else received. Still, even this is far short of what was anticipated; "nous verrons";[2] in the meantime you must be sensible from what I have told you that I pursue the most rigid economy, that I may, if possible, accumulate a little sum for your permanent benefit and that we need not be quite so straightened as we have been. If I can accomplish this, it will be something.

By the last steamer I enclosed a little note for you in a letter I wrote Wm. Aspinwall—this was aside from my main letter by the steamer....

I sent you, or for your use, by last steamer to care of Mr. Gilman, 300 dollars in gold dust, and shall send more ere long. Goodbye, my best love, embrace all my darlings for me and believe me, truly and faithfully, your affectionate husband.   *D. W. C.*

1. The first part of this letter is missing.
2. This term, "nous verrons," we shall see, was a cant phrase of the period.

My dear Harriet,   *San Francisco, November 11th, 1849*

I wrote you in the last days of October by the steamer of the 1st inst., and another steamer to sail on the 15th again affords me this pleasure. It is said that the letters by this opportunity will meet no detention on the Isthmus and that they will arrive in the United States in a shorter period of time than any which have previously left here. The steamer *Panama* arrived here from Panama, bringing a mail from New York just after I had written the letter above referred to, and I had again the greatest of all the pleasures I experience here in the receipt of another of your letters, of 24th August. I am glad to learn that you have experienced so little alarm in regard to that terrible scourge, the cholera, which has had so many victims in some particular locations, as at St. Louis, Sandusky, etc. The sins of a people, not excepting our own people, seem to call for these visitations of Providence, but how little, after all, they are regarded. We live here in the midst of a most corrupt and wicked people where the restraints which keep even bad men within some bounds amongst us at home are thrown aside, and I expect nothing less than to see the place visited with some signal judgment from Heaven ere long.

Even this sacred day (I write on the Sabbath) is little regarded by the great mass of people, and many who have been accustomed at home for the sake of respectability or of decency to pay some outward deference to it seem here to think it uncalled for and show themselves under their true colors. In going to church this morning, I could not but be impressed with this state of things. A large house near ours in the stage of building had some 40 or 50 carpenters engaged at work upon it. The peddlers' stands and shops about the public square were all, or a large proportion of them, occupied as usual, and the immense gambling establishments—the most seductive and at the same time the vilest of all vile places—had their golden hoards spread out as usual. In the evening the temptation will be increased by musical bands, serenades, and perhaps balls.

I was wending my way to my usual place of worship, the tent where the Presbyterian congregation under the charge of the Reverend Mr. Williams meets, when I met a friend who told me they had no service owing to the inclemency of the weather for the past day or two.[1] Then we turned our steps up the hill to the Baptist meeting house, under the charge of the Reverend Mr. Wheeler,[2] where I had heard a most charitable and I must say eloquent discourse the past Sabbath, which put me quite in love with the man. The subject was, "The unity of the spirit in the bond of peace," or at least this was the pith of the text. In discoursing on this topic he took occasion to say that there was a broad platform on which all evangelical Christians could meet and be united heart and hand, then embraced the leading essential

---

1. In farewell sermon to his congregation in 1854, Mr. Williams wrote: "During the months of November and December, in consequence of heavy rains, religious services were somewhat irregularly attended; and at the close of the year 1849, they were no longer attempted in the tent." Albert Williams, *Farewell Discourse, op. cit.*, pp. 15–16.

2. Osgood Church Wheeler, a native of New York, born in 1816, slender and only five feet, two and one-half inches tall, made up in vigor and zeal what he lacked in physical stature. He was the first pastor of the Baptist church in East Greenwich, Rhode Island, achieved great success, and then was sent to a more important charge in Jersey City, New Jersey. There he did equally well, but within a year, the American Baptist Home Missionary Society called on him and, in November, 1848, said, "We want you to go to California as our Pioneer Missionary." On December 1, he and his wife sailed on the steamer *Falcon*, via the Isthmus, boarding the *California* at Panama on January 31, and reaching San Francisco on February 28, 1849. There, he began to preach, at first in the home of Charles L. Ross, but in July, 1849, he bought a lot on Washington Street for $10,000, built a church in 22 working days, and thus "completed and dedicated the first Protestant church edifice in California." *First Steamship Pioneers* (San Francisco, 1874), pp. 307–335. As can be imagined, these early church structures were very simple, sometimes partly in tent form. See also O. C. Wheeler, *The Story of Early Baptist History in California*, pp. 11–15; Introduction, p. 17.

doctrines of the gospel. As to mere forms and ceremonies, they were altogether of minor importance, thus setting aside that doctrine in regard to baptism which we consider so uncharitable, but which most of his profession affect to consider of such vital importance.

Arrived at the church door, a notice posted on it informed us that here again, for the same reason as in the other case, there was no service. The building, although pretty large, is of the slightest construction, covered with cloth so as to lead to the fear that a strong gale might make a heap of ruins of it, thus admitting a heavy rain pretty freely into its interior. Baffled here, we determined to ascend the hill, which here rises pretty abruptly to the Methodist Church, where we learned there was service, and somewhat to my surprise I found that an Episcopal Church had, within a few days or weeks, sprung up right alongside of it. The services of this church had been for some time past held in a large private house a little back of the town. I had heard of Mr. Miles,[3] the rector of this church, and having had desires to hear him, I was now gratified.

These new churches, you must understand, are temporary structures of the most simple construction, sufficient to contain some 500 people. This was rough-boarded, with a very insufficient roof, I should think, for so the wet benches testified. These benches were but pine boards planed, stretching from the passage through the center to the walls on either hand. A little pine railing enclosed the sofa and a small desk where the clergyman officiated, and a rude low pulpit outside the railing on one side completed the whole arrangement. I have forgotten a material part, the choir, which was by the side of the pulpit and gave us most excellent music to the accompaniment of a small organ, or perhaps piano.

The congregation was for the most part of well-dressed, mostly young, persons—men, of course, there being not above half a dozen of the other sex. I was much pleased with the whole service. Mr. M. read admirably that interesting chapter in the Gospel of John where so graphic an account is given of the blind man, miraculously restored to sight by our Savior, and then preached an admirable sermon from the passage of Scripture. "So then, everyone must give account of the deeds done in the body."

The two churches of which I have just made mention have the most picturesque location that can well be imagined. On the crest of quite a high hill, in a fresh spot of ground, the bushes not yet removed from the vicinity, the town now much extended, stretching far away below to the bay; here, a dense belt of shipping laying off at anchor, a mile or more in extent; beyond, a lofty and picturesque island; and in the distance, lofty mountains bounding the view. This is the appearance on one side only. As you turn in other directions the views are infinitely varied and interesting. This is altogether a unique site for churches in a city, and I must endeavor to take a sketch of them, with the landscape, of course, attached, to make a new feature in my sketches of San Francisco.

The rainy season has set in a month or two earlier than usual, to the very great annoyance of such as were living in very slight houses or tents or, indeed, to such as were in the act of constructing better ones. We have already had three spells of two or three days each of this rain and the damage done has really been quite serious. Many goods, for which there was no storeroom, have been almost totally destroyed. Hence, building and rents, and I may add lots too, suitable for building are at

[*Remainder of letter missing*]

3. Reverend Flavel S. Mines; see Introduction, p. 18.

My very dear wife,   *San Francisco, December 30, 1849*

This always pleasant day, the Sabbath, has come round again, rendered doubly so at present by the receipt of your welcome letter of 8th ulto., with the best of all news that you and our friends generally were well. True, you say the boys were confined by indisposition, but in the way you speak of it, it would appear to have been slight and I doubt not our good Dr. Haile would soon put them all right.

The steamer arrived only yesterday morning and the one intended to sail, going tomorrow or early the following morning, I was very uncertain whether I should get my letters seasonably to answer them so promptly, as it takes days to get the mails sorted, and the delivery to most persons is still more tedious, but I have an excellent friend in the Post Office who is pretty sure to serve me on these occasions, albeit it is against rules. So about 9 o'clock, just as I had finished my solitary breakfast of chocolate and was about dressing for church, his well-known tap at the door was heard and in came the Colonel.

Now I must introduce him to you—Colonel Poor—for he is rather an extraordinary man and a right good friend of mine, which must be my apology for the introduction.[1] He is a thorough Yankee from the interior of Massachusetts where, I am told, he has a large and interesting family. His last occupation, that of a farmer, and something of a farmer he must be, too, to possess one of the most attractive and finest prize farms in that state. Well, all this (and with means, too, as is said), he has left to come to California in person. The Colonel is fully 6 feet high, of strong, powerful frame and iron constitution and, I am sure, of indomitable courage and resolution—just the man I would select for a traveling companion through a country filled with dangers and privations. He is, besides, a most amusing companion. He has a peculiar and quaint way of relating things, and some of his anecdotes of his own life (he is about 50 years of age), although without polish, are equal in point and effect to the very best stories of Willis.

But I am wandering too far astray with the Colonel. As I said, he came in and, with a significant caution to the prudent and not reveal family secrets, he slipped some 6 or 8 letters into my hand, telling me he had not been in bed through the whole night, but had been hard at work assisting Mr. Moore, the Postmaster,[2] to sort the mails that he might have the satisfaction of securing his own letters at an early moment and those of a few friends. I spoke of him as being in the Post Office, but he is now only occasionally there, when there is much need of his services, having got an engagement in the way of business, promising, I am glad to say, a handsome competency in a year or two with which I sincerely hope he may be enabled to return to his family and home.

The last steamer, that of the 1st December, sailed just as the present steamer arrived, or so immediately after that few persons received their letters from home in season there to answer. Mine were at that time also brought me by Colonel Poor, and it was also Sabbath morning, a most dismal rainy day, with mud half a leg deep in the streets. I got at that time two letters from you, one of 24th August and another of 17 September. Afterwards still another came to hand of 12th October. This, with your present letter of 8th November, completes your correspondence, as I presume, up to the last date. . . .

I got a letter also today from Brother Perit and from Brother Gilman. The latter tells me that the articles from Mexico had at length arrived and that you had requested they might remain unopened till you went down to New York to have that pleasure yourself. That was

---

1. Probably Colonel Benjamin Poor, listed in Charles P. Kimball's 1850 directory of San Francisco, with the address: "Com whf, Clark's Point."
2. Jacob C. Moore. See Kimball's *Directory*.

quite right, for there is something quite exciting and agreeable in opening curiosities from abroad, howbeit I am afraid these may disappoint you—I mean the tapestry and also the paintings. They, of course, are in the worst possible condition to be seen and those who knew nothing about the matter and how far they are capable, with proper treatment, of being restored would, I well know, be much inclined to turn up their noses and pronounce them trumpery.

The hangings are very full of dust; they are also broken in a great many places; they are also more or less faded, but all this is capable of being in a very considerable degree remedied. I think you will be able to have nothing done with them in New York except perhaps putting tobacco into them to keep the moths out. In the spring, if I am not home seasonably, you might have them taken to Norwich and there properly, though carefully, beat and dusted and then folded up to await my return.

The paintings are most of them in a very bad state, though *all capable of restoration*, and it would be better that they were not opened (certainly those rolled up) or disturbed as every movement is likely to injure them. They may, indeed, be so rolled up as to spoil them. Recollect that to roll an oil painting properly the painted side must be the *outside*, or come on the outside. For instance, you have a painting to roll up. Well, spread it out on the floor *with the painted side to the floor* and then roll up. If, on the contrary, it be laid with the painted side upward and you thus roll up, at all tightly, the painting must unavoidably be badly cracked as the inner side of the canvas in rolling must necessarily be contracted, and that cracks the paint and often ruins the painting, more particularly if it be a very old one and the paint dry and brittle, as is often the case. Perhaps you may not need this caution. As to the sketches, they will probably please you as [your] husband's work better than the others. As to pleasing others, that is quite another question. I can only say they are generally slight things.
[*Remainder of letter missing*]

My dear wife,   *San Francisco, January 14th, 1850*
It is just a fortnight today since my last was written when I acknowledged the receipt of no less than four, I think, of your always precious letters which had come in upon me nearly together. The last of these was under date 8th November when you were planning your arrangements for leaving home, all of which, as far as you mention them, appear altogether judicious. I take it for granted that you finally left the boys with Mrs. Edgerton who, I trust, will exercise sufficient authority to make them entirely obedient. At the time of your writing, they were both confined to the house by indisposition. You speak of it lightly, however, and I hope your next, which I am now looking for by the *Panama* (steamer) daily expected, will tell me that they were both quite well again.

I think you put off your passage through the Sound too late. I don't like the idea of your passing that stormy place in winter, and shall be relieved to hear that you are safe in your comfortable winter quarters in Clinton Place. Neither is it necessary for you to leave New York too early in the spring. The middle of April is quite early enough—sooner the roads do not get settled and passable. Jones, who I take it for granted will remain with you as usual the ensuing season, can commence his work as early as circumstances may seem to require, certainly by first of April. You will, of course, have at once an understanding with him, if you have not already done so, as to his engagement through the summer and as to any matters which you may wish him to attend to before you go on.

You see, I am not planning to be with you myself, and I assure you it makes me heave a sigh when I say so, and that I am obliged yet to leave this matter in doubt. I finally gave my letters to you—I mean my last letters—in charge of Mr. Alfred Robinson, who has had the agency of the steamers here, and went to New York in the last.[1] Attached to my letter was a little parcel of gold dust, intended, as I wrote you, for a New Year's present to Jones' wife, which is richly merited by his attention to you and his general faithfulness. He shall not be a loser by it. I sometimes wish I had him here and, were it not for depriving you of his services, I really think I should send for him. I could employ him here advantageously for myself, while I could put him in the way of making money for *himself*, but the thing is out of the question.

I heard a most capital sermon this morning from Mr. Milne, the Episcopal clergyman.[2] I forget whether I have before mentioned that I have been much in the habit of late of going to hear this gentleman. The fact is I feel here a little more at liberty than I should do at home to go where I can hear the best preaching and be the most instructed and edified. I was accustomed during the summer to attend the Presbyterian Church where I heard with pleasure the Reverend Mr. Williams, an excellent and amiable man for whom I have a great regard, but as the winter season approached and it became wet and chilly, a tent was not a very inviting or comfortable place of worship and I felt constrained to change my place. As to my own proper church, the Congregational, I confess I have pretty much deserted it. Mr. Hunt, who officiates there and who I believe is a very estimable and good man, seems to have an idea that any very particular arrangement or preparation in his sermons is uncalled for, perhaps with special reference to California hearers, so he extemporizes a good deal, or preaches with a bare apology for notes, for which he is utterly incompetent. Now it is pretty hard work for a man of only common abilities to address an audience for three-quarters of an hour on any subject without due preparation, and so Mr. Hunt finds it, for from the start he labors like a ship in a gale of wind by rising on his toes, twisting his feet, swaying awkwardly his body backwards and forwards, gesticulating much with head and arms, while his language is oftentimes confused and ungrammatical, in fact floundering through what he has to say, not greatly to the edification of any one. This is not uniformly so, for I have sometimes heard the gentleman when he has appeared much more to advantage by a well-studied, written discourse, showing that at least he has the ability to do better if he would.

1. Alfred Robinson was one of those sturdy New Englanders who came to California before the American conquest. After several trips to the West Indies, he was hired by Bryant and Sturgis in 1828, at the age of 21, as clerk on the *Brookline*, bound for the California hide and tallow trade. Later, he managed several of this company's ships as resident agent on the California coast. This experience gave him an unusual opportunity to visit every part of the region and to obtain an intimate acquaintance with its affairs. In January, 1836, he married the 15-year-old Ana María de la Guerra, daughter of the influential José de la Guerra of Santa Barbara, tying him more closely to the California scene. When Bryant and Sturgis dissolved their business in 1841, much of it was taken over by William Appleton and Company, with Robinson as advisor in its business operations.

After twelve years of these experiences, Robinson left California, in 1842, never to return, but he wrote a marvelous account called *Life in California*, published in 1846, containing personal experiences, political history, and the people and resources of the country, altogether one of the most worthy books of this kind. It has been reprinted several times.

2. This was the Reverend Flavel S. Mines, the first Episcopalian minister in San Francisco, who arrived in the summer of 1849. He soon organized Trinity Church, and about January 1, 1850, had built a small chapel on Powell Street between Washington and Jackson. Rev. Mines died August 5, 1852. Taylor, *California Life*, p. 67; Willey, *Thirty Years in California*, p. 38; San Francisco *Alta California*, August 7, 1852; Kimball, *City Directory*, p. 127; Fletcher J. Hawley, *A Tribute to the Memory of the Rev. Flavel S. Mines* ... (St. Croix, W.I., 1853).

How striking is the contrast with Mr. Milne, with infinitely more of ability to extemporize, never trusting himself to do so—his gestures simple and natural, his delivery solemn and impressive, his sermons well digested and written so as never to offend the most fastidious taste, while they are addressed with great power and eloquence to the consciences of his hearers, enchaining the most undivided attention and carrying conviction, as it would seem they must, to the mind of everyone. He strikes me as one of the most orthodox and uniformly impressive speakers, as an Episcopalian, that I have ever heard. His discourse this morning was from II Corinthians, 4th chapter, and part of second verse: "But by manifestation of the truth, commending ourselves to every man's conscience in the sight of God."

I took a stroll after church this morning to the new burial ground about half a mile back from the densely settled part of the town. It lies on the slope of one of the high hills in the neighborhood, having a commanding view of the bay, the shipping and the distant mountains. I knew there had been many deaths, but I was quite unprepared for the solemn spectacle of so great mortality as presented itself. It appeared to me there could not be less than a quarter of an acre closely filled with ranks of fresh-made graves—only think, a quarter of an acre in nine short months or since I have been here!—but very few had any monumental stone or tablet or railing, or were likely to have any to register the name even of the occupant. The few which there were designated young men generally from one or other of the different states. I observed but a single female name. What a mournful commentary on the uncertainty of life, and disappointed hopes and prospects.

They told me during the summer that I should find the winter warmer than that season, but it is no such thing. Without much frost, there is a great deal of wet, raw, uncomfortable weather calling for fire almost as much as severe cold, and yet for the most part people are obliged to do without. I am sorry to say I am in that unfortunate predicament, and having been writing this with fingers benumbed in my little attic, I am really glad to find my paper used up and that I am enabled to go to bed to get warm. So goodnight, dearest, with much love to all,
Faithfully and affectionately your
D. W. C.

My dear wife,   *San Francisco, April 30th, 1850*
Having just concluded the business part of my correspondence for the present steamer, I come to a more agreeable duty, that of answering the delightful family letters which have reached me within a few days, particularly your own, valued above all others, of the 11th and 14th March. All your previous letters I believe I have acknowledged except that missing one of 1st January or about that time. That I put down now as utterly lost, and I regret it the more, as I may have before said, because I am sure it must have made mention of the drawings and possibly of the pictures. Your last letter does refer to the tapestries, and if it were not giving Sister Perit too much trouble, I would gladly accept her offer of receiving them at Bloomingdale and retaining them there 'till my return.

I have been disappointed that Brother Gilman has made no mention of these articles. I wished to have known whether they incurred duties and indeed what the whole expenses on them, freight from Vera Cruz, etc., etc., has been. He tells me that he had received $200 on my account from a certain source recently, $100 of which he had used in paying expenses on the articles sent me, and that he would pay you the remaining $100. This, I take it, must be in addition to the $170 balance which your letter speaks of as remaining on hand. Otherwise

I should fear you might run short in the expenses you must incur on returning to Norwich before you can receive another remittance which I propose to make you at this time.

In my last to you on the 20th inst., I mentioned George Thomas being here. A Mr. Gages, son of the gentleman of that name who resides at The Landing,[1] came with Mr. Thomas and they both now propose to return home by the present steamer to Panama. This Mr. Gages appears a very businesslike, correct young man, and as he will go straight to Norwich and from thence to Fall River (I think it is), where he resides and, moreover, as he will pass by our door, I determined to give him this letter and the remittance spoken of, which, unless some unforeseen circumstance prevents, he will hand you in person.

Mr. Thomas, I am sorry to say, is far from being one of the fortunate visitors to California. He most unfortunately bought in Valparaiso a large quantity of lumber and brought it here, on which he will lose, or rather has lost, more money than he will make, I think, in a very long time. He talks of retrieving his bad luck by making another adventure here on his return home. I can't help thinking, however, that it may in the end prove sending good money after bad. I don't think him very well adapted for these "diggings," and I hope his father may discourage his coming out again. Mr. Gages had an offer to remain here to conduct some agency business which would have given him $300 or more per month, but preferred returning home.

The articles sent by the Isthmus—which cost you so much trouble to prepare and to which other very dear and attentive friends kindly contributed—arrived in perfect order, and I am in the full enjoyment of them. If there is any place in the world where it is not exactly "idle and ridiculous" to send a friend a few knick-knacks such as these, this is that very place, and it does not become those to censure, as it strikes me, whose tables are daily loaded with every luxury that the best market and the most finished cooks can provide, while they and their friends are indulging to satiety. It is a little in character with Washington Irving's fat alderman who, himself gormandizing daily on turtle and venison and other like choice things, when visiting some charity or poorhouse and touching his lips to the soup prepared there, pronounced it "*excellent* food for the *poor*."

I find it after midnight and must therefore get a little sleep . . .
[*Remainder of letter missing*]

1. See letter of September 15, 1850, note 1.

My very dear wife,   San Francisco, May 23rd, 1850

I wrote you on the 30th April by Mr. Gages who, with Mr. George Thomas, was returning by the steamer [*Panama*] of 1st inst. to Norwich. Again I wrote you on the 14th inst. by the steamer *Isthmus*, being the first vessel of the new line between this [city] and Panama (an opposition to Howland & Aspinwall's line). . . .

Letters coming through this channel are pretty sure to come into my hands a day or two sooner than when they have to wait the regular mail delivery, which meets with much delay owing to the great numbers of letters. These are constantly increasing with the increase of population; there were upwards of 140 mail bags on the present steamer, constituting the largest mail yet received.

Mr. Bailey was very attentive in bringing me my Mexican letters, which were of unusual interest, covering as they did bills of lading of $70,000 in gold and silver coin to my address, making me on this occasion the largest consignee on the steamer's manifest. It is gratifying to perceive that the prompt manner in which the business entrusted to me here has been conducted is now beginning to tell somewhat more advantageously than in the early stages of my being here, and it is further gratifying to reflect that in the rather larger amount of my transactions for my Mexican friends during the past year, not only no fault or objection has been made, but the most entire satisfaction expressed. Neither has the smallest mistake or error occurred in my accounts rendered; indeed, I should have filled the station of principal for so long a mercantile life to little purpose were I now unable to perform the duties of an *agent* with tact and with efficiency. I must tell you that I now consider it exceedingly fortunate that our friends, Howland & Aspinwall, did not accept the propositions for business which I made them from Mexico. It would certainly have involved me in great responsibilities, given me hard labor, with many annoyances, and with the uncertainty after all of giving satisfaction.

As it is, I have been entirely my own master, which, with one of my age and habits, is something at least. Then I have had an exceedingly easy position as to labor, with no responsibilities that I was unequal to or afraid to grapple with, and in a pecuniary point of view I certainly have lost nothing.

Did I ever tell you an admission that was made to me long ago (I think it must have been in the early part of winter) by one of Howland & Aspinwall's employees? It came, too, from almost the only person in the establishment whose opinion I should have much valued. I refer to Dr. Farnham, a gentleman from the Mint at Philadelphia who the house sent out especially with relation to their gold-dust business as assayer, etc., etc. Well, the Doctor (a most intelligent high-minded man, as exact in all that relates to fidelity and truth as in his mechanical operations of assaying), a few days before he left to return to the United States, told me that he had written to the house in New York that my selection of gold dust would give three per cent better result than such as they had had made, and he added further, "If your Mr. Coit had had the sole management of Howland & Aspinwall's bullion account since he has been here (a period then probably of nine or ten months), in my opinion he would have saved them $20,000."

I think you did not see Mr. Bissell[1] when he was in New York—he made a very short trip of it—and immediately on his return commenced his operations for Howland & Aspinwall at Benicia which are to be of an exceedingly important character to bring that place into notice. It is determined to make it the grand depot for the steamers instead of this port. This involves a great outlay of money in building warehouses, wharf docks, etc., which will require not less than $200,000. Now in consideration of this heavy expenditure, the principal proprietors of the town concede some of its most valuable parts to Howland & Aspinwall or the Steam Company, and I have heard the opinion expressed that this grant, improved as they propose, will soon be worth half a million of dollars! Neither would this be strange, seeing the great natural advantages of the place and the attention which it is now beginning to attract. Perhaps you don't know that *you* have a small interest in this matter yourself, and for this reason I have gone somewhat more into particulars than I otherwise should have done.[2]

Soon after I came here, impressed with the geographical position and the other claims which Benicia had to become a place of importance, I possessed myself of some choice lots there (what would be the equivalent of some eight or ten New York building lots), but the then proprietors were cramped for means to act. This place [San Francisco] was then all the rage, and Benicia for a time was almost lost sight of. This state of things continued pretty

1. Evidently George W. P. Bissell. See Letter of April 29, 1849.
2. Among the chief promoters in the scheme to make Benicia a metropolis were Dr. Robert Semple, Mariano Guadalupe Vallejo, and Thomas Oliver Larkin. From Coit's letter, it appears that Howland & Aspinwall were also deeply involved in this enterprise. Cf. Hammond, *The Larkin Papers*, Vols. VII, p. vi, and VIII, pp. xii–xiii.

much through the year, and I more than once regretted that I had not made a more fortunate investment, but now, as you will perceive, Benicia lots begin to be appreciated. They would at this moment sell for three times what they would have brought six months ago, and as they are yet at comparatively moderate prices, there is margin for much advance; "nous verrons."

What a strange eventful life mine has been, do you not sometimes think, dearest? And the last new chapter in it the most strange of all. But little more than two years ago, long retired from all intercourse with men of business and lost sight of, or, if thought of, perhaps considered incompetent, or already too old for an active life; without credit or property—or comparatively none—submitting to much irksome toil and labor, to which I had never been accustomed, rather from necessity than choice. And now how changed. Enjoying the unlimited confidence of mercantile houses of very high standing in the world, whose acquaintance is quite recent and accidental (amongst others I have been employing funds for the Rothschilds, and should have had a large share of their business but for a relative and agent of theirs unexpectedly coming here), with the control of large specie funds and credits on different parts of the world, handling gold coin and gold dust with as much *sangfroid* as a little time ago I did my garden seeds or the very soil that received them. I say, are not these rapid changes and contrasts truly astonishing? How wonderfully has an ever-presiding and gracious Providence watched over me, and directed all my footsteps for good.
[*Remainder of letter missing*]

My dear wife,   *San Francisco, June 17th, 1850*
I wrote you a couple of sheets by the last steamer, one under date of 28th May and the other a few days later, and have since nothing of yours to acknowledge, though as the regular steamer is now due and daily expected, I trust I shall not be many days without hearing agreeable tidings from you. I have again a chapter of incidents of no little interest to relate. After the frequent mention my letters have made of the imminent danger we are constantly living in from fire, it will not greatly surprise you to learn that this dreadful calamity has again befallen this doomed city, and on this occasion even to a greater extent than previously.

It was three days ago that I had risen and was about breakfasting when that appalling cry of fire reached my ear. I ran immediately to the scuttle on the roof of the house, which overlooks the intervening blocks between the public square and the bay or shipping, when I saw the smoke curling up from about the center of what was then the largest and most valuable and densely built block of the city. At the moment it seemed as if a few buckets of water, well applied, would have put the fire out, and I watched with intense interest to see if this would be so—otherwise, it was clearly evident, the conflagration would be a most extensive and dreadful one.

I was not long kept in doubt. A column of flame soon burst out, and I then reflected on the probabilities of its again reaching the public square and my own residence. They were certainly in my favor, as I was well to windward and living, as I have before told you, in an insulated and comparatively safe position. I, however, prepared to some extent to move, in case it should become necessary, and then, taking my key in my pocket, sallied out to the more immediate scene of action.

What a scene! It baffles all description. Men, women, and children running in all directions to escape the flames in the utmost confusion and dismay. As many as could do so were endeavoring to reach the square with the few articles they were able to snatch away with them, the streets offering no manner of protection. The fire, however, so rapid was its spread on all sides, gave little time to save either furniture or merchandise, which of course soon became a prey to the flames to a very large extent—the greater because the part of the town now burned (consisting of four large blocks) was occupied by the largest importing and wholesale dealers, who had time to remove but very few of their effects. By almost superhuman efforts of the inhabitants, the fire was prevented from crossing the streets to other blocks which were in imminent peril, but to leeward it went quite through to the water's edge, and was finally, after about two or three hours, got under entire subjection.

I am sorry to number not a few of my friends and acquaintances among the sufferers, and you will regret to learn that our friends, Howland & Aspinwall, are in this category. Their store in which were the offices of the Steam Company, and filled besides with merchandise, was burned to the ground, they having barely had time to remove their money, books, valuable papers, etc., but none of their goods. Indeed, the clerks told me that they had not even saved their clothes, except what were on their backs. Poor Beach, I am exceedingly sorry to say, was burned out and his loss must be a very serious one as he had covered his lot with buildings, the rear having been occupied as a hotel, giving him $1,000 per month rent. It is said that the fire originated in a back kitchen to this house from a naked stovepipe which had been carelessly conducted through the roof.[1]

Two young men in the hardware business, one a son of Mr. Lester of New Rochelle, and the other a son of Mr. Brewster, were among the sufferers. My friend, Mr. Willis, the banker, with whom I have had much business, was another, but as he had only his books and money to remove, which he accomplished in a very satisfactory manner, he lost nothing.[2] Finley Johnson & Co., friends of mine,[3] lost their store and some goods in it, but as these were for account of shippers in the United States, they will not lose much. The merchandise consumed will, much of it being on consignment, fall very heavily on our merchants at home, as well as those of other countries. These constantly occurring losses by fire will be a great damper to shipments to this country from whatever quarter. There must have been in the three fires little if any short of a total of $10,000,000 property destroyed, entirely consumed and gone. More, I am sure, than all the gain that has occurred here. Many, very many, must be again among the ruined.

Some very curious developments have been made by this fire, but one in particular is so very extraordinary and at the same time so very dreadful (almost too much so to commit to paper), that I cannot refrain from giving it to you. It is, after all, nothing more than the short career of a young man throwing off, on arrival in this country, the restraints which had kept him within some bounds, while among friends in a different state of society and giving himself up to the unrestrained indulgence of his worst passions and appetites.

The name of this person was Vail, as I am told, of respectable connections in Troy. He was

1. This was San Francisco's third great fire. It broke out on the morning of June 14, scarcely six weeks after the fire of May 4, yet rebuilding had proceeded speedily. This one started at 8 o'clock in the morning in a small wooden shack, a bakery, according to *The Annals*, in the rear of the Merchants' Hotel between Sacramento and Clay streets. The wind was high, and the flames soon spread on all sides. In a few hours, the entire area between Clay and California streets and from Kearny down to the water's edge was a mass of flames. The loss was estimated at more than $3,000,000. *The Annals*, pp. 277–278; Bancroft, *History of California*, Vol. VI, pp. 202–203.
2. Possibly H. P. Willis, listed by Kimball as a member of the firm of Fay, Peirce & Willis, commission merchants on the corner of Clay and Montgomery. Or, if Coit actually meant that he was a banker, it might have been Wells, or Welles, of the firm of Wells & Co., who were bankers. Cf. Coit's letter of October 10, 1851, describing how Willis was burned out in the fire of May, 1850, and also personally suffered severe burns.
3. Finley, Johnson & Co., *i.e.*, John M. Finley and Chas. H. Johnson, on the corner of Washington and Montgomery streets. Kimball's *Directory*, 1850.

a tall, stout, and what would be called a fine-looking young man. It appears that he arrived not many months ago in Valparaiso, having in his possession some $7,000 or $8,000 in ready money. Here he commenced a very notorious course of indulgence in every species of dissipation. Soon afterwards, coming here, he pursued much the same course, until finally he went to the mines, and although from all accounts there is quite as much dissipation in the small towns of the interior in proportion to their numbers as here, yet the broader field of operations at this point probably having more attraction, he returned here, gave himself more entirely up to debauchery than ever, lost all his money, and finally died some weeks ago of delirium tremens. This is sufficiently shocking of itself, but it is the fate of so many young men who come to this country in pursuit of gold that if the wretched remains had been simply sent with decency to their last resting place and there deposited, it would have scarcely attracted notice, but mark in how extraordinary a manner a retributive Providence has singled out this reprobate and pointed him out in the most sickening and revolting possible manner to the public gaze. It appears that after his death his friends here were desirous of sending the corpse to his family in the United States, and for that purpose it was enclosed in a cask with spirits. [*Remainder of letter missing*]

My dear wife   *San Francisco, September 15th, 1850*

I take pen in hand this pleasant Sabbath morning to hold a little intercourse with you before going to church. The fact is that I have been so much occupied for the past three or four days that I have again delayed answering your last letter of 25th July until now, just when the steamer is about to sail. . . .

One after another of our Norwich people are returning back to their homes by almost every steamer. I mentioned in my last (under date of 31st ult.) that two carpenters from The Landing,[1] Fanning and Greenman, were then returning, though I believe with the intention of coming back again.[2] I think, as their profession has been one of the best, master carpenters, and as they have had a good share of business, they must have done well, but there is an instance of another of the craft now returning on the steamer who has met with incredible success. I refer to a Mr. Wright, also, as I understand, of The Landing. His business has been, although carpenter's work, of a peculiar kind—that of having piles driven and piers or wharves made out into the harbor. In this he was a pioneer, and being evidently a shrewd man, more so probably than he ever had credit for until circumstances elicited the trait in his character, he has acquired a large fortune, at least for a man of his habits. It is said no less a sum than $60,000 to $70,000!! Very few, very few men, indeed, even with the best advantages, have accomplished so much. You will understand, of course, that this was not entirely the result of his own labor or even of his contracts for work, but as he acquired money from those sources it was judiciously invested in property, mostly, as I am told, in steamboat property

1. Norwich Town dates from the late 17th century. As the business of the young community expanded, it was found desirable to ship by boat. The old landing place was near the Falls, which are in the center of the town. Hence a committee of citizens selected a spot at the mouth of the Shetucket River for "a public landing place." While the merchants lived in Norwich Town, they built wharves and warehouses at "the Landing," and it was commonly known as such. Frances M. Caulkins, *History of Norwich, Connecticut* (Hartford, 1874), pp. 302–308.
  Fanning was probably a member of the Thomas Fanning family who owned a store located between the town and the Landing. Ledyard Bill, *History of the Bill Family* (New York, 1867), p. 183.
2. Kimball lists an H. T. Fanning, cabinet maker, on Bush Street between Montgomery and Kearny, but no Greenman.

on the rivers where, or in which business, investments have frequently been doubled in three months....

It is believed that great suffering exists amongst the immense population who have taken up their march from the western states, across the continent to this Land of Promise—I say this Land of Promise, but it is quite as proper to call it a Land of Blasted Hopes and of Utter Disappointment, for such it truly is to many—perhaps it may be said to the majority of those who come here. Would you believe that numbers of those who have made so great sacrifice of their comfort and of their property in crossing the country have been so utterly discouraged on completing their tedious journey and arriving at the mines that, with the least possible delay, they have come straight down here and taken passage home via the Isthmus, where, indeed, they had the means to do so, which all were not provided with, or had any means of obtaining.

There is the strangest contradiction in the experience of different people here as to the results of their labors, as there will be in their reports of the country and of the gold region on their return. There are no less than 300 passengers returning on the steamer, the *Tennessee*, which takes this letter, and I cannot help contrasting in my mind the position of the only two of the number which I chance to know.

One I have already pointed out to you—Mr. Wright, so wonderfully favored and prospered. Just imagine the pride and exultation with which he will meet his family and friends and the deference which will be paid him in consequence of his altered position, and then turn your thoughts to the other individual I have referred to and reflect what must be *his* feelings on returning to his family. He is a Bostonian of very good family, his father a merchant of high standing, a tall, handsome young man of perhaps two and twenty years. Happening in at Welles and Company banking house yesterday,[3] my attention was called to him from a conversation between him and the principal of the house, Mr. Skinner,[4] to this effect: "Well," said Mr. Skinner, "I have taken a passage for you on the *Tennessee*" (steerage, I suppose, of course), "but I suppose you'll want clothes, too, won't you?"

"Yes, sir," said the young man, in a voice hardly audible from shame and mortification. (He had on simply a pair of thin trousers, with check shirt and a California hat.)

"Well," said Mr. Skinner, "come in by-and-by and we'll see you provided."

After he had gone out, Mr. Skinner told me his recent history. He had come to California eight or ten months ago with high hopes and expectations of the speedy acquisition of wealth, and had gone to the mining region and tried the miner's life, and though he had labored, as it would appear, thus long, had barely made enough to pay his expenses and had finally got back here with simply the clothes on his back. Neither would he have had the means of getting back to his family but through the kindness of Mr. Skinner, who was well acquainted with his father. He told Mr. Skinner that many persons in the neighborhood where he had been had met with no better success than himself. This is the scheme of the great California lottery—a few brilliant prizes, many smaller ones, but the greater portion blanks.

I enclose a check for $100 which please endorse and get the money for either through one of The Landing cashiers or by sending to Brother Gilman.

Much love to all. In haste, affectionately and faithfully yours,   *D. W. Coit*

3. Kimball lists Wells & Co., bankers, corner of Clay and Montgomery streets.
4. Kimball gives Lucien Skinner, of the firm of Wells & Co., bankers, corner of Clay and Montgomery.

My dear wife,   *San Francisco, September 17th, 1850*

Although I wrote you but two days ago by the regular steamer then leaving for Panama and although I have been very busy all morning, first, in watching the incidents to a very large fire and next in despatching goods from the customhouse, yet I have just time before the closing of another mail for the Isthmus to write you a few lines, which I feel the more called on to do as you will again be likely to have your anxieties awakened on my account in reading of another of those calamities with which this place has been afflicted.

The fire broke out about daylight, and although it commenced more than a block from the public square, it soon found its way there, burning all the new buildings, some of them large and costly, which had been erected on the previous burned district.[1] It has never, however, reached the side of the square [Portsmouth] (the west side) where I reside, though I am not, as I have before told you, in the identical house I before occupied.

At the first glimpse I got of the light, I found it was in a direction where I had placed goods in a commission store for sale. I therefore lost no time, taking a man with me, in hastening to the spot. As we came near, we found several buildings in flames, but a single one intervening between them and that with the goods. We rushed in through a crowd who had just begun emptying the store, and I, knowing where my goods were placed, was not long in helping myself to them and in making good my retreat without loss. And this is all I can say, for my time is up. Once more with best love to you all.   *Most affectionately yours,*

D. W. Coit.

1. Bancroft states that the fire broke out at 4 A.M. in the Philadelphia House, on the north side of Jackson Street, between Dupont (Grant) and Kearny, near Washington Market. The section burned was about equal to the preceding one, but it was covered mostly by one-story construction, so that the loss did not exceed half a million dollars. *History of California*, Vol. VI, p. 203.

My very dear Harriet   *San Francisco, October 31, 1850*

I have just concluded a long letter to our good friend, Mr. Adams, and now turn to say a few words to you, though I have no letters of yours to acknowledge since I wrote you about the middle of the month. This will unquestionably find you in New York comfortably settled, I trust, for the winter with all that may contribute to your happiness. . . .

We have had some very exciting events here within the past few days, joyous on the one hand, and most sad on the other. The news from Washington which reached us recently of the admission of California into the Union of States was received on all hands with demonstrations of joy.[1] Balls, processions, illuminations, fireworks, all testified to the general sentiment which prevailed, but in the very midst of this rejoicing a loud explosion was heard at one of the principal wharves. Half the population who were in the streets rushed to the spot only to witness one of the most appalling sights. A steamboat bound up the river with about 120 or 130 souls on board, just in the act of hauling out, had blown up with a frightful loss of life.[2] You may well suppose that the scene presented at the moment was revolting and shocking

1. San Francisco celebrated the occasion in gala fashion on October 29. Bancroft, *History of California*, Vol. VI, pp. 343–350; *The Annals*, pp. 293–295. A more recent account is William H. Ellison's, *A Self-governing Dominion: California, 1849–1860* (Berkeley and Los Angeles, 1950), pp. 78–101.

2. This was the river steamer, *Sagamore*. In his *History of California*, Vol. VII, pp. 130–135, Bancroft gives a full account of the development and importance of river transport. About 30 or 40 persons were killed in this explosion. *The Annals*, p. 295.

THE JETTY AT BENICIA, 1850

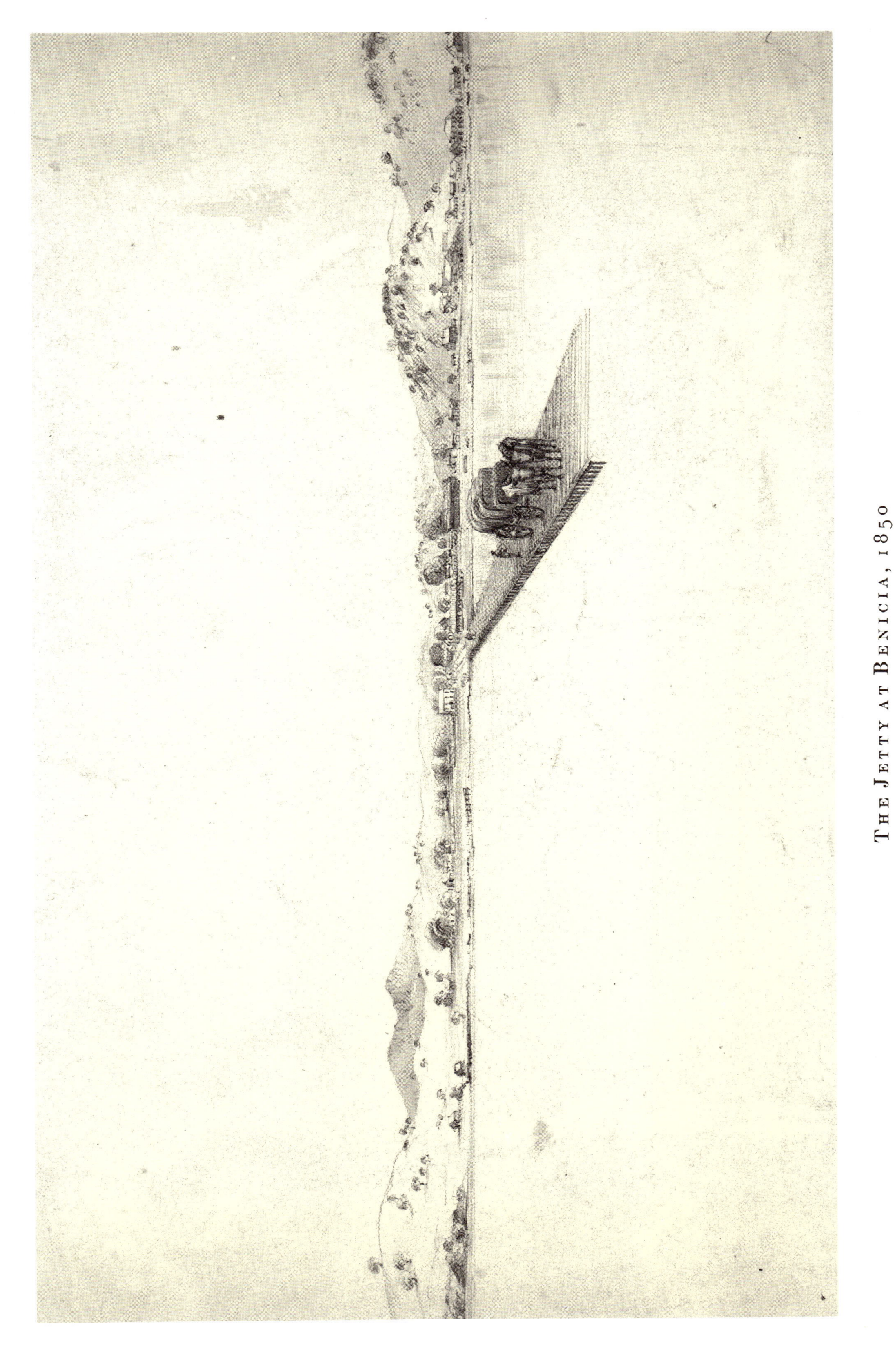

"Benicia, California, Looking Down the River," 1850

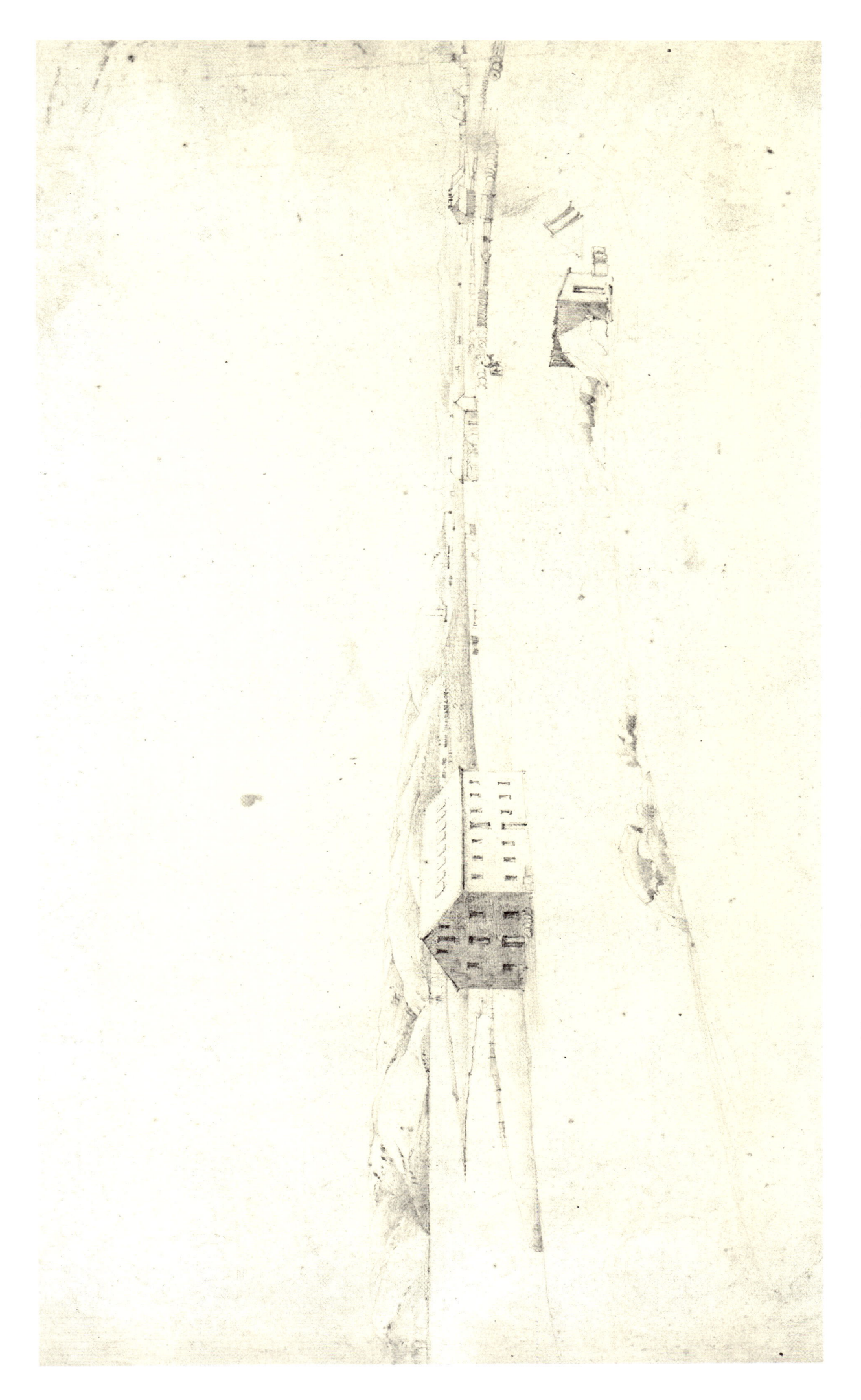

"Sketch Above Benicia — Government Property," 1851

San Francisco in 1851: Clay Street at Montgomery

beyond anything that language can describe. I send a newspaper containing some particulars if you can make up your mind to read such sickening details.

The following night after this accident we were again alarmed by the cry of fire. It was found to proceed from a house owned and occupied by a notorious courtesan who is said to have accumulated here no less than $50,000. The fire was directly in our rear, and I hastened to it, presuming at first that we were in some danger. It being rather remote from the more thickly settled part of the town, people were rather slower than usual in arriving at the spot. When I got there not many were present and I approached near the building, from the doors and windows of which the flames were just beginning to issue.

The scene which presented itself to my view was a curious one, to say the least of it. The house had been furnished at great cost with the richest description of bedroom and drawing-room furniture, and here it lay, thrown on the ground in one promiscuous heap—French bedsteads, mirrors, carpets, silk curtains, hangings, toilet furniture, rich female apparel, etc., etc. On one side and occasionally moving about with perfect composure and affected dignity, the proprietor of all this rich furniture—a tall, showy woman, not very youthful or very pretty, but yet in a full rich plain black satin dress with the light shining strongly upon her, a very striking object at the moment. It was not many minutes before the sparks and burning shingles or pieces of them began to shower down upon the rich furniture and trappings. When they were roughly removed to a greater distance by the crowd, something in this new movement suddenly disturbed the equanimity of the frail lady. The mock dignity was lost sight of and the cauldron of rage, which was boiling but stifled within, burst forth and vented itself upon a most inoffensive glass chandelier, which was kicked and trampled to pieces in a moment.

But I am losing sight of the fire, which, I regret to say, had rather a tragic termination. Immediately in the rear of the building described stood the city hospital, owned by the City Physician, Dr. Smith, but rented by the town.[3] This was filled with the sick in every stage of disease. It was evident from the first that this building could not be saved and the utmost despatch had to be used in getting the poor wretches (for such very many of them truly are) into a place of safety; safety from the flames, but not from the cold and much exposure, as they could only be laid on cots in the open air with insufficient covering.

What sufferings do not men hastily rush into, wherever there is a prospect of collecting a little gold without the ordinary industry, economy, and labor which is generally called for in its accumulation. The vicissitudes and exposures to which men are sometimes called in this "El Dorado" are strikingly exemplified in the case of some of these invalids I have been speaking of. Not a week ago they were here in high health and spirits, bound for the mines. Well, probably with all their worldly effects (it might be so), they went aboard one of the steamers bound up the river. This steamer was run into by another larger coming down and instantly sank, barely giving time for the passengers to escape with their lives. Arriving here, some of them immediately took passage on another steamer just about leaving for their destination. This was the unfortunate one blown up at the wharf already referred to, and now those of our adventurers who were not killed outright are carried, scalded and maimed, to the hospital where, within forty-eight hours, they have another hairbreadth escape. What a succession of disasters—truly the events of years in other countries transpire here in days. . . .

We have had *talk* of cholera cases here for three weeks past, but it occasions no alarm. Mr. Dorr of New York brought me a letter from Gorham and, you probably know, returns on this steamer to New York and possibly may take this. I have had very pleasant intercourse with

3. Kimball gives a Dr. P. Smith as the proprietor of the City Hospital. It was located on Clay Street. Kimball's *Directory*. This was Dr. Peter Smith. *The Annals*, p. 295.

him. He leaves few behind him his equal in intelligence, refinement, and true gentlemanly deportment. These qualities do not over-abound here, at least in my walks. Mr. Dorr has promised to call on you to answer any inquiries you may have to make after me that I do not anticipate.

Much love to your father and mother, Henry and Sarah, to my sisters and their families when you may see them, and to all our numerous circle of friends a kind remembrance. Kiss dear Libby for me, and believe me faithfully and affectionately yours,   D.W.C.

My very dear wife,   *San Francisco, November 15th, 1850*

I was glad to avail myself of an opportunity of writing you a few lines three days ago by a young man by name of Hyatt, a carpenter by trade, who has been living in the same house with me and who has promised to deliver my letter in person so that if you want to make any verbal inquiries about me you will have opportunity. More people seem to be returning to than coming from the Atlantic states at present. Some 250 persons went on the small steamer *Antelope*, by which Mr. Hyatt took passage, and some 300 now go on the *Tennessee*, by which I write. Some of these have accomplished the objects for which they came, to a tolerable extent—I mean the acquisition of gold. A few have been *very* fortunate, and take home quite large sums of the precious metal, but by far the greater number, I have reason to think, return disheartened and disappointed—not a few even poorer than they came, while others who would gladly turn their faces homeward have not even the means to meet the expenses of getting there.

As it is most pleasant to dwell upon the cares of the fortunate few, I will just mention the success which has attended the labors of three individuals since the first of the past month of September only. One of these gentlemen is a Mr. MacIntire, a clergyman, too, from whose own lips I had the recital. I met him at Willis and Co.[1] where the pile that the trio had exhumed and brought here to be sent home on the *Tennessee* was exhibited preparatory to being packed and shipped.

It appears that the little spot of ground on the side of the Yuba River where this gold was deposited had been discovered the past year by three men, and the space or claim which they were authorized to occupy and avail themselves of just covered the whole of it. The riches of the spot (of course not *fully* understood at the time) was ascertained only just before the rains of the past winter set in, and it was not until September, little more than two months ago, that the waters had subsided sufficiently to permit the miners' work to commence. One of the three original proprietors was obliged to go away from some cause, and Mr. MacIntire, happening to come along at the proper moment, bought his interest.

Well, the three *then* proprietors set to work, as I have said, early in September, digging into the sand and gravel between the edge of the river and the bank, not very many yards in extent. They soon came to a very rich deposit, and, anxious to realize as fast as possible, they called in the aid of eight or nine laborers whom they paid from eight to ten dollars per day. Having got through the first layer of gold (which by means of two common rockers only was washed out as fast as collected), on digging another foot or two deeper, they came to a second deposit, similar to the first, and finally to a third, which brought them to the solid rock and here their work was ended, amounting in all to some 30 or 35 days' work of the dozen men.

1. See letter of June 17, 1850, note 2.

The result was a pile of the most beautiful pure gold I have seen in the country, weighing about 250 or 260 lbs., and of the value of $60,000!!

Now, this extraordinary success is just sufficient to turn the heads of thousands at home, who will only look on the bright side of the picture and lead, probably, when it comes to be widely circulated in the newspapers, to a new impulse in immigration which, in the aggregate, will lead to greater disappointment and suffering than all that has preceded it, for as a general rule the success of mining operations as a means of acquiring much wealth speedily is becoming more uncertain and precarious daily.

I send by the *mail* two of our daily newspapers addressed to you at No. 4 Clinton Place, where I have no doubt this also will find you, though as I am writing Wm. Aspinwall a long letter, I shall slip this into the envelope and by this means get two or three hours grace in writing, the post office closing a considerable time before the letters of the *house* are sent on board. One of the newspapers contains, as you will notice, an article on the subject of the new port of Humboldt which I think William[2] will be pleased to see. When you have done with it, send or hand it to him, calling his attention to the article; the other paper send to Jones, addressing it to him through the post office. I do not write him by this opportunity, having nothing special to say.

We have had the cholera with us for some two weeks past, but it is not of a very alarming nature, having been confined, to a very great extent, to persons of dissipated habits or who have lived in exposed situations, and many of the deaths which have occurred from it have been owing to the most criminal neglect of medical men, even of such as are selected to preside over the hospitals—so says Dr. Coit. Mr. McNulty is better, though yet confined to the house. . . .

I have done little with my pencil since I have been here, though the early sketches I took are somewhat curious now as showing the great advance which the place has made within the year.

Yours faithfully and affectionately,
D. W. Coit

2. William H. Aspinwall.

My dear wife,   *San Francisco, December 1, 1850*

The steamer sails this afternoon for Panama and I have not much time remaining for writing you. I did mean to have attended to this last evening, this being the Sabbath, but after writing a good part of the day and until well on to midnight, I really felt too much fatigued to attempt to fill another sheet. . . .

The winter has now fairly set in upon us; it is not the serious affair as with you, with the absence of vegetation, extreme cold, with the consequent inconveniences attending it. Here warm rains take the place of the snows with you, and vegetation, which had been parched up and destroyed by the drought of summer, returns *with* the winter. It was certainly somewhat of a serious business to be wading and floundering through the mud in getting from one part of the town to the other last winter, but now, with capital planked streets and sidewalks, all dread of the winter is banished, howbeit the rain does pour down here in earnest some times.

Yesterday was our Thanksgiving Day and religious services were observed in two or three of our churches. I was at the Baptist Church of the Reverend Mr. Wheeler,[1] where clergymen of the Congregational and Methodist persuasions united in the worship. A capital discourse was delivered by one of the Methodist preachers, taking the 67th Psalm as his subject. I doubt if dinner tables were bending under the weight of turkeys and fowls and all manner of nice pastry as they would have done in New England, for it is no joke to be obliged to pay seven or eight dollars for a fat turkey. Neither are the other appliances by any means as accessible and abundant as there. Indeed, a single mince pie, which had been almost, I may say, miraculously brought here and preserved to this occasion, created a sensation in a private party of seven or eight gentlemen who were dining together, such as you would scarcely have imagined a single pie to have had the power to do. As a Yankee, you may make a guess if you have a mind to, where that pie came from. . . .

We have the cholera here, but it does not occasion much alarm. Our friend, Dr. Coit, seems to have as much as he can turn his hand to, which is saying that he is making money faster than he ever did before. I hope he will have the prudence and good sense to keep it. Much love to all friends.   *In haste, faithfully and affectionately yours,*

D. W. Coit

---

1. Located on Washington Street. See letter of November 11, 1849, and Introduction, p. 17, and notes cited therein.

DIGGING FOR GOLD—WITHOUT A SHOVEL

My very dear Harriet,   *San Francisco, January 31, 1851*

Another packet day has come round again, reminding me that I can have the pleasure of an hour's intercourse with you. I wrote you last on the 15th inst., and since then have been again favored with another of your letters, under date 11th December. I doubt not that your family gatherings, which you refer to in anticipation, at the close of the old year and the beginning of the new, were delightful, particularly to the young folks. Libby no doubt enjoyed herself to her heart's content.

Your last asks for more particulars as to my own movements and doings. Well, I have had some little variety of late in my usually monotonous way of living. Mr. Welles,[1] who has recently returned from his visit to the East, was ten days ago making a visit to Sacramento with a few friends and invited me to make one of the party. It does not cost a small fortune to make a trip now in a steamer, as it did a year ago, so I joined in, and we had a very nice time of it. Although there was nothing in the place itself worthy of being noted, it is situated on the river in the midst of a great plain, or I might almost say marsh, of many miles in extent, which in the spring season is liable to be inundated. You may recollect to have seen statements in the newspapers last summer of the whole town [of Sacramento] being under water and how all outdoor intercourse was carried on in boats.[2] It must have been quite a novel event for the ladies there to have gone by water to their tea parties and to have been ushered by their friends into their bedroom windows. At the time I speak of, when the waters were up, property, real estate, was at most unheard of prices, and even the calamity they were suffering did not seem to affect it materially. It was said that as people could not get about with ordinary convenience to attend to business, they made a sort of real estate exchange of their house tops where many lots, then under water, changed hands.

A sad revulsion, however, has come over the place, and many who counted their wealth by hundreds of thousands at that period are either ruined or under serious embarrassment. Although most descriptions of property are very much depressed and unsalable, yet the price of living in the *best* hotels is still dear enough. In the house we stopped at, for instance, the charge was $2 for a bed and the sheets rather suspicious even at that. Then a very simple breakfast $1-$1.50 (if you indulged in a couple of eggs a dollar extra), dinner $1.50, and supper about the same—this, besides, for the most simple food. If you were to indulge in the luxury of poultry, game, or any such thing, it would add at least a dollar to the meal. There are *eating* houses, however, where you have a pretty full "carte" of plain meats and vegetables and indifferent dessert of your choice at $1, and these houses now are generally resorted to. I was absent a couple of days, and with my curiosity abundantly satisfied, so far as Sacramento was concerned, was glad to get back to my quiet rooms in the "iron post office building," as it is called.

You have probably heard from our friends, the Gilmans, of Mr. Willey, a Congregational clergyman,[3] a particular friend of Edward's. I had intended for some time to make his acquaintance, but living, as he does, a good way from me, in the outskirts of the town, it is

---

1. It seems plausible that this was Thos. G. Wells of Wells & Co., bankers, whose offices were on the corner of Clay and Montgomery.
2. The rains began on November 2, 1849, and continued, with intermissions, to about March 22, 1850, with over 36 inches. By Christmas, water covered the lower parts of the city; by January 9, four-fifths was under water, and patrons entered the second story of the City Hotel by boat! "The country presented a sheet of water for miles around, save here and there a knoll or ridge, and the dottings of trees and houses.... The average rise of water within the city was 4 feet." Bancroft, *History of California*, Vol. VI, p. 453.
3. The Reverend Samuel H. Willey arrived in Monterey on the steamer *California*, February 23, 1849, and later moved to San Francisco. See Introduction, p. 18; Willey, *Thirty Years*, especially chapters 7 and 8; and note 53 of the Introduction.

but recently that I fell in with him. Learning that a few of his friends intended to pass an evening with him to make what I think is termed a donation visit, I thought it a good opportunity to present myself and was gratified in meeting quite a large party with not a few ladies (indeed, your sex are not quite the curiosities they were a twelve month since). I found both Mr. and Mrs. Willey pleasant, well-bred people, and I must say here that they have one of the most lovely babes I ever saw—a magnificent head, a model for a painter. The party went off extremely well. They were able to exhibit over here a supper table for 36 or 40 persons that would have done credit to any housekeeper in New England, and not the least important part of the affair was that the donations (as I heard) amounted to about $300, which, considering the pressure of the times and that there were no *rich* contributors, was very well.

My own health, I am happy to say, is uniformly good. I don't know how frequently it has been remarked, within the past six months, "Why, how well you're looking!" This, it will be observed, is said with reference to a person being on the wrong side of 60 years.

Dr. Coit and his brother William are well. I think the former ought to be laying up money, for he certainly has a good practice, and with visits at $9 and living economically, he cannot but accumulate.

Tracey Bill is now here and looking well; he has called on me two or three times. I am afraid he has not been successful in his operations, as I find he has left the country where he was, is here out of employment, and wants a situation. I don't believe a word of his being married, as you hint, though I have not put the question to him.

Ever affectionately and faithfully yours,
D. W. Coit

My dear wife, San Francisco, February 28th, 1851

Your two letters of 24th December and 9th January both came into my hands at the same time, the former having somehow got delayed on one steamer. They prove of unusual interest, though I was prepared in a great measure for the sad intelligence of your dear father's death, your previous letters having foreshadowed that event. . . .

I am truly grieved at what you tell me of dear cousin Abby Wolcott's critical situation. When her regular physicians despair of her, her case would really seem wellnigh hopeless. I learn that your Uncle Sam, after passing a very short time at the Havana, had returned to New York, and that Woolsey Aspinwall had done the same. He probably thought it too great a sacrifice to leave his family for the time that would have been requisite to visit this place, though for the reasons before stated to you, I still think it would have been judicious for him to have come here. Steamboat interests, in which I learn he is deeply interested, are not by any means what they have been. At present there is a very spirited opposition, and transportation and passage on the rivers are reduced as low as with you. A year ago a passage from here to Sacramento City and back cost $50, at present only $2!!

You say you wish to know more about myself and that other information is comparatively of little value. It is so recently that I went into these details and so little does my life change from one week or from one month to another, that it would meet the case pretty well to tell you to read one of those letters over again; the only novelty you need look for now is in the form of words, not in the events of my daily life.

First, I enjoy and have enjoyed uninterrupted health, indeed with such an unexceptionable climate as the past autumn and winter have been there is the least possible exposure to illness to those who with good constitutions live sober, quiet, regular lives, with their minds undisturbed, and this has been very much my case.

I have heretofore told you that I have rooms in the Post Office Building on the public square[1] consisting of a small parlor, which serves at the same time for an office, with a bedroom adjoining. These rooms are papered and carpeted and plainly furnished—the rent, $50 per month, I finding furniture. This would pay the rent of a tolerable house in New York. I rise about seven o'clock, shave and dress with much more regard to appearances than for the first year after my arrival, and then determine whether I shall take my own cup of tea at home, for which I have facilities, or otherwise go to Delmonico's for a cup of coffee, bread and butter, which, with a mutton chop or some like simple thing, costs a dollar. The daily papers, of which we have now half a dozen, are to be found here, and having looked them through I generally drop in at one or another of two or three stopping places I have, particularly Welles & Company's banking house, and get the news.

If I have any business or writing, I now proceed to that, or I look in at an auction room to observe the sacrifices being made, my mind reverting very naturally to the poor sufferers at home (by the bye, I am told some of our Norwich people—I don't know who—have been building or perhaps purchasing a large steamer to send out here, which I am sorry to hear, as they can only, as I think, make a losing business of it). Two o'clock soon comes, reminding one of dinner, and here I may select from between 30 and 40 restaurants. The dinner may cost from $1 to $10. You may suppose that, bearing in mind the value of a dollar at home, I don't go in for luxuries; indeed, one may dine perfectly well for a *single* dollar upon fresh salmon, wild geese and ducks and venison, with all the domestic meats, and a tolerable dessert. If the cooking was as good as the material, there would be hardly anything to desire, but the salmon is the only thing properly cooked as that requires only simple boiling. Poultry—turkeys, fowls, tame ducks, quails, etc.—are excessively dear and quite out of the question for economists.

After dinner I write or read or take a stroll and ten o'clock generally finds me in bed. It would not be difficult, I believe, to make acquaintances in families where there are ladies, but I have no desires to make new acquaintances, and so I pass the evenings almost uniformly at home alone, which to me is far more agreeable than to mix with those of uncongenial habits or that I do not fancy. As to my present place of worship, I have not been in the Episcopal Church for six months past. Mr. Mines, I understand, has gone on a visit to New York. I now attend regularly the Congregational Church.

[*Remainder of letter missing*]

1. Descriptions of San Francisco's post office and of the lively scenes that took place there when the mail steamers arrived are given in Taylor's *El Dorado*, ch. 20, and in *The Annals*, pp. 259–261. In addition, nearly every gold miner had much to say on this matter in his letters home.

My dear wife, San Francisco, March 15th, 1851

I have no new letter of yours to answer since I wrote you on the 28th February, neither have I any one new thing to communicate of interest. I am now daily looking for the arrival of certain iron warehouses, which were ordered from England more than a year ago.[1] They were planned by me for certain friends of mine who propose to erect them as soon as they arrive. They are very large, entirely of iron, and of course fireproof, and when put up will be the most extensive and commodious buildings for the storage of entire cargoes of any that exist here. It is this business which has kept and still is keeping me here, and until it is finally disposed of, I mean turned over to other parties, I cannot leave. You will of course ask when this is likely to be. This, as it depends upon others and upon so many contingent circumstances, I cannot exactly say; but a very few months will bring it about, though. Suppose it should take place in midsummer, or even in the latter part of summer, I should not think it judicious or prudent to cross the Isthmus at that time, but should by all means prefer to wait till the early part of October for leaving here, and thus taking a very favorable month for my arrival home —November—until when I think you had better not make up your mind to see me.

This, I think, will find you on the point of returning to our home at Norwich, if you should not already have arrived there. I sent you by the last mail a remittance of $150 which you will require on arriving there. I may possibly enclose the *second* of the draft, as also the *second* of the draft which preceded it. These, you will recollect, are only duplicates to take the place of the firsts in the event of any accident happening to them, and if the firsts have been paid these must be destroyed. If you are in any doubt in the matter, refer it to Brother Gilman, who will put you right. . . .

Captain John Perit is here and now out of employment. The steamer *Santa Clara*, in which he came out from New York, belonging to our cousin Woolsey Aspinwall, was burned at the wharf and nearly a total loss of some $60,000.[2] I hope he was insured. Fortunately for Perit, he was not in her at the time. He got a letter a day or two since from Perit Huntington on the Umpqua River in the southern part of Oregon. He writes in good health and spirits and like a person who understands himself, and I doubt not will do well. Let his father and mother know this and remember me to them. I have written Perit fully on some information he wanted and intend now to write him again. Captain John, in the absence of anything to do here, will, I think, return home.

Remember me to Mr. Thomas' family, to Mr. Arms,' Mr. Spauldings,' not forgetting dear Aunt Lathrop and her children, to George Ripley particularly, and last though not least, dear Cousin Mary Woodhull and Elisabeth. Alas, how sad the reflection that the mention of these dear friends awakens. How many breaches have been made in our family circle in the short three years of my absence. I have just heard of another which took me quite by surprise. Cousin Emily Woolsey is said to have lost one of her little boys.

I had a few lines from Mr. Perit by the last steamer in which he makes very gratifying mention of our dear Elisabeth. Business is exceedingly depressed here, and property, both merchandise and real estate, sold, when not particularly wanted, at ruinous sacrifices. Somebody at home has got to bear all this, and sooner or later it will be known who, I am thinking.

1. See Introduction, p. 16. As already noted, these iron warehouses failed to live up to expectations, but they marked a step toward more permanent construction. Coit's warehouses did not suffer from fire, but from the unstable San Francisco sand hills, which broke loose and slid down, causing much damage both to buildings and contents. Chas. W. Coit in *Autobiography*, pp. 51–52.
2. "March 3d.—The steamers Hartford and Santa Clara were burned this morning at Long Wharf." *The Annals*, p. 321; the *Santa Clara* was a total loss. Bancroft, *History of California*, Vol. VII, p. 136; for further details, see the *Alta California* for March 3 and 4, 1851.

I stood by this morning and saw an elegant oil cloth carpet packed in a case 20 feet long, said to have cost $2.25 in the United States, sold for 62½ cts. per yard. Persons are actually buying goods now to take back to the United States and teas are said to have been ordered back from here to Canton.

Embrace our dear children for me, for I fancy you all united again, and believe me faithfully and affectionately yours,

D. W. Coit

My very dear wife, San Francisco, April 14, 1851

Notwithstanding what you are pleased to term your "stupid feelings," when you sat down to indite your last letter to me, I mean that of 25th February, you rarely have been more successful in the variety and interest of your communication.

I began to despair of getting the promised daguerreotype of our dear Libby which you entrusted to the care of Mr. Godard, when on entering my apartments yesterday I found his card saying that he had left it at the office of the Pacific Mail Steamship Company, where I hastened to get it and have been highly delighted in gazing upon those beloved features so rapidly maturing into womanhood. The change within the past year, or since the former daguerreotype was taken, is truly wonderful. I can hardly realize that it is the same dear, sprightly, little Libby that I left three years ago, and when to this improvement in personal appearance is added the still more important advance in mind and in character of which you are enabled to give me such gratifying testimony, I must say we have abundant cause for gratitude. I have written her in answer to her letter, though before I received the daguerreotype, which of course was not referred to.

You asked me some time ago after our cousin Tracy Bill and desired to be informed if he was really married.[1] I can at length answer your enquiries. He is now living here and his wife with him. I am sorry to say that he does not appear to have been among the successful. He was for a twelve-month in one of the interior towns, but not finding it satisfactory, he came down here and is now living as clerk with Mr. Atwell, formerly of New York, who keeps a fancy store of pianos, musical instruments, etc., in a part of the Post Office Building where I live. He gets here $100 per month only, which I presume as a man of family will barely support him. I think I can procure him, if he wishes, a situation as storekeeper in one of the custom-house bonded warehouses at a salary of $150 per month, but he seems in doubt whether to accept it, though it is a situation that hundreds of men, and of those some very competent, would jump at. I have not yet seen the lady, though I am told that I am to have an invitation to tea one of these days when they get matters and things fixed a little.

Mr. McNulty suffers with most others in the general depression of business—his business has fallen off greatly. Indeed, the auctioneers are the only people who seem to be doing an active business and making money, and that is done at a terrible cost to other people. Many people who, without much solid capital, have gone extensively into the shipments to this country from New York and other places, must be ruined. Good staple articles are now selling daily so low at the auctions that purchases are made to great advantage frequently to ship back again to the United States. I happened accidentally into one of these places the other day where some goods were being sold at one-quarter their value in New York. They were black

1. Curiously, his name does not appear in Chapman's genealogy of the Coit family.

twilled worsted goods, very little used here, and no bidders for them—or almost none. As I thought they would make a very good remittance, I bought several bales, which I shall now ship by a vessel direct for New York, and they will come in very well, or the proceeds will, for your use some 5 or 6 months hence—not that you will have to depend on them, for I shall take care of your wants in the meantime.[2]

This reminds me that I met the Reverend Mr. Willey, a friend of Ed. Gilman's, this morning who wished me to take his draft on the Home Missionary Society at New York for fifty dollars and give him the money for it, which I did, and now send it to William Gilman for collection who will, when collected, hold the amount at your disposal. I will send you a further sum very shortly. On the 1st March steamer I sent you $150 in Welles & Company's draft, which I trust you received seasonably for your return to Norwich.

You ask why it is, if young Meredith is a man of so much *note*, that I do not make more mention of him?[3] If, by being a man of note, you mean a man of business capacity, I think there is a great mistake in this. The notice taken of him in the papers, etc., grew out of a desire of his particular friends to make him some returns for the nice parties and balls he had afforded them in excursions on board the steamers to Benicia. The ladies also had a debt of gratitude to pay on this account, but it appears that the parties who had interests at stake, *i.e.*, the steamboat proprietors, took a very different view of things, and very summarily dismissed Mr. Meredith, being highly dissatisfied with what had occurred during his agency—in a word, he got the affairs of the company into a terrible mess, the books and even the cash account in such a state that neither head nor tail could be made of them; this I have directly from Captain Knight, who superseded him and who appears to understand his own position well.

I was always on friendly terms with Mr. Meredith, not intimate, for that was hardly to be expected with one so young as he was and with such different associates and habits. I always gave him credit for being honest in his intentions and doing as well as he knew how, but that was by no means enough to fill with credit the responsible situation he had. He went directly home, evidently much mortified, on Captain Knight's assuming the direction, and although he said he should return, I do not expect he ever will. . . .

Remember me to neighbor Thomas. Tell him to hold on a little longer, and he will see me back again at my old stand in the garden and the fruit yard, entering with renewed zest into those employments again. Tell him further that I shall have a good long yarn to spin for him. Remember me also to George and Hannah Ripley, and tell George I shall be right glad to take him by the hand again one of these days, not very remote, I hope. My love to my dear Aunt Lathrop, who I am glad to hear retains her health so well, also to dear Cousin Maryann Woodhull and Elisabeth. My best regards to Mr. and Mrs. Arms and to our Landing friends; tell your Aunt Coit that the Dr. and William are well and appear to be doing well in their temporal affairs; that William is highly esteemed amongst his church brethren as a devoted Christian endeavoring to do his duty here as faithfully as at home. I must say to you, too, that on a nearer acquaintance with him than I ever had at home, he has gained much in my estimation. I have barely left room to add my best love to your mother, as well as a large share to yourself and our dear children.

Ever affectionately,
D. W. C.

2. Coit had previously noted the glut of the market on certain occasions and the depressed prices at auction sales. See Introduction, p. 15.
3. Kimball's Directory of San Francisco lists a Gilmore Meredith, with Robinson, Bissell & Co., on the Sacramento Street wharf.

I enclose you the draft referred to and you can send it to Brother Gilman for collection just as it is.[4]
D. W. C.

4. After this letter a gap of nearly four months exists in the correspondence, though it is evident from the next letter printed that Coit kept on writing during this time. One reference to him has been found in the summer of 1851. A letter written by John Bensley in Sacramento to R. A. Harris in New Orleans, July 14, 1851 (original in the possession of Mrs. Lisa Galluccio, Washington, D.C.), includes this mention of a joint acquaintance: "Mr Danl Coyt is Still in San Francisco in the Broker Business in Small way dont know how he is doing."

My dear wife,   *San Francisco, September 6th, 1851*

I write the present not that I have anything new to add to what I wrote on the 1st by the regular steamer to Panama, but that you may have news of later date and to test at the same time the despatch on the new line or, in other words, Vanderbilt's line via Nicaragua.[1] They do pretend that they mean to put the passengers through in twenty-five days, but that I doubt very much, though I think it is not improbable that the time will be shorter than by the other route so that you may possibly receive this before you do my letter above referred to.

We have just gone through an election here which has been attended with all the excitement which usually accompanies such an event in New York. An attempt has been made to put in a more honest class of legislators and other officers, and I trust with some success. Parties are pretty nearly equally divided, Democrat and Whig, though the latter in the city have a decided majority.[2]

Another steamer of the regular line is now due from Panama so that I may hope for later advices from you perhaps tomorrow. The precarious health of several of our immediate connections occasions me much solicitude as to the tenor of your communications.

The summer having now passed, the weather has undergone a considerable change for the better. We have much less of those disagreeable winds (to me one of the most unpleasant things about our climate), and in their place have a cloudy atmosphere threatening rain, which indeed has begun to show itself by some slight showers.

I renew the expressions of my best love to you all. *Remaining ever affectionately yours,*
D. W. Coit

1. "The story of the Panama steamers between 1851 and 1860 was one of exciting, if also ruinous, competition," writes Kemble. Service via Nicaragua began in 1851. The passage from New York to San Francisco required 31 days, sometimes a day or two more, and it is not at all clear that travel on the Vanderbilt line was an improvement over that of their competitors. Kemble, *The Panama Route*, p. 58 *et seq.*
2. The contest for city offices in San Francisco in 1851 is described in *The Annals*, pp. 348–350.

My dear wife,　　　　　　　　　　　　　　　　*San Francisco, September 30th, 1851*

... In my last I referred to your arrangements for the approaching winter, taking it for granted that you would again close the house, place Daniel with Charles at Mrs. Cooley's, and calculate to take up your own abode with your mother in New York until my return, which, I trust, at any rate, will be before you will have occasion to go to Norwich again. The facilities for travel between this city and the Atlantic states are now so much increased that it will not at the utmost require more than four weeks for the return home by the time I am ready to go. The Nicaragua route is still laboring under some difficulties, though nothing, I am persuaded, that will not be easily removed, causing that, then, to be the favorite way, and certainly the shortest by some six or seven days. I should not like to express this as my opinion to our friends whose interests and sympathies are of course all in the other route. It is said to be very sickly at this time at Panama and Chagres.

I am not at all surprised at it; a malignant fever, similar to yellow fever, always prevails in a greater or less degree in this, the season of greatest exposure from heat and rain, but these considerations do not seem to weigh with the multitude anxious to get home. They rush down from the mines, crowd the steamers which go loaded to their utmost capacity, and, as to the rest, there is much uncertainty. It is to be feared that many will make a much longer journey than they bargained for, and land where their gold will be valueless, indeed.

Captain Knight (who, I believe, I formerly mentioned to you as having come here from New York as agent for the steam company) has asked permission to return home. He has been sorely afflicted in the loss of his eldest daughter and hardly less so by the illness and melancholy of his wife, occasioned by that misfortune. He will probably leave in a few weeks, and you may have an opportunity of seeing him at William Aspinwall's, when he would probably tell you that we have been on terms of pleasant intercourse.

Mr. Meredith, having returned here, is now very much engaged in a gold quartz vein in which he has an interest with others. Machinery for working the quartz has already been erected and is in active operation, and I learn from a disinterested and very judicious person who has very recently visited and examined the works that the speculation promises excellent results. For my own part, although I never doubted that some of the mining companies which might be judiciously managed would be successful and amass much wealth, yet it was a business which I did not understand and, moreover, I have a great aversion to connecting myself with companies and putting myself thus in the power of men that I could not know well. I have therefore kept aloof from all mining operations, never having taken an interest of a dollar in one of them, and it is rather late now to do so, whatever advantages they may offer.

I sent you by the last steamer (in my letter of 15 inst.) a check on New York for $100. I also gave an order on George Thomas for $50, though perhaps there may be demurrage in paying this (there ought not to be), and I now send to William Gilman still another check for $100, which I order him to hold at your disposal. Mr. Thomas, the elder, will doubtless have received sometime since from me $808, which I trust he has had a favorable opportunity of investing in some good bank stock in your name to be handed you, as I requested him to do. About this time, or at any rate before the present gets to hand, there should have arrived in New York a small shipment which I made from here last spring by the ship *Pacific* to the consignment of Mr. Gilman—when you get to New York and chance to see him, you can ask about it. The proceeds I expected to be about $500, though it may be more or less. This, if duly realized, you had better also have put in stock, presuming that you will not have occasion to use it for expenses, as I will keep you provided by remittance for that purpose. Now, make due mention of these items severally for my government.

I continue to be sufficiently pleased with my boarding house and the gentlemen I meet there; it is true there are not at least more than one or two such as I would select as associates, but I have knocked about the world and mixed with all classes and descriptions of men too long not to accommodate myself to circumstances, and even to submit to much ill-breeding and some grossness without showing that I am often annoyed and sometimes thoroughly disgusted with it. For instance, my seat at table is unfortunately next to a gentleman, of good family connections too, who is incessantly blowing a most troublesome nose in a most disgusting manner, tucking his not over nice bandanna under his arm for the convenience of frequent recourse, and who, in addition to this, for some reason best known to himself, never swallows above half his food, but after mastication bolts it out upon his plate with the other aliments not yet submitted to this course of treatment. Then the gentleman on my other side has his peculiarities—I might say ill-breeding—of quite another character. He has certainly never been taught to sit at table or feed himself properly. When he commences eating (quite a large and tall man), he seems really afraid of trusting his fork or knife with their appropriate duty of carrying the food to his mouth in the ordinary position of eating, but doubling down his body, he drops his chin as near to his plate as he can possibly get it, and fixing an elbow on either side, on the table, sets to work most industriously. Now, tell me, do you think me too comfortably situated and that I shall be grieved to break away from such agreeable associations whenever I am enabled to leave?

My best love to the dear children and to other friends who care enough for me to make the communication proper, and believe me, as ever, faithfully and affectionately yours,

D. W. Coit

My dear wife,   *San Francisco, October 10th, 1851*

What a precious treat I have just had in the receipt of your August letters, for that which was missing, as my last informed you, has now come to hand by the present steamer, that of the 9th with that of the 23rd together. They have afforded me quite a budget of news and good tidings which I have read over and over till I have it pretty well by heart. I was pleased to hear that you had indulged yourself with a jaunt to your friends in the neighborhood of New York which had proved in all respects so agreeable. I hope the young beau you had to attend you acquitted himself with credit on the occasion.

At length I have a very satisfactory letter (or I should rather say letters, for I have two under the same date) from Brother Gilman, in which he gives me his account of monies received and paid over to you since the present year's came in. I am relieved to find that the small amount entrusted to Mr. White had not been left on the beach and lost, as I formerly wrote you I supposed it had been, but had arrived safely and been handed to Mr. Gilman; one payment which you speak of, of $100, and another, which at the time of your writing it appears you were not advised of, amounting to $106.95, but which Mr. Gilman writes me under date of 25th August he had remitted you. These two sums together, $206, with the balance you had in hand would doubtless be all that you would require to pay up everything square before leaving Norwich to go to New York. My last informed you that owing to the failure of Mr. Willis, sundry drafts which I had taken from him on his banker in New York, amounting in all to about $1,000 and which was intended for you, would, in all probability, be refused payment and be returned here under protest. Two hundred dollars of this sum was intended especially for your expenses; to replace this, I sent enclosed in the letter above referred to a fresh draft of Page, Bacon & Co. on their bankers in New York for $200, which I trust you will have received ere the present gets to hand.

You may be anxious to know whether the $1,000 referred to is like to prove a loss. No doubt *some* loss will occur, though exactly what I am not prepared to say, possibly three or four hundred dollars, but here again, I consider myself as peculiarly fortunate that it is not a much larger amount.

I feel truly great sympathy for my friend Mr. Willis.[1] I have rarely met with an instance of more sudden, unlooked for, and overwhelming disaster than has befallen him in the short space of a year. I wrote you, I think, last winter that he had gone home to visit his family who reside in Massachusetts. At that time he supposed himself quite independent and it was his intention, after another year's residence in this country, to retire to his home, which I understand is a beautiful spot in the interior of the state, there to pass the remainder of his days. How much truth in the saying that man appoints and God disappoints. On his way back he took the Panama fever in crossing the Isthmus and was exceedingly ill on the voyage up, so that his life was despaired of. Sometime after this he regained his health when that dreadful fire of May came and burned up his large and costly block of stores, supposed to be thoroughly fireproof. This must have swept off at a blow for him, in one way or other, full $100,000—but not this alone, he was very nearly burned alive. For weeks he laid in a most agonizing and critical situation and even now, after so many months, is not entirely recovered. Then, to complete the catalogue of disaster, his friends in Boston, Willis & Company, protest large amounts of his bills drawn upon them, obliging him to close his doors and to make an assignment for the benefit of his creditors. I learn today that he will return home tomorrow by the steamer, which is doubtless the best course for him to pursue—his health is by no means restored, his wounds yet unhealed, his face disfigured, and although he has stood up manfully against his misfortunes, yet if he were to remain under all the perplexity and mortification which would be inevitable, he might sink under it after all.

I have been highly gratified to learn that you have had visits from my sisters and so many of our New York friends and that they have found the old place to retain many of its charms to them. Libby must have had a delightful summer of it with her young friends and will be prepared to go back to Mr. Abbott's school in New York with renewed satisfaction. If you left Norwich the first of October as you proposed (though it strikes me as earlier than usual), you must be ere this again fixed for the winter in Clinton Place. . . .

It is barely possible that Mr. Willis' drafts remitted may be paid, either in whole or in part, though lest they should not, and to guard against disappointment to you, I sent by last steamer a remittance to Brother Gilman of $200 as already mentioned, which I trust will be received and made available for your use. *Yours as ever, faithfully and affectionately,*
D. W. C.

1. Presumably H. P. Willis, of Fay, Peirce & Willis. See Coit's letter of June 17, 1850, note 2.

My very dear wife,   *San Francisco, December 13, 1851*

I take pen in hand to write you at this time, not in the best humor at having been deprived of your last letter, which should have been written somewhere about the 25th October. I received that of the 8th October and answered it on the 4th inst., when it became my painful duty to communicate to you the death of our friend, Mr. McNulty. I went into much detail, as my letter was intended equally for his family, particularly for my dear cousin, Betsey Brinckerhoff.

As I do not send a copy of that letter (although I have one in my possession), it may be well to give you the substance of it in the event of its miscarriage. I stated then that Mr. McNulty, having suffered long under the effects of diarrhea, went into the interior to a large mining town called Nevada for the improvement of his health. There he became immediately much worse, his complaint resulting in dysentery. Under the effects of this disease, he sank rapidly for about a week, when he died. The moment I heard of his severe illness, I went immediately to him, a journey of 200 miles and upwards, but was too late—the funeral had taken place the day before my arrival. I satisfied myself, however, that every kindness and attention had been shown him during his illness by his excellent correspondent and friend, Mr. Holt, by his two physicians, and the nurse that was employed.

On my return to town I found a will had been left by which his cousin, Mr. Marvin (just returned here from New York), together with myself, had been appointed executors. I am not even yet prepared to give an opinion in regard to the estate, or whether there will be anything for the orphan children after the debts are paid; unfortunately for them, there is quite a long list of creditors in new and I fear large indebtedness. We have written to learn the extent of these claims, and until we get an answer must remain very much in the dark. I wrote to Cousin George at Matanzas, giving him the substance of the foregoing and requesting to be furnished with his account against the estate, which I have reason to think will be some $4,000 or more.

Let me now go back to your cheerful pleasant letter which afforded me the greater pleasure as it fixed you again in Clinton Place for the winter. I always feel relief when that journey, which you have to make by yourself through the Sound, is accomplished, either one way or the other—I mean whether going or returning. Keep up your courage but a little longer, and I promise you a very experienced beau for the future.

I was delighted with your account of the family movements. Won't they have a nice time of it for the winter, or rather for the year?—for they can hardly take less time, if they mean to make the grand tour, as I suppose they will, passing the winter probably in Naples. Keep me advised from time to time, as you may hear of their whereabouts. I shall follow them with interest, the more so as there is scarcely a place of interest they will be likely to visit where I have not been. What a host of the young fry are growing up to be men and women within the last few years (I am startled whilst I write the period of my absence and reflect on its strangeness), becoming manageable and setting off on foreign travel.

Brother Gilman has quite reinstated himself in my good opinion as a correspondent, having written me no less than three letters lately, explaining what I wished to know of my remittances and their disposition. As to funds for your future use, this appears to be the position of them: first, a draft drawn by Willis on Boston for $100 had been paid early in November; next, he had received on my account from a Mr. Kilbourn, $177—this makes already in his hands, certain, $277. Next, I remitted in October another bill for $200, which I have no doubt whatever will be paid, and if the other draft of Wells' also for $100 should be paid the total at your disposal will be $577. This will, I think, abundantly meet all your wants till my return, even should that be delayed till April next. Mr. Gilman further informs me that two cases of goods of the value of $400 or $500 had also arrived safely.

We are creeping into the winter nicely, with fine bright days, as yet with very little rain, not by any means as much as the miners would like to see, and the temperature so that I find it quite pleasant writing this in the evening in my rooms, as I am doing, without a fire. The entire winter the past year was of this character. It is too much to expect that the present one will be equally pleasant although, as I have said, the beginning promises well.

Another steamer from Panama will be due in a couple of days, which should bring New York dates to 10th November. Of course, I shall get a letter from you, and I hope in addition the missing letter of October. How is it that my newspapers come so irregularly? I do not get one-half the numbers of either the *Home Journal* or the *Independent*. Do be a little more regular in sending them, and more prompt, too, for I generally read other people's before I get mine.

You got quite an exaggerated account of my indisposition, which was nothing more than a cold with a slight attack of fever which confined me to the house for a day. My general health never was better and my activity certainly equal to what you have ever known it. Shall I prove it? Well, then, Captain Knight mounted me on a very spirited saddle horse for a short ride with him the other day, when we trotted off 15 miles in little more than a brace of hours. By the bye, tell Cousin W. H. A. that he has at length got the right kind of man to manage his steamboat affairs, one that will save the company as much money in a couple of years by economy and good management as was previously lost in the same period of time by the extreme opposite, and *that* will be no small amount, either.

We have a rumor that William is talking of paying us a visit in a month or two. There was a time when I thought his presence was of infinite importance to put things right, though that urgency no longer exists, owing to the wiser counsels which prevail, as I have hinted above.

And now, my dearest dear, my paper is drawing to a close and I must bid you for a little time adieu, trusting that your dear mother (to whom I desire my best love) may continue so well that you may enjoy a very pleasant winter. Give my best love to dear Libby, who will not, I am sure, deprive me of a letter at least once a month when she knows the pleasure it affords me. If possible, I will enclose a few lines for her. My love to the boys, too, from whom I hope you have favorable news. Further, love to Sarah and Henry and to all my dear sisters and nieces, and accept for yourself always the largest share.

Faithfully and affectionately yours,
D. W. Coit

P.S. Do not rob me of that last or fourth page of your sheet when you write, please, madam.

INDEX

Alamo, The: at San Antonio, 1
American Antiquarian Society: acknowledgment to, 20
American Star, The: 31n.
Annals, The: cited, 12n., 17n., 79n., 81n., 82n., 93n., 96n., 103n., 104n., 107n.
Antelope: passengers returning on, 98
Anthony, Elihu: Methodist minister, 18
Armistice: between the United States and Mexico, 27
Arms', The: of Norwich, 76, 104, 106
Armstrong, Charles: 24
Aspinwall, William H.: businessman, 3, 5; interest of, in Panama Railroad and Pacific Mail Steamship Co., 5-6, 75, 99
Aspinwall, Woolsey: 102, 104
Astor House: in Mexico City, 7, 31
Atherton, Faxon Dean: 61n.
Atherton, Robert: tells of gold mines, 61-62
Atwell, Mr.: 105
Auction houses: in San Francisco, 15, 75n., 104-106
Avery, Benjamin Parke: cited, 39n.

Bailey, Mr.: 90
Baldwin, J. L.: engineer, at Isthmus of Panama, 5, 22n.
Bancroft, H. H.: cited, 2n., 5n., 6n., 16n., 40n., 46n., 56n., 69n., 73n., 75n., 78n., 93n., 96n., 101n., 104n.
Bandits: *see* Guerrilla bands
Baptist Church: in San Francisco, 80, 84, 100
Barron, Forbes & Co.: 73
Beach, Mr.: 76, 80-81; burned out, 93
Beale (Beals), Lt. Edward F.: brings news of gold discovery to Mexico, 1, 11, 48-50
Becker, Robert H.: acknowledgment to, 20
Belle Union Hotel: in Mexico City, 31
Bemis, Samuel F.: cited, 2n.
Benicia: promotion of, 91-92
Bensley, John: 107n.
Biddle, Charles: negotiates for Isthmian railway, 5
Bidwell, Charles T.: cited, 6n.
Bieber, Ralph P.: cited, 48n.
Bill, Ledyard: cited, 94n.
Bill, Tracey: 83, 102, 105
Bissell, George W. P.: 12, 58, 72-73, 91
Bolton: bound for California, 63
Bolton, Herbert E.: cited, 2n.
Bonsal, Stephen: cited, 48n.
Brannan, Sam: 17, 18, 78
Bretnor, Helen Harding: acknowledgment to, 20; cited, 80n.
Brewster, Mr.: burned out, 93
Brinckerhoff, Betsey: Coit's cousin, 111
Buchanan, James: 48n.
Budd, Captain: 75
Bustamante, Gen. Anastasio: defeats Paredes, 42
Butler, Col. Pierce: 30
Butler, Gen. William O.: succeeds Scott in command of American Army in Mexico, 8; departure of, 39

Byrne, Marie: acknowledgment to, 20

Calderón de la Barca, Frances Erskine: cited, 38n., 50n.
California: gold discovery in, 1, 6; extent of gold fields, 49, 57; extraordinary accounts of, 56-57, 61-62; gold mining in, 74-75, 77; admission of as state, 96-97
California: launched, 5; first voyage of, 6; on Pacific Coast, 69, 73, 84n.
Castañeda, C. E.: cited, 2n.
Castillero, E. J.: cited, 5n.
Catherwood, Frederick: with Stephens, 23n.
Caughey, John W.: cited, 49n., 56n.
Caulkins, Frances M.: cited, 94n.
Chapman, Frederick W.: cited, 41n., 65n., 79n.
Chase, Lee: acknowledgment to, 20
Chase, Victory Van Dyck: acknowledgment to, 20
Chauncey, Henry: 5, 23n.
Chileans: attacks upon, in San Francisco, 78
Cholera: danger of, 84; talk of, in San Francisco, 97, 99, 100
Churches: in San Francisco, 16-18, 80; *see* individual denominations
City Hospital: burned, 97
Clifford, Nathan: peace commissioner and minister to Mexico, 9-10, 11, 34, 37, 46, 52-53, 54, 62-63
Coins: shortage of, in California, 56-57
Coit, Dr. Benjamin B.: 69, 76, 79, 99, 100; and brother William, 102
Coit, Dr. Charles G.: acknowledgment to, 19
Coit, Charles Woolsey: son of Daniel W. Coit, 4
Coit, Daniel Lathrop, and Lydia Lathrop: family of, 41n.
Coit, Daniel Wadsworth: Autobiography of, cited, 3n., 4n., 104n.; character of, 1, 7; letters of, to his wife, 21-112; sketches by, 1, 6-7, 10-12, 18, 19, 36, 42, 51-52, 64, 69-70, 85, 87; business agent in Peru, 3-4; student of art, 4; children of, 4; moves to Norwich, Conn., 4; buys property in Michigan Territory, 4; business agent in Mexico for Howland & Aspinwall, 4-6, 37-38; voyage of, to Jamaica, 24; experiences storm in Gulf of Mexico, 25-26; arrival at Vera Cruz, 26-27; Vera Cruz to Mexico City, 7, 26-30; description of the City, 31; lives in Drusina home, 31, 38; moves in elite circles, 8; daily routine, 32-33, 50-52, 102-103; observes Pillow and Scott courts of inquiry, 8-9; witnesses departure of American troops, 10; visits churches of Mexico, 10-11, 44-45; drive to Drusina ranch at San Antonio, near Churubusco, 35-36; learns of gold discovery, 11; plans purchase of gold dust in San Francisco for silver coins, 1, 12-13; Howland & Aspinwall decline Coit's offer to buy gold, 64-65; Coit accepted as agent of Drusina & Co., 66, 70; off for California via San Blas, 13-14, 67; appearance of traveling party, 67-69; arrives in San Francisco, April 1, 1849, 67; description of San Fran-

INDEX

cisco, 69–70; experiences of, as gold broker, 14–15, 90–91; has rooms in Post Office Bldg., 15, 103; describes churches of San Francisco, 16–18; complains of irregularity in receipt of letters, 50, 53, 58; asks T. S. Cooper to publish his sketches, 53; obtains tapestries, 64; returns home, 1852, 19

Coit, Elizabeth: daughter, 4, 19, 33, 74, 75, 98, 104; daguerreotype of, 105, 110, 112

Coit, Harriet Frances: marries Daniel W. Coit, 4

Coit, Joshua: brother of Daniel, 4n., 11n., 41, 53n., 75

Congregational Church: in San Francisco, 17, 18, 73–74, 88, 100

Cooper, Thomas Sidney: influence of, on Coit, 11; Coit proposes publication of his sketches by, 53

Coronel, Antonio Franco: buys gold dust, 12; cited, 57n.

Cortina, Conde de: 54

Cosío, J. Miguel: supports Paredes revolt, 40n.

Coulter, Edith: acknowledgment to, 19

Cushing, Caleb: organizes volunteer regiment, 23–24

Daguerrotypes: received by Coit, 75, 76, 105

Dakin, Susanna Bryant: acknowledgment to, 20

Daniels, Matthew: 31n.

Davidson, Benjamin and Lionel: 52, 53, 62

Delmonico's restaurant: 103

Derbec, Etienne: cited, 15n.

Deserters: from American Army, 46–47

Devotion, Colonel: 80

Dictionary of American Biography: cited, 23n., 34n., 39n.

Dolphin: catch of, 21–22.

Dorr, Mr.: of New York, 97

Douglas, John W.: minister in San Francisco, 18

Doyle, Percy W.: British representative in Mexico, 9

Drusina & Co., William de: German firm in Mexico, 4n.; Coit obtains rooms with Drusina family, 7–8, 50–51; description of Drusina family, 35–36, 42, 51; friends of General Paredes, 41; Coit dines with, 52; offers to send Coit to California to buy gold, 14, 58, 65; agent of Rothschilds, 62; Drusina gives Coit folding bed, 69; Coit buys gold dust for, 70, 83

Du Coin: merchant, 44

Duncan, James: in Pillow scandal, 8–9

Dyer, Brainerd: cited, 34n.

Edgerton, Mrs.: 87

Ellison, William H.: cited, 96n.

Emory, Col. William H.: leads escort to Mexico City, 7, 29

Episcopal Church: in San Francisco, 85, 88, 103

Eugenia: at Vera Cruz, with gold seekers, 63

Falconer, Rema: acknowledgment to, 24n.

Fanning, H. T.: 94

Farnham, Dr.: 91

Ferrier, William Warren: cited, 17n., 18n.

Faulk, Odie B.: cited, 2n.

Faulkner, William: Norwich editor, 80

Finley, Johnson & Co.: 93

Fires: in San Francisco, 15–16, 81, 92–93, 96–97, 110

Fleming, Sandford: cited, 17n.

Forbes, Alexander: 73

Gages, Mr.: 90

Galluccio, Mrs. Lisa: 107

Gambling: in Mexico City, 31; in San Francisco, 78–79, 84

Garber, Paul N.: cited, 44n.

Gilman, Daniel Coit: donor of sketches, 19

Gilman, Edward: 18

Gilman, William C.: Coit's brother-in-law, 19, 41n., 65, 66, 70, 75, 83, 86, 89, 95, 101, 104, 106, 108, 109, 111–112

Goddard, Mr.: 76

Gold discovery, in California: 1, 6; news of, reaches Mexico, 11, 48; *see* California

Gold dust: low price of, 56–57

Gran Sociedad Hotel: Coit at, 7, 10, 31, 33, 42, 47; American troops at, 37

Grand Rapids, Michigan: Coit property in, 4

Greenman: carpenter, 94

Guadalajara: Coit sketches, 71

Guadalupe Hidalgo: treaty signed at, 9; cited, 9n.

Guerra, Ana María de la: daughter of Jósè de la Guerra, 88n.

Guerrilla bands: in Mexico, 2, 7, 27–29, 30, 40–41, 49–50, 55; between Guadalajara and Tepic, 72

Hargous, Louis Eugene: New York merchant in Mexico, 11, 33; center of social group, 43, 44, 46, 52; financial agent for General Scott, 44n., 46, 52–53, 54; Coit dines with, 62

Hargous, Peter A.: 44n.

Hargous, Stanislaus: 44, 46

Hargous & Co.: business firm in Mexico, 3, 44n.; claims of, against Mexican government, 46

Harris, Arnold: sells interest in Pacific Mail contract to Aspinwall, 5

Harstad, Peter T.: cited, 2n.

Hartford: burned, 104n.

Henry, Robert S.: cited, 8n., 9n., 10n., 27n.

Herrera, President Jósè Joaquín de: 48

Home Missionary Society: 106

Honolulu: 17

Hounds, The: 17, 77–79

Howard, W. D. M.: 17, 78

Howard & Mellus: 75

Howland, Gardiner Greene: founder of firm, 3, 5

Howland, Mrs. L. L.: 41

Howland, Louisa: 67

Howland, Samuel Shaw: founder of firm, 3

Howland, William Edgar: businessman, 3

Howland & Aspinwall: New York business firm, 3; send Coit to Mexico, 4–5, 11, 36, 37–38; business of, satisfactory, 43; Coit proposes the firm send him to California, 58–59; reply delayed, 62–63; reject Coit's offer, 64; interest of, in Benicia, 91n.

INDEX

Hughes, Col. George W.: leads escort to Mexico City, 27
Hunt, Timothy Dwight: minister in San Francisco, 17–18, 78, 80; sermons of, 88
Huntington, Perit: 76, 86, 104
Huntingtons, The: of Norwich, 76
Huth & Co., Frederick: German firm, represented in Peru by Coit, 3–4, 65
Hutton party: experience of, in Mexico, 71–72
Hyatt, Mr.: returns East, 98

Immigration: to California, 79, 98
Indians: employed in gold mining, 61
Isthmus: 90
Iron warehouses: in San Francisco, 16, 104
Irving, Washington: 23n.

Jarauta, Cenobio: revolt of, 40; shot, 42–43, 46
Johnson: brings letters for Mrs. Coit, 69
Johnson, Kenneth M.: cited, 16n.
Jones: Coit's hired hand in Norwich, 45, 87, 88
Jones, Com. Thomas ap C.: dispatches of, 11, 48

Kaufman, of Drusina & Co.: home of, as social center, 33, 51–52
Kemble, John Haskell: cited, 5n., 6n., 13n., 107n.
Kennedy, Alfred: acknowledgment to, 20
Kennedy, Lawton: acknowledgment to, 20
Kennedy: of New York, in Jalapa, 27
Kingsley, James L.: cited, 41n.
Knight, Capt.: 106, 108, 112

Landing, The: 90, 94, 95; Coit friends at, 106
Lansing, Arthur B.: 43
Larkin, Thomas O.: reports on gold discovery, 11, 48, 57n., 91n.
Larkin Papers: cited, 9n., 16n., 57n., 91n.
Lathrop, John: 76
Lawton: of New Rochelle, 67
Leavenworth, Thaddeus M.: alcalde, 17, 78
Lee, Lt. Robert E.: in Mexican War, 43
Leland, Warren: cited, 80n.
Leonidas: article by, 8
Lester, Mr.: of New Rochelle, 83, 93
Lynden, Fred: acknowledgment to, 20

MacIntire, Mr.: extraordinary success of, 98–99
Mail day: in San Francisco, 77, 80, 86, 90
Mail service: New York to San Francisco, 66
Mason, Gov. R. B.: visits gold region, 57, 69
McCarthy: Episcopal minister in Mexico, 37
McCormac, Eugene I.: cited, 32n.
McEniry, Blanche Marie: cited, 47n.
McNulty, Mr.: improved, 99; business of, 105; death of, 111
Meredith, Gilmor: 13–14, 67–69, 73, 106, 108
Methodist Church: in San Francisco, 17–18, 80, 85, 100
Mexico City: described by Coit, 31; rainstorm in, 38–39; climate of, 41, 63

Mexican War: government demoralized, 2–3; treaty negotiations, 34; peace treaty concluded, 36–37
Miller: Englishman, 44
Mines (Milne, Miles), Flavel S.: Episcopal minister in San Francisco, 18, 85, 88–89, 103
Miranda, Roque: bandit, 47–48
Moore, Jacob C.: postmaster, 86
Morgan, Dale L.: acknowledgment to, 20; cited, 56n., 57n., 79n., 81n.
Mormons: in San Francisco, 80

Nasatir, A. P.: cited, 15n., 16n.
Naylor, Charles: 43
New-York Historical Society: acknowledgment to, 20
New York Public Library: acknowledgment to, 20
Norwich, Conn.: Coit family home at, 4
Norwich Courier: quoted, 24n.

Ohio: 11
Oregon: launched, 5; Coit on, 14; 72–73; Rev. Williams on, 17, 74; goldseekers on, 75
Otis, F. N.: cited, 5n., 6n., 22n.

Pacific Mail Steamship Co.: incorporated, 5; Aspinwall's interest in, 5, 6
Page, Bacon & Co.: 110
Palmetto Regiment: 30
Panama: launched, 5; in Pacific, 75, 79, 84, 87, 90
Panama, Isthmus of: railway across, 5; goldseekers stranded at, 6
Panama Railroad: construction of, 6
Paredes, Mariano: leads revolt, 40–42, 46
Parker House: 79n.
Patterson, Robert: 43
Paul, Rodman W.: cited, 49n.
Peña y Peña, Manuel de la: acting president, 2; negotiates treaty of peace, 9
Perit, Capt. John: 104
Perit, Peletiah: 41n.
Philadelphia House: 96n.
Pillow, Gen. Gideon J.: center of Army scandal, 8–9, 31–32, 34; friend of President Polk, 8
Placer mines: 73–74, 77; *see* California
Plata piña: 49
Polk, President James K.: supports Gen. Pillow; replaces Gen. Scott, 8–9
Poor, Col. Benjamin: 86
Portsmouth Square: 15, 17, 78, 79, 96, 103
Prendergast, John: English artist, 70
Presbyterian Church: in San Francisco, 17–18, 80, 84, 88
Prescott, William H.: 23n.
Priestley, H. I.: cited, 73n.
Probst: of Howland & Aspinwall, in San Francisco, 69, 73
Pronunciamento: of General Paredes, 40; danger of, 46–47; report of, 66

INDEX

Quaife, M. M.: cited, 39n.
Querétaro: description of, 71

Radepont, Marquis de: 53
Rebec, Estelle: acknowledgment to, 20
Regulators, The: 17, 77–79
Reilly (Riley), John: deserter from American Army, leads renegade Americans, 47–48
Resh, Richard W.: cited, 2n.
Revere, Joseph Warren: cited, 57n.
Ripley, George: 33, 104, 106
Rives, George L.: cited, 9n., 27n., 37n.
Roberts, William: Methodist minister, 18
Robinson, Alfred: brings letters for Mrs. Coit, 88
Rodríguez, Ruth: acknowledgment to, 20
Romero, José Guadalupe: cited, 54n.
Rosenstock, Fred A.: acknowledgment to, 20
Ross, Charles L.: 75, 84n.
Rothschild & Sons, N. M.: 52n., 62, 65n., 92

Sacramento: flooded, 101
San Francisco, City of: effect of gold boom on, 1, 74; sketched by Coit, 14; description of, 15, 69–70; lawlessness in, 77–79; danger of fire in, 15–16, 81; climate of, 81, 100; cost of labor in, 82; fires in, 16, 92–93, 96–97
San Francisco, Convent of: sketched by Coit, 10, 36n., 51–52
San Antonio: Drusina's country estate, 10
San Antonio: Texas, founding of, 1
San Patricio Division: 47–48
Santa Anna, Antonio López de: 2, 27n.
Santa Clara: burned, 104
Santo Domingo, Island of: 22
Scobie, James R., cited, 56n., 57n., 79n., 81n.
Scott, Gen. Winfield: captures Mexico City, 2; submits to court of inquiry, 8–9; at Pillow trial, 31–32; leaves Mexico, 34, 43
Seaman's Friend Society: 80
Semple, Dr. Robert: 91n.
Sevier, Ambrose H.: peace commissioner to Mexico, 9–10, 34, 37, 39
Shaw, Stephen W.: 38
Ships: deserted in San Francisco Bay, 56, 62–63, 75
Skinner, Lucien: 95
Smith, E. Kirby: cited, 2n.
Smith, Henry: 76
Smith, Justin H.: cited, 27n., 28n., 32n., 53n.
Smith, Gen. Persifor F.: 14, 32, 39n., 43, 69
Smith, Dr. Peter: 97
Spaldings (Spauldings), The: of Norwich, 76, 104
Starbuck, Captain: of Howland & Aspinwall line, 54, 59–60
Steam Company: 91, 93
Steinberger: San Francisco real estate agent, 80
Stephens (Stevens), John Lloyd: writings of, 5; interest of, in Panama railway, 6, 21, 22n., 23–24
Stephenson, Nathaniel W.: cited, 2n.

Stewart, Major: 43
Stickles, Arndt M.: cited, 8n.

Tapestries: Coit acquires, 64; received, 87
Taylor, Bayard: cited, 56n., 103
Taylor [Francis?]: 43
Taylor, Gen. Zachary: 2, 34n.
Taylor, William: Methodist minister, 17; cited, 18n.
Tennessee: passengers returning on, 95, 98
Texas: annexation of, as cause of Mexican War, 1; pioneer settlements in, 2
Thanksgiving: in San Francisco, 100
Thomas, George: 90, 108
Thomas family: of Norwich, 104, 106
Tompkins, John Barr: acknowledgment to, 20
Trade winds: 21–22
Trigaros, Señora: 44
Trinity Church: in San Francisco, 18
Trist, Nicholas P.: American representative in Mexico, 3, 9, 24, 33n.

United States Army: in Mexico City, 7; departure of, 37, 39; deserters from, 46–47

Vail: spendthrift, 93–94
Vanderbilt steamers: 107
Volunteers: in Mexican War, 28, 31
Von Hagen, Victor Wolfgang: cited, 23n.
Vos, Mr.: in Mexico, 33, 43, 44, 52; summer home of, 55, 64; going to California, 61

Wallace, Edward S.: cited, 23n., 47n.
Walsh: U. S. chargé in Mexico, 62
Ward, Frank: 78
Warehouses: lack of, in San Francisco, 75n.; of iron, 104
Weller, John B.: Boundary Commissioner, 34n.
Wells, Thos. G.: 101
Wells (Welles) & Co.: bankers, 15, 95, 103, 106, 111
Wheeler, O. C.: Baptist minister in San Francisco, 17, 84, 100
Willey, Rev. Samuel H.: 18, 88, 101–102, 106
Williams, Albert: Presbyterian minister in San Francisco, 17–18, 74, 80, 84, 88
Williams, Mary Floyd: cited, 78n.
Willis, H. P.: failure of, 93, 109–110, 111
Willis & Co.: of Boston, 110
Wolcott, Abby: 102
Wool, Gen. J. E.: 27n.
Woolsey, Ed.: 24
Worth, Gen. William J.: demands court of inquiry, 8, 9; sketch of, 23n., 43; leads last American troops out of Mexico City, 37, 39
Wright, Mr.: made a fortune, 94–95
Wright & Co., Elin: 24

Zamacois, Niceto de: cited, 40n.